Employment Law
Explained

First edition January 2012

ISBN 9780 7517 9663 6

British Library Cataloguing-in-Publication Data
A catalogue record for this book
is available from the British Library

Published by

BPP Learning Media Ltd
BPP House, Aldine Place
London W12 8AA

www.bpp.com/learningmedia

Printed in the United Kingdom

Printed on paper sourced from sustainable, managed forests.

All our rights reserved. No part of this publication may be reproduced, stored in a retrieval system or transmitted, in any form or by any means, electronic, mechanical, photocopying, recording or otherwise, without the prior written permission of BPP Learning Media Ltd.

©
BPP Learning Media Ltd
2012

Contents

Page

1 Advertising and recruitment

1	Introduction	1
2	The Equality Act 2010	1
3	Recruitment and selection	11

2 Appointment and contracts of employment

1	Introduction	21
2	Key elements for a binding contract to be formed	22
3	Who is an employee?	25
4	How can employment status be determined?	27
5	The terms of the contract	33
6	Express terms of the contract	35
7	Specific express clauses	39
8	Duties of the employer	43
9	Employer's obligations at common law	44
10	Duties of the employee	47
11	Confidentiality	48
12	Restraint of trade	50
13	Garden leave	52
14	Atypical contracts	53
15	Dismissal and waiver clauses in fixed-term contracts	55
16	Temporary and casual contracts of employment	56
17	Annual hours and zero-hours contracts of employment	57
18	Rights of part-time workers	58

3 Information

1	Information	61
2	The Data Protection Act 1998	61
3	Data protection principles	69
4	Regulation of Investigatory Powers Act 2000	73
5	Telecommunications (Lawful Business Practice) (Interception of Communications) Regulations 2000 (SI 2000/2699) (Regulation 3 amended by Regulation 34 of The Privacy and Electronic Communications (EC Directive) Regulation 2003)	75
6	Data protection related matters	77
7	Recommended course of action for employers	79
8	Employee information in relation to recruitment and selection	81
9	Medical information	98
10	Information relating to equality in the workplace	102
11	Occupational pension schemes	103
12	Information which may or may not be lawfully protected under the Public Interest Disclosure Act 1998 (Whistleblowing)	103

4 Pay and benefits

1	The meaning of pay	107
2	The employer's duty to pay wages	110
3	Deductions in wages	111
4	Pay in lieu of notice payments	113
5	Recovery of wages	114
6	Non-contractual and discretionary payments	115
7	Other forms of 'pay'	116
8	Introduction guarantee payments	117
9	Statutory rights	117
10	Contractual rights	118
11	Eligibility to receive a statutory guarantee payment	118
12	Redress for non-payment	119
13	Statutory Sick Pay	119
14	Statutory Maternity Pay (SMP), Maternity Allowance, Paternity Pay (SPP) and Adoption Pay	124
15	The National Minimum Wage Act 1998	125
16	Equal pay	129
17	Bringing an equal pay claim	130
18	How a claim is dealt with by the Employment Tribunal	132
19	Discussions about pay	137
20	Gender pay gap information	137
21	Individual rights for time off	137

5		Statutory benefits	
	1	Maternity rights	141
	2	Maternity leave provisions	142
	3	Statutory maternity pay and maternity allowance	147
	4	Paternity leave	149
	5	Paternity pay	152
	6	Parental leave and time off for dependants	152
	7	Adoption leave	155
	8	Adoption Pay (SAP)	159
	9	Right to request flexible working	161
6		**Ongoing employment**	
	1	Introduction	167
	2	Changing a contract	167
	3	Variation of the contract	169
	4	Continuity of employment	174
	5	The Working Time Regulations 1998	176
	6	Sunday working	189
	7	Discrimination legislation	189
7		**Transfer of undertakings**	
	1	Transfer of Undertakings (Protection of Employment) (TUPE) Regulations 2006	205
	2	Regulations explained	208
	3	Dismissals connected with a transfer	209
	4	Consultation on transfers	209
	5	When do regulations apply?	211
	6	Legal considerations of a transfer	213
8		**Termination of employment**	
	1	Introduction	219
	2	Outline of the provisions	219
	3	Unfair dismissal	228
	4	Redundancy	238
	5	Retirement	251
	6	Some Other Substantial Reason (SOSR)	252
	7	Fairness of the dismissal	253
	8	Procedural fairness	256
	9	Termination involving dismissal at common law	260
	10	Termination without dismissal	261
	11	Dismissal with notice	265
	12	Dismissal without notice	265
	13	Summary dismissal	266
	14	Unjustified dismissal without notice	267
	15	Damages for breach of contract	267

9 Trade unions, employee communications and participation

1	Introduction	269
2	Recognition	270
3	Rights of independent recognised trade unions	272
4	Trade union membership and refusal of employment	277
5	Detriment on trade union grounds	277
6	Dismissal for trade union reasons	278
7	'Compulsory' trade union recognition (introduced by the 1999 Employment Relations Act)	279
8	The rules on seeking compulsory collective bargaining rights	284
9	De-recognition	285
10	Summary time-scale of the recognition procedures	286
11	Industrial action and picketing	288
12	The economic torts	289
13	Secondary industrial action	292
14	Unofficial industrial action	293
15	Ballots for industrial action	293
16	The Citizen's Right of Action – s 235A	297
17	Picketing	297
18	Remedies for employers	300
19	The meaning of industrial action and 'protected' industrial action	302
20	Employee Information, Participation and Consultation with Employee Representatives – Pensions and the Companies Act 1985 (amended and repealed in part by the Companies Act 2006)	304
21	Employee participation and information	305

Introduction

This book is intended to help Line Managers navigate their way through the employment legislation that is associated with managing people. It assumes that you are aware that legislation exists but need guidance as to what to consider, what to avoid and other useful points to be aware of.

Whilst this book makes reference to and explains various pieces of legislation, it is not designed as a definitive explanation. It focuses on what you need to be aware of.

It is designed to follow the typical 'life cycle' of engaging people. Therefore it starts with advertising and recruitment and finishes when someone's employment is ended.

Advertising and recruitment

1 Introduction

In order for the employer to increase or replace their workforce they will inevitably go through a process of recruitment. This may involve asking current employees to recommend people or engaging people who speculatively apply. Alternatively, there may be a more formal process with the use of advertising or a recruitment agency followed by interviews and a selection process.

Very little legislation exists regarding the actual mechanical process of advertising and selection. There is however plenty regarding the fairness of these processes. Therefore we start with anti-discrimination legislation.

2 The Equality Act 2010

Whilst you maybe familiar with many of the major component parts of the laws that have come into effect over recent decades eg Equal Pay Act, Sex Discrimination Act, Race Discrimination Act, 1 October 2010 saw the introduction of the Equality Act. This Act is a major revision of the anti-discrimination legislation and replaces previous legislation. The Act is so profound that it needs to be considered in its own right, not least because it introduces several new concepts. However, as with any new Employment legislation currently the only reference material is the legislation. As yet none of the provisions have been tested in an Employment Tribunal and so as time elapses the interpretation of the tribunals will be more evident. That said, it should not be overlooked that the new legislation has evolved from the previous statutes which may be based on previous tribunal findings.

The Government Equalities office summarises the changes implemented by the Equality Act as follows:

- The basic framework of protection against direct and indirect discrimination, harassment and victimisation in services and public functions; premises; work; education; associations, and transport.

- Changing the definition of gender reassignment, by removing the requirement for medical supervision.

- Levelling up protection for people discriminated against because they are perceived to have, or are associated with someone who has, a protected characteristic, so providing new protection for people like carers.

- Clearer protection for breastfeeding mothers.

- Applying the European definition of indirect discrimination to all protected characteristics.

- Extending protection from indirect discrimination to disability.

- Introducing a new concept of 'discrimination arising from disability', to replace protection under previous legislation lost as a result of a legal judgment.

- Applying the detriment model to victimisation protection (aligning with the approach in employment law).

- Harmonising the thresholds for the duty to make reasonable adjustments for disabled people.

- Extending protection from third party harassment to all protected characteristics.

- Making it more difficult for disabled people to be unfairly screened out when applying for jobs, by restricting the circumstances in which employers can ask job applicants questions about disability or health.

- Allowing claims for direct gender pay discrimination where there is no actual comparator.

- Making pay secrecy clauses unenforceable.

The Equality Act 2010

Due to the Equality Act being new it is necessary to review the legislation that has gone before it. This is important for two reasons. First because this is currently the best source of information to help interpret the meaning of the legislation. Second because the Equality Act sought to 'harmonise discrimination law, and to strengthen the law to support progress on equality'. So whilst the legislation is new, and introduces some new provisions, it does not seek to consign to history what has gone before. The principles of these are still pertinent. The previous legislation where relevant is covered in Chapter 6 – Ongoing employment.

1. Protected characteristics

The Equality Act effectively consolidates all the previous equality legislation and aims to bring consistency into the definitions and terms. However it also introduces some new concepts, the most notable of these being **'protected characteristics'**:

- Age
- Disability
- Gender reassignment
- Marriage and civil partnership
- Pregnancy and maternity
- Race
- Religion or belief
- Sex
- Sexual orientation

These 'characteristics' are protected by the provisions contained in the rest of the Act.

Age – see Chapter 6 Ongoing employment

The legislation concerning age discrimination is unchanged. However the Act does allow it a unique characteristic; it allows employers to justify direct discrimination if the employer can demonstrate that it is a proportionate means of meeting a legitimate aim.

The Act allows employers to have an employer justified retirement age (EJRA) as the old Default Retirement Age (DRA) was phased out over a transitional period running until 30 September 2011. This means that the last notice of retirement under the old scheme could be given up to 5 April 2011.

Disability

Disability is subject to a new definition and other changes.

The Act does not give specific examples of what would be considered a disability. Under the Act, a person is disabled if they have a physical or mental impairment which has a substantial and long term adverse effect on their ability to carry out normal day-to-day activities.

The meaning of 'impairment' here is where day-to-day activities are affected, for example, mobility, manual dexterity, physical co-ordination, continence, lifting, carrying or otherwise moving everyday objects, concentration, vision, speech, learning/understanding and perception of danger.

Gender reassignment

The Act provides protection for transsexual people and the term transsexual person is given new definition. A transsexual person is someone who proposes to, starts or has completed a process to change his or her gender. The Act also **no longer** has the requirement for the person to be **under medical supervision** to be protected.

The Act also provides protection for a person in the following circumstances.

A person who was born physically female decides to spend the rest of her life as a man. He starts and continues to live as a man. He decides not to seek medical advice as he successfully 'passes' as a man without the need for any medical intervention. He would have the protected characteristic of gender reassignment for the purposes of the Act.

It is discrimination to treat transsexual people less favourably for being absent from work because they propose to undergo, are undergoing or have undergone gender reassignment, than they would be treated if they were absent because they were ill or injured.

Transgender people such as cross dressers, who are not transsexual because they do not intend to live permanently in the gender opposite to their birth sex, are not protected by the Act.

Marriage and civil partnership – see Chapter 6 Ongoing employment

There is no change in this category.

Pregnancy and maternity – see Chapter 5 Statutory benefits

There is effectively no change to this category. During any statutory maternity leave, a woman is protected against discrimination on the grounds of pregnancy and maternity. During this period, pregnancy and maternity discrimination cannot be treated as sex discrimination as it has been acknowledged that pregnancy is a unique condition.

In cases of direct discrimination because of pregnancy or maternity, the test is whether the treatment is **unfavourable** rather than less favourable. Unlike direct and indirect discrimination, this form of discrimination does not require the use of a comparator to establish less favourable treatment.

Race – see Chapter 6 Ongoing employment

There is effectively no change to this category. 'Race' includes colour, nationality and ethnic or national origins. A racial group could be 'black Britons' which would encompass those people who are both black and who are British citizens.

Religion or belief – see Chapter 6 Ongoing employment

There is effectively no change to this category. In the Equality Act, religion includes any religion. It also includes a lack of religion, in other words employees or jobseekers are protected if they do not follow a certain religion or have no religion at all. Additionally, a religion must have a clear structure and belief system. Belief means any religious or philosophical belief or a lack of such belief.

A philosophical belief must be a genuinely held 'belief and not an opinion or viewpoint based on the present state of information available; be a belief as to a weighty and substantial aspect of human life and behaviour; attain a certain level of cogency, seriousness, cohesion and importance; and be worthy of respect in a democratic society, compatible with human dignity and not conflict with the fundamental rights of others'.

Denominations or sects within a religion can be considered a protected religion or religious belief. Humanism is a protected philosophical belief but political beliefs would not be protected. Discrimination because of religion or belief can occur even where both the discriminator and recipient are of the same religion or belief.

Sex – see Chapter 6 Ongoing employment

There is no change in this category.

Sexual orientation – see Chapter 6 Ongoing employment

There is no change in this category.

2. Prohibited conduct

There were no single definitions of direct and indirect discrimination under previous legislation. These have been defined and the definition of harassment has also been clarified.

Direct discrimination

Direct discrimination occurs when someone is treated less favourably than another person because of a protected characteristic they have or are thought to have, or because they associate with someone who has a protected characteristic.

This definition of direct discrimination applies to all protected characteristics. In relation to the protected characteristic of age, direct discrimination can be justified if it is a proportionate means of achieving a legitimate aim.

Discrimination arising from disability

The Act includes a new protection from 'discrimination arising from disability'. This states that it is discrimination to treat a disabled person unfavourably because of something connected with their disability (eg the need to take long breaks). In such cases the reason for the treatment does not matter, the question is whether the disabled person has been treated unfavourably because of something arising in consequence of their disability.

Unlike direct and indirect discrimination, discrimination arising from disability does not require the use of a comparator to establish unfavourable treatment. It is only necessary to demonstrate that the unfavourable treatment is because of the something arising as a consequence of their disability.

It is, however, possible to justify such treatment if it can be shown to be a proportionate means of achieving a legitimate aim. For this type of discrimination to occur, the employer or other person must know, or reasonably be expected to know, that the disabled person has a disability.

There is no change in the Act concerning the duty on the employer to make reasonable adjustments for staff to help them overcome any disadvantage of their disability. The protections of direct and indirect discrimination continue to apply.

Associative discrimination

This is direct discrimination against someone because they associate with another person who possesses a protected characteristic. Prior to the Act this already applied to race, religion or belief and sexual orientation. The Act extended this to cover age, disability, gender reassignment and sex. However associative discrimination does not include marital status or civil partnership. This is because those protected characteristics are outside the scope of European discrimination legislation.

Perceptive discrimination

This is direct discrimination against an individual because others think they possess a particular protected characteristic, even if they do not possess the characteristic.

Discrimination by perception was previously prohibited on grounds of sexual orientation, age, religion or belief or on racial grounds. However this is now extended to include sex, gender reassignment and disability discrimination.

As with associative discrimination the protected characteristic of marital status or civil partnership is not covered.

Indirect discrimination

Indirect discrimination is where a provision, criterion or practice is applied to all employees and those with a particular protected characteristic are placed at a disadvantage. It is the phrase 'provision, criterion or practice' which is important here. It can be interpreted to mean any formal or informal policies, rules, customs and practices, arrangements, criteria, qualifications or provisions.

Indirect discrimination already applied to age, race, religion or belief, sex, sexual orientation and marriage and civil partnership. The Act extends the cover to disability and gender reassignment.

If the provision, criterion or practice cannot be justified as 'a proportionate means of achieving a legitimate aim', it will be unlawful. Being proportionate is interpreted as being fair and reasonable, including demonstrating the consideration of 'less discriminatory' alternatives to any decision being made.

It should be noted though that indirect discrimination does not include maternity or pregnancy. However a pregnant woman who is adversely affected by a provision, criterion or practice may be able to bring a claim of indirect sex discrimination.

Harassment

The Equality Act identifies and prohibits three types of harassment.

A. Involves unwanted conduct which is related to a relevant characteristic and has the purpose or effect of creating an intimidating, hostile, degrading, humiliating or offensive environment for the complainant or of violating the complainant's dignity.

B. Sexual harassment which is unwanted conduct of a sexual nature where this has the same purpose or effect as the first type of harassment.

C. Treating someone favourably because he or she has either submitted to or rejected sexual harassment, or harassment related to sex or gender reassignment.

Harassment applies to all protected characteristics except for pregnancy and maternity and marriage and civil partnership.

The main change from the previous legislation is that unwanted conduct can be just 'related to' the protected characteristic. Therefore the Act will protect someone who associates with a person who has the protected characteristic.

A. Unwanted conduct

The unwanted conduct can include any kind of behaviour, including spoken language or written words or the portrayal of imagery, gestures or conducting practical jokes affecting a person's surroundings. The conduct does not have to be directed at the person, it can include creating an environment that has the overall effect.

Protection is also provided where someone is subjected to harassment related to a protected characteristic even where it is **known** that they do not have that characteristic.

B. Sexual harassment

Sexual harassment occurs when a person engages in any unwanted verbal, non-verbal or physical conduct of a sexual nature which has the purpose or effect of:

- Violating an individual's dignity; or
- Creating an intimidating, hostile, degrading, humiliating or offensive environment for that individual.

The unwanted conduct includes sexual advances, touching, sexual jokes, displaying pornographic photographs or drawings or sending emails with material of a sexual nature. The legislation is not limited to people of the opposite sex but equally applies to incidents of people of the same sex.

C. Less favourable treatment for rejecting or submitting to unwanted conduct

The third type of harassment occurs when someone is treated less favourably because they have submitted to or rejected:

- Unwanted conduct related to sex or gender reassignment as described above or
- Conduct of a sexual nature, as described above.

Third party harassment

Employers may be liable for harassment of their employees by third parties, such as customers and clients, where:

- An employee has been harassed on **at least two** occasions (whether by the same person or different people), and
- The employer is aware harassment has taken place but fails to take reasonably practicable steps to prevent it happening again.

Third party harassment already applies to sex. It has now been extended to cover age, disability, gender reassignment, race, religion or belief and sexual orientation.

Victimisation

Victimisation arises when the employer subjects the employee to a detriment because the employee has done a protected act or because the employer believes that the employee has done or may do a protected act in the future. 'Protected acts' in this context means supporting or raising a grievance under the Equality Act. So if an employee makes a complaint under the Act, they must not suffer a detriment as a result. Detriment will include any actions which the employee reasonably considers changes their position for the worse or put them at a disadvantage. Only an individual can claim for victimisation.

A person making a victimisation claim no longer requires a showing of 'less favourable treatment' in comparison to someone who has not made or supported a discrimination claim.

An employee is not protected from victimisation if they have maliciously made or supported an untrue complaint.

Combined discrimination: dual characteristics

The Equality Act introduces the new claim of combined discrimination. This occurs when an employee is treated less favourably because of a combination of two protected characteristics. The protected characteristics which may be combined are age, disability, gender reassignment, race, religion or belief, sex and sexual orientation.

In order to bring a claim for combined discrimination, each characteristic does not have to be able to stand scrutiny as a claim in it own right, indeed a person can bring a combined claim and a direct discrimination claim.

For combined discrimination, disability is treated as a single characteristic, consequently someone with a combination of disabilities would not be able to rely on these for a combined discrimination claim.

Positive action

The new provision allows an employer to take positive action where they reasonably think that:

- People who share a protected characteristic suffer a disadvantage connected to that characteristic;
- People who share a protected characteristic have needs that are different from the needs of people who do not share it; or
- Participation in an activity by people who share a protected characteristic is disproportionately low.

Employers may take action to achieve one of three legitimate aims, directly corresponding to the three situations described above:

- Enabling or encouraging people to overcome or minimise disadvantage
- Meeting different needs
- Enabling or encouraging participation

Positive action means providing training or support in development to enable the individual to overcome their disadvantage. The action that the employer takes should be proportionate to allow the individual to overcome that disadvantage or to encourage participation.

Positive action is not a requirement, the legislation simply says that it is not prohibited. Any employer using positive action will need to be able to demonstrate that there is good reason for the action, for example under-representation, and that their action is 'proportionate'.

The only exceptions to this are disability and age where discrimination can be justified in limited circumstances.

The steps an employer takes will be reasonable if there were no further reasonably practicable steps they could have taken.

Employees will be personally liable for unlawful acts which they commit during the course of employment where the employer is also liable. Employees may be liable for their actions even when their employer is able to rely successfully on the 'reasonable steps' defence.

3. Recruitment and promotion

The Act allows positive discrimination in situations of recruitment and promotion purposes. They apply where two candidates are equally qualified for the role and the situation is balanced. In such circumstances the employer may prefer the candidate with the protected characteristic. This is not a requirement however the provision allows for the employer to take such action.

To recruit a less well-qualified candidate from an under-represented group will remain unlawful. The emphasis on this provision is that the candidates are as equally qualified as one another.

Liability of employers

An employer will be held liable for the actions of their employee during their employment, whether or not they knew the employee was engaged in the action. However where the employer has taken all reasonable steps to prevent such acts, they will not be liable for unlawful acts committed by their employees.

The steps an employer takes will be reasonable if there were no further reasonably practicable steps they could have taken.

Employees will be personally liable for unlawful acts which they commit during the course of employment where the employer is also liable. Employees may be liable for their actions even when their employer is able to rely successfully on the 'reasonable steps' defence.

The Equality and Human Rights Commission provide a useful 'Guidance for employers about their rights under the Equality Act 2010'.
www.equalityhumanrights.com

ACAS also publish the 'The Equality Act – What's new for employers?' guide.
www.acas.org.uk

3 Recruitment and selection

3.1 Avoiding discrimination during the recruitment and selection process

Ensuring that discrimination does not enter the process is critical in effectively managing the employment relationship. Care must be taken from the beginning with recruitment/selection right through to termination of contract. Regarding the 'protected characteristics' and prohibited conduct, job applicants, not just employees, may make claims to the Employment Tribunal. Former employees can claim that discrimination has taken place after the employment has ended (for example, in references).

While allegations of discrimination can arise at any stage in the employment relationship, the early stages of recruitment and selection are particularly prone to pitfalls. These can often be as a result of the subjective methods of selection adopted by managers. To overcome the risk of accusations of subjectivity an objective approach should be taken with setting the job criteria, treatment of candidates, questions asked, short listing criteria and any tests undertaken.

Applications regardless of any characteristic, pregnancy, maternity leave, union membership or age etc should be processed in exactly the same way. Careful records of interviews should be kept, where practicable, showing why applicants were or were not appointed.

3.2 Arrangements for recruitment and selection

For many employers the recruitment process can take a number of approaches from the highly informal to the highly formal. The risk is that discrimination can occur at any point, however the main areas of risk are:

- Informal methods of recruitment
- Job descriptions, person specifications and competency frameworks
- Selection criteria
- Job advertisements
- Application forms
- Interviews
- Testing

3.3 Informal methods of recruitment

This is potentially one of the most discriminatory employment practices. This method can include:

(i) Recruitment by 'word of mouth' from friends and families of existing employees

(ii) The supply by a trade union of job applicants by use of a 'list' or 'word of mouth'

(iii) Filling vacancies through unsolicited letters from applicants

(iv) Recruitment by internal appointments or transfers

The primary risk with 'word of mouth' is that if the workforce consists predominantly of one sex or race this method of recruitment prevents members of the other sex or race from applying. These informal 'networks' are likely to exclude women, ethnic minorities, and the disabled, and their use is likely to result in imbalances in the composition of the workforce.

It should be emphasised that not all of the above methods are unjustifiable by employers. For example, a small employer may rely on an unsolicited application when filling a single post. For employers of all sizes internal appointments may be perfectly justifiable when 'ring-fencing' vacancies in a redundancy exercise or when attempting to provide internal career paths to retain good calibre staff. But, employers must be careful not to allow these methods to become standard for all vacancies, and to justify them on sound 'business' grounds.

The Equality and Human Rights Commission (EHRC)

The EHRC replaced the former Commission for Racial Equality, the Equal Opportunities Commission and the Disability Rights Commission. Launched on 1 October 2007, broadly, the EHRC:

(a) Promotes equal opportunities and anti-discrimination policy

(b) Keeps the legislation concerning discrimination under review, and advises the government on developing the law

(c) Works with employers, service providers and organisations to develop best practice

(d) Conducts enquiries into alleged discrimination

(e) Where necessary uses their powers to enforce the law

(f) Undertakes research and publishes advice and guidance

(g) Issues Codes of Practice

The EHRC will assist some applicants in Employment Tribunal proceedings with advice or legal representation.

www.equalityhumanrights.com

EHRC guidance on recruitment

It is unlawful for an employer to discriminate against a candidate for a job because of their age, disability, race, religion or belief, sexual orientation or gender in any part of the recruitment process – in job descriptions, person specifications, application forms, during interviews, in tests, or in shortlisting.

For example, application forms should not ask for details that are not relevant to the job, such as country of birth or sexual orientation (except where such questions are contained in monitoring forms that are separated from application forms before assessment). During interviews, questions about a woman's plans for starting a family, or asking an applicant whether they think that they will 'fit in' with the organisation, may also be evidence of discrimination.

However, an employer can ask if the person has a disability so they can make special arrangements for them to attend an interview.

Evidence of discrimination

There is no obligation on an employer to show that they have selected the best candidate for the job. However, all employers are recommended to keep records that allow them, if challenged, to justify their decisions to select particular candidates and reject others. The former Commission for Racial Equality's code of practice on employment contains useful information on this and other areas, which may also be relevant to issues other than race.

Employers need to be able to show that each selection is based on objective evidence of a person's ability to do the job satisfactorily, and not on assumptions or prejudices about race, gender, disability, sexual orientation, religion or belief, or age. An employer is unlikely to say that they rejected the person for these reasons. But if the person believes there is evidence of discrimination, they may be able to make a case.

3.4 Job descriptions, person specifications and competency frameworks

Job descriptions and person specifications should be drafted using factual, objectively gathered information. Likewise competency frameworks should be drafted in a similar fashion ensuring that any cultural bias is involved.

Qualifications and personal attributes sought in candidates should be appropriate to the job, otherwise direct discrimination could result. For example, a good standard of English for a manual or unskilled/semi-skilled job could discriminate against those with English as a second language. Generally speaking, the requirement for higher qualifications such as a degree, is not discriminatory.

The sensible employer will not use 'sexually connotated' job titles. As the job description and person specification are often subsequently used to create advertisements and selection criteria, avoiding these at the start reduces future risk. Examples of these are storeman becomes storekeeper; cameraman becomes camera operator.

3.5 Job advertisements

It is unlawful to advertise a job vacancy in a way which indicates the job is only available to members of one group based on sex, racial origin, age, disability, marital status, religion/belief, and sexual orientation.

Just as with the job descriptions and person specifications the emphasis should be on skills, competencies and relevant experience. Consequently advertisements should avoid age limits or ranges, and the use of words that imply age for example 'young' or 'mature'. It can argued that words such as 'bright' and 'lively' imply an intention to discriminate by recruiting younger people, just as 'mature', and 'dependable' imply a preference for older workers.

Placing a job advertisement in a certain publication could amount to indirect discrimination, for example advertising a job in a magazine aimed at young people may constitute discrimination on grounds of age. Additionally the inclusion of photographs of only one group could also lead people to conclude that only one type of applicant is being sought.

Where a role requires a particular ability, the advertisement should focus on the requirement for example 'a very high standard of written and spoken English', or, alternatively, 'fluent English', rather than wording which invites applicants only who speak English *as their mother tongue*. This phraseology discriminates indirectly against people who speak English fluently, but not as their first language.

If the employer is using a recruitment advertising agency the agency should be able to provide advice on copy and visual work that will achieve the commercial objectives and avoid infringing anti-discrimination legislation.

Employment and recruitment agencies

Employment agencies will not avoid liability under the anti-discrimination statutes because they simply relied on a statement by the employer that an advertisement was not unlawful. Such a reliance must be reasonable, so where it is clear and obvious that an advertisement is discriminatory the agency should query it, and if necessary refuse to handle the advertisement unless it is amended. The same process should be applied where instructions are received from the employer, for example 'do not put any women forward for interview'.

3.6 Selection criteria

The criteria chosen should be clear, objective, fair and relevant. Proper job analysis and an objective assessment of higher performing employees should proceed the drawing-up of selection criteria. Subjective 'gut feelings' about whether people will 'fit in' or not should definitely be avoided.

Conditions or requirements which may have a disproportionate effect on one sex, or racial group, or those with disabilities should be avoided. It is possible that applying unnecessary height requirements (eg, no applicants under 5 foot 6 inches (1.7 metres), or no applicants over 5 feet 6 inches (1.7 metres) could indirectly discriminate, in the first example against women, and in the second example against men.

In the Equality Act the general principle is that health-related inquiries are not permitted until a job offer has been made. However the recruiter is allowed to ask questions to establish whether the candidate is able to perform the tasks and functions 'intrinsic' to the work. This would allow questions relating to a person's ability, for example, to lift and carry where that would be necessary for the job, but would not permit questions about general impairments, for example past mental illness. It should not be overlooked that the employer still has a duty regarding reasonable adjustments.

3.7 Application forms

Questions on the application form should not suggest that the employer will take into account any factors which could amount to discrimination. Only questions that are relevant to the job should be asked. If the information required is justifiable and relevant, it must be asked for all applicants regardless of sex, racial origin, age, disability, marital status, religion/belief, and sexual orientation.

It is recommended that questions on marital status, responsibility for children and domestic obligations are not included. If it is necessary to obtain information relating to the applicant's family for example, for pension purposes, these questions should be asked **after** the successful applicant has been selected.

Where employers are monitoring information such as sex, racial origin, age, disability, marital status, religion/belief, and sexual orientation etc then this should be included on a tear-off slip which is removed before those involved in the selection process review the application form. The existence of monitoring or its absence may be taken into account in tribunal proceedings.

Employers who require applicants for certain types of job to demonstrate irrelevant and unnecessary skills may indirectly discriminate.

The Equality Act 2010 makes it **unlawful to ask health questions** – including questions about disability – of any job applicants **prior** to making a job offer. However there are exceptions. Health questions will still be allowed where:

- The employer is establishing whether the applicant will be able to comply with a requirement to undergo an assessment or establishing whether a duty to make reasonable adjustments will apply

- The employer is establishing whether the applicant will be able to carry out a function that is intrinsic to the work concerned

- The employer is monitoring diversity in the range of persons applying for work

- The disability is a genuine occupational qualification

It also creates a presumption of direct discrimination on grounds of disability if an employer relies on the reply to a health-related inquiry.

3.8 Interviews

Research studies over a number of years have demonstrated that the interview as a predictive device is an extremely fallible method. Nevertheless, they have also shown that **trained interviewers** produce better results than untrained interviewers and are less susceptible to **bias** and **stereotyped** perceptions. No interviewer is totally free from bias but they should realise this and attempt to minimise any tendency towards their personal preferences.

The Equality Act allows that where an employer has taken all reasonable steps to prevent employees from discriminating against people, they may not be liable for unlawful acts committed by their employees.

To achieve selecting the 'best' candidate the employer should:

- Focus on the skills, abilities, competencies, potential and the enthusiasm of candidates when making shortlists and selection decisions.

- Ensure interviewers are trained to avoid age-related bias in questioning and suppress any stereotypes of older (or younger) persons they hold; indeed, training on equal opportunities should include age diversity, and should help them to ask appropriate, probing questions.

- Use, wherever possible, a mixed age interviewing panel.

- Finally, select on merit, based on the application of each candidate and their individual performance during the selection process.

Model guidance for interviewers

Selection panels or individual interviewers must be particularly careful not to treat people less favourably based wholly or partly on their sex, race, or age etc. Candidates must be assessed solely on their qualifications, relevant knowledge, experience and personal qualities relevant to the job. Identical standards should apply in assessing all candidates based entirely on the individual's suitability for appointment. Disabled candidates should be assessed equally with all others after **reasonable adjustments** have been taken into account. Equally, all candidates should be assessed on the basis of the same job related criteria regardless of marital status and domestic responsibilities.

Any criteria adopted for the assessment of candidates should not discriminate indirectly against women, eg, length of experience in particular types of work which women may not have had because their working lives have been interrupted by periods of domestic responsibility. Subtle and subconscious discrimination can result from general assumptions being made about women's capabilities, characteristics and motivation, for example, a preconception about their ability to supervise men.

When considering candidates for future potential and promotion ability, interviewers should avoid unwarranted assumptions about the potential of men or women or their motivation to advance in the organisation. Each individual's potential should be assessed on the same objective criteria, and should not be influenced by stereotypical preconceptions.

If the decision not to appoint a candidate was based upon answers to these kinds of questions, then the employer may have discriminated unlawfully. If the question is not intended to influence the interviewer(s) decision in any way, then there is no point in asking for this information as it will lead applicants to **suspect** the employer of having an intention to discriminate, which in turn could lead to a complaint of unlawful discrimination. Questions which are relevant to the job – for example, about the candidate's ability to undertake shift work – should be asked of both men and women. All questions should be justified.

In summary, the following type of questions must be avoided:

- Marital status and marriage intentions
- Children/other dependants and child-care arrangements
- Future family intentions/traditional male/female role models
- Sexual preferences
- Religion (except in special religious establishments)
- Personal beliefs that are not connected with the work in question
- Ethnic origins

It is worth noting that the candidate cannot take the prospective employer to an Employment Tribunal on the basis of asking questions that are prohibited. However, if the interviewer does ask such questions and does not employ the candidate, should that person bring a claim, the burden of proof will be on the employer to demonstrate that they had not acted in a discriminatory manner.

It is also worth noting that concerning questions on disability and health, a candidate cannot complain to an Employment Tribunal but they can complain to the Equality and Human Rights Commission.

3.9 Selection tests

Selection tests are normally used in recruitment to measure the attitudes, abilities and interests of job applicants and achieve a profile of their personality to achieve a 'best fit'. Tests of personality are more properly referred to as 'personality questionnaires'. The ability tests include measuring literacy, numerical reasoning, spatial awareness and trainability. If tests are carefully chosen, professionally designed and properly used by trained administrators they can minimise bias in the selection process and be a valuable tool for employers in making recruitment decisions. Their key strength is bringing enhanced **validity, objectivity** and **reliability** to the selection process.

Irrelevant questions in tests should be avoided, particularly if they are about matters which may be unfamiliar to applicants from different ethnic backgrounds, for example, questions which assume a knowledge of English history. This important characteristic of tests is known as being **'culture fair'**.

Other examples of unfairness would be using national or regional colloquialisms which might confuse people who have not spent many years living in the UK.

Information should be collected on the way that men and women and members of different racial groups perform in comparison to each other. This is known as **'norm referencing'**. For example, if the test to be used is to select personnel managers it is inappropriate to use a test norm referenced with engineers. This process should assist employers to assess whether the tests adversely affect certain groups.

3.10 Other issues relating to recruitment

In Chapter 3 – Information – there is a section on employee information in relation to recruitment and selection. This includes:

- The right of foreign persons to work in the UK
- Information relating to criminal convictions including Criminal Record Bureau checks
- Monitoring – information relating to equality in the workplace

Pre-employment health checks

As described in the section regarding application forms an employer is prohibited from asking health related questions until the candidate has been offered a job or is in a pool of successful candidates. The exceptions to this were outlined earlier in section 3.7.

Appointment and contracts of employment

1 Introduction

The contract of employment is probably the example of a contract that most people are familiar with. The contract is at the heart of the employment relationship and sets out the rights and obligations of both the employer *and* employee. This chapter looks at the principles of law of the contract and the popular clauses, and associated pitfalls, that are usually incorporated.

1.1 A binding contract

Despite the growth in the employment law field, the common law principles of contract continue to provide the basis of the employment relationship. The relationship between the employer and employee is, like all contracts, in principle, subject to the general contractual rules.

Otto-Kahn-Freund once stated that the contract of employment was 'the cornerstone of the edifice of the employment relationship'. Whereas the common law rules of the contract of employment can be traced back to the 19th century, individual **statutory** employment protection only developed significantly from 1963 (with the Contracts of Employment Act). Today most rights and obligations in the employment relationship are determined by legislation. However the common law rules of contract continue to exert a very strong influence on that relationship.

Generally speaking, there are no special formalities required for entry into a contract of employment. An employment contract, with a few exceptions may be written, oral, implied or a mixture of all three. There are clearly advantages in having a written contract; moreover, the law requires that most employees are entitled to receive a **written statement of main terms and conditions** relating to their employment. However, it is important not to confuse the contract with the written statement.

2 Key elements for a binding contract to be formed

2.1 Key elements which must be present

Formalities of the contract (Requirements for a valid contract)

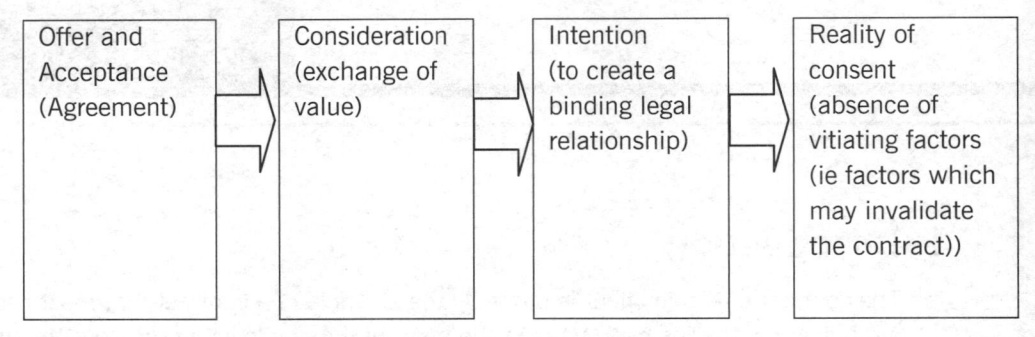

Offer and Acceptance (Agreement)	Consideration (exchange of value)	Intention (to create a binding legal relationship)	Reality of consent (absence of vitiating factors (ie factors which may invalidate the contract))

2.2 Agreement – offer and acceptance

There must be an **agreement** between the parties consisting of a **definite offer** (of a job) and an **unconditional acceptance** of that offer (by the job candidate) for a contract to be formed.

Since a contract does not have to be in writing, if a verbal offer of employment is made at the job interview and accepted, a contract will normally have been concluded at that point; and, therefore anything stated in the interview may be used to interpret the contract terms or to constitute the express terms of the contract itself. It is therefore essential that at the interview stage the prospective employee is given a totally accurate picture of the terms and conditions under which s/he will be engaged. It is both sensible and good practice for an employer to take accurate notes of job interviews and what is subsequently offered to the successful job candidate. If there is any subsequent conflict between verbal and written statements the latter will usually prevail, but not if the latter does not state the true intention of the parties.

A job advertisement does not in law constitute an offer; however, statements in the advertisement may be classified as legal representations. False representations which **induce a contract** constitute a misrepresentation and the person misled could seek a legal remedy such as damages. Thus, an employee who enters into a contract of employment as a result of a false statement made in the job advertisement may be able to claim damages from the employer. In some circumstances the courts have held that a statement in the job advertisement becomes a term of the contract and that non-compliance with such a term is a breach of contract.

The offer of employment will usually be made after consideration of a CV or an application form which has been completed by the prospective employee. The employee has **no duty** to volunteer information which is **not** requested by the employer in the recruitment process. Even if the employee is deliberately dishonest this will **not necessarily** render any subsequent dismissal based upon the untruth as fair.

A conditional offer may or may not lead to a contract being formed.

It is advisable to apply a time limit as to how long the offer of employment is open. Without a time scale confusion can occur when the candidate has not accepted the position, yet to unilaterally withdraw the offer would be deemed as unreasonable given no timescale was ever provided.

2.3 Consideration

Each party to the agreement must provide **consideration** (ie something of value). In a contract of employment the consideration is the promise to pay wages on the part of the employer, and the promise to provide services, ie, to work on the part of the employee.

2.4 Intention to create a legal relationship

The parties must **intend to create a legal relationship** (a legally binding agreement). The tribunal or courts will normally presume that there is such an intention unless it can be proved otherwise.

The contract may be formed through explicit or implicit means. Explicit is where the employee returns the contract signed as requested. Implicit acceptance is where the employee does not return the paperwork yet attends work on the day indicated during the offer process. Assuming that they start work without being given any indication to the contrary, both parties will be considered to have entered into the contract. Should the latter be the case it is important to realise that a **written statement** of the **principal terms of employment** must be supplied to any person who is employed for at least one month or more within two months of commencement of employment (see section 6.2).

Once the contract has been formed the courts or tribunals will enforce it immediately in the absence of **vitiating factors**, that is, any factor which in law will affect the validity of the contract. Thus, where an offer of employment has been made and accepted, if the employer changes their mind before the date on which the employee has agreed to commence work they must terminate the contract in accordance with the agreed terms, ie, they must give the employee the required notice or payment in lieu even though the employee has never carried out any work for the employer.

2.5 Vitiating factors

Vitiating factors may affect the validity of the contract. These factors are defects in the contract, which may make the contract void (invalid), voidable (avoidable by the person misled) or unenforceable in the courts. Vitiating factors include **duress, misrepresentation**, and (in particular in relation to the employment contract) **illegality**.

The courts will not normally enforce an illegal contract, and this aspect of the common law has been relied upon in a number of unfair dismissal cases to prevent a party to a contract tainted by illegality from enforcing a right under that contract. In particular consideration will be given not to whether the employee knew of or participated in the illegality, but, rather whether he or she obtained a personal advantage from the illegality.

The common law doctrine of **restraint of trade** provides a further example of illegality in contract. This doctrine was established to stop individuals or bodies (including employers or unions) from preventing free trade or business. Restraint **covenants** in employment contracts are designed to restrict ex-employees from working in, or setting up in, a competing business or soliciting ex-customers. These clauses are *prima facie* void. Such clauses may, however, be valid under the test of **reasonableness**.

In reaching conclusions on these matters, the courts have recognised **two** different principles:

(a) In the course of employment, in fact as an essential element in the employee relationship – an employee will develop **skills** which the individual can use later in other employment. The courts will, as a matter of principle, resist curtailing this future use.

(b) The second principle is different because there is **specific knowledge of the employer's business** and in particular, confidential information relating to customers or trade secrets (such as contact numbers, customer preferences or special ingredients or formulae). The courts will protect the employer in the latter case.

2.6 Privity of contract

The last issue to consider is that of the doctrine of **privity of contract**. The doctrine states that only parties to the contract may sue or be sued on the contract. Thus, an employee will not be able to force the employer to comply with the provisions of a collective agreement made between the employer and a trade union unless the provisions are **incorporated** into the employee's contract.

3 Who is an employee?

For both individuals and employers, **employment status** is critically important. For individuals the difference in status between being an **'employee'** and a **'worker'** is that, as an employee they are protected by a wide range of employment protection legislation.

Employees also have rights and obligations in respect of non-statutory terms of the contract of employment, such as the implied terms.

For their part, employers must fulfil responsibilities in respect of deducting tax and National Insurance contributions, and upholding a range of statutory obligations.

The UK labour market has seen a growth in so-called 'atypical' employment since 1980. This has largely been associated with different forms of flexibility, particularly numerical, temporal and distanced modes of flexibility. The decline in full-time employees with 'open-ended' contracts of service (sometimes referred to as 'permanent' contracts of employment) has been partly matched by different forms of part-time, casual and temporary employment, but also by individuals who are not hired as employees at all but as self-employed 'workers' on *contracts for services*, eg, consultants, contractors, agency staff and those on performance-only contracts. It is yet to be seen whether this trend will now be reversed as a stream of legislation, some of it emanating from the EU comes into force, extending statutory employment protection to specified groups of 'workers'. This can be seen by looking at the categories of 'employees' and 'workers' to whom various pieces of legislation extend employment protection.

3.1 Distinctions between status of employee/worker

Significance of being employed on a contract of service.

- Central to the distinction between being employed and self-employed is the 'contract of service' (for employees) and the 'contract for services' (for self-employed workers).

- From a practical employment perspective.

It is necessary to have some clarity as to the position of employee and worker in relation to a number of specific issues, including those in the following table:

Vicarious liability

An employer is vicariously liable for the acts of his or her employees which are carried out 'during the course of their employment'. The employer/organisation is vicariously liable even if it did not instruct, authorise, approve or even know of the act. Liability extends to the negligent, dishonest or mistaken acts of employees even where the employer has instructed that the work be done carefully, honestly or correctly.

The employer will have certain health and safety liabilities and common law liabilities. Otherwise the individual is liable for his or her actions and would be best advised to take-out third party liability insurance.

Employment protection rights

Only employees enjoy the full range of employment protection rights provided by the Employment Rights Act 1996 (these include unfair dismissal, rights to a redundancy payment, not to have unlawful deductions made from pay, to be given a statement of principal terms and conditions). This also extends to (under certain conditions) statutory sick pay and statutory maternity pay and paternity pay. Obligations in tort and under health and safety rules are also placed on employers. Anti-discrimination legislation applies to employees and workers alike. Employers are empowered to restrict certain benefits, such as employee share schemes, profit-related pay and benefits-in-kind to employees with service of more than one year.

Self-employed workers enjoy the protection of the Equality Act 2010, but there are very few other areas of protection. (The anti discrimination legislation does extend to those who 'contract personally to execute any work or labour.')

Since 1998 government policy has been to extend protection to 'workers', ie, National Minimum Wage Act 1998 and the Working Time Regulations 1998.

Illegal contracts

The validity of a contract may be vitiated by illegality. In other words, a contract of employment which is tainted by illegality (and is known and understood by both parties to be tainted) cannot be enforced. This means that because the individual is not employed on a contract of service s/he cannot claim employment protection rights. Tribunals will refuse to hear such claims.

Illegality of contract may affect the rights of both parties, but it does not change the worker's status.

Taxation

Employees are taxed under Schedule E as part of pay-as-you-earn (PAYE) scheme for 'emoluments from any office or employment'. The employer must have arrangements to make these deductions and for trade union subscriptions to be collected by the 'check-off' system.

The self-employed are taxed under Schedule D on 'profits and gains' from any trade, profession or vocation and are generally assessed (by self-assessment) on a yearly basis. There is a less rigorous regime for determining expenses. However, this has become less attractive to the individual because HM Revenue and Customs (HMRC) requires the 'self employed' to pay estimated tax 'on account' before the actual assessment takes place.

It should be noted that the tax schedule that someone is administered under is not an indication of their employment status as HMRC applies different legislation to assess taxation and National Insurance liability.

4 How can employment status be determined?

Despite the importance of this question, there is no satisfactory statutory test or definition. The Employment Rights Act 1996 provided for the first time a definition of an employee: '...an individual who has entered into or works under a contract of employment, which means a contract of service or apprenticeship'.

This definition provides little guidance, so to determine employment status in law it has been necessary to rely on a number of **tests** developed by the courts over several decades. But no one single test is persuasive. As Lord Denning MR stated:

'...it is often easy to recognise a contract of service when you see it, but difficult to say where it lies'.

This has become known colloquially as the 'elephant test' – in other words you know one when you see it, but it is difficult to describe!

Definitions of a 'worker' are by comparison relatively common being found in the Trade Union and Labour Relations (Consolidation) Act 1992 (s, 296), and the Employment Relations Act 1999 (s, 13).

4.1 The test of control

This test was one of the first to be developed in the nineteenth century. It requires an examination of the extent and degree of control which the employer has over the individual. Not only what the individual does but the manner and method in which they do it is important. The greater the evidence that the individual takes orders from the employer in exactly the same way as other employees, and works to a regime determined by the employer, the greater is the likelihood that the individual will be **an employee**.

4.2 The organisational or integration test

With the changing nature of work giving employees more discretion and autonomy (particularly those working in a professional or highly skilled capacity) it was thought that a broader test to determine the extent that an individual was integrated into the employer's business would be sufficient. The question to be assessed here is whether the individual is essential to the running of the business or ancillary or independent to it, such as performing the role of contractor or consultant. This was increasingly viewed, however, not as a decisive factor, but **one** potential factor in determining an answer.

4.3 The multiple-factor or pragmatic test

Rather than one single test the approach which still retains a high degree of validity is the weighing-up of **all the relevant factors** to determine employment status. It should be noted that no one single factor is decisive in determining the status and indeed not all the factors have to be evident for consideration.

The factors of importance can be ascertained by examining whether:

(a) There is any **mutual obligation** on the employer to provide work and the individual to perform work

(b) The individual or the employer **provides the tools, equipment and premises**

(c) The parties **intended** to be bound by a contract of service

(d) The employee performs exclusive work for the employer

(e) Tax and NI is deducted at source under the PAYE scheme

(f) There is an opportunity for the individual to profit from the performance of the organisation

(g) The individual takes any financial risk, and

(h) The individual has any responsibilities for investment and management.

While the intention is not that an individual 'chooses' their status it is worth considering the merits of being an employee versus being self employed.

(a) (i) Advantages for staff	
Employee contract of service: Security and an 'open-ended' contractual relationship – obligation to offer work and to pay regularly; • Tax and National Insurance deductions handled by employer • A range of employee benefits available; employment protection in respect of a wide range of legislation available • Common law implied terms of the contract provide for a number of protective obligations on the part of the employer • Employer is vicariously liable for the employee's acts and omissions; employer takes responsibility for directing work, and • Eligibility for sick pay, contractual maternity pay, holiday pay and leave.	Self-employment: Choice and flexibility – no ongoing obligations to work for same employer in the same capacity; • Tax benefits (eg, allowances against premises, equipment and facilities, and part-delayed payment of Income tax under self-assessment rules) • Control over own means and methods of work • Can hire others to assist in their work or appoint deputy • Can enjoy a profit from their own work, and • Variable periods and hours of work.
(ii) Disadvantages for staff	
Contract of service: • Obligation to personally regularly perform work for the employer at times set by the employer • Lack of choice and flexibility over type of work • Reduced tax allowances, tax benefits and regular payment of Income tax • Inability to directly profit from their own work (dependent on employer's willingness to give pay rises and bonuses and benefits) and	Self-employed: • Lack of security of work and income • Need to find and secure work on a transitional, assignment basis • Responsibility for carrying-out and completing work • Liability in respect of others – need to obtain third party liability insurance • Absence of sick pay, maternity pay, contractual/statutory paid holidays and contractual/statutory special leave

• Working under the control of others – lack of autonomy.	• Working hours not protected by regulations relating to working time • Limited health and safety protection and • Limited employment protection (anti-discrimination rights the only principal rights available).
(b) (i) Advantages for employers	
Contract of service: • Secured, long-term workforce: opportunity to train, develop and retain a loyal committed workforce – individuals integral to the business • Obligations from employee to work regularly in accordance with the contract and • Opportunity to control the work of the individual.	Self-employed: • Individuals hired on a performance only basis – when assignments completed the individual is no longer needed and leaves • No liability in respect of employment protection rights (other than primarily in anti-discrimination); and workers: working time and minimum wage • Limited liability in respect of third parties • Limited liability in respect of health and safety • Many self-employed require little or no supervision (control) • No obligation to provide ongoing work or pay • Simple pay systems – usually lump sum payments, with no responsibility to deduct tax or National Insurance • No responsibility to pay sick pay, maternity pay or paid holidays or provide special leave

	- The individual can hire their own helpers when additional assistance is required and - The individual may provide all or most of their own tools and equipment.
(ii) Disadvantages for employers	
Contract of service: These are mainly opposite to the advantages shown in (a) (i) above. Overall, there is the cost and time involved in recruitment, pay and training administration. Also: - The cost of industrial relations and HR and other support services – employee overheads and - Ongoing obligations to provide work.	Self-employed: These are mainly opposite to those shown in (a) above. Overall, there is the lack of any permanent employment relationship that has trust, loyalty and commitment at its centre. These factors are often important for establishing and maintaining product and service quality. Also: - The possible high fees of consultants - Lack of control over work – the self-employed worker may leave a job unfinished or in an unsatisfactory condition which may not become apparent until after the assignment has finished and - Because there is no mutual obligation the self-employed may finish the work in-hand before the assignment is satisfactorily completed.

HMRC guidance

The HMRC website provides a useful amount of information on tax and National Insurance including an Employment Status Indicator Tool. (*http://www.hmrc.gov.uk/calcs/esi.htm*)

'As a general guide as to whether a worker is an employee or self-employed; if the answer is 'Yes' to all of the following questions, then the worker is probably an employee:

- Do they have to do the work themselves?
- Can someone tell them at any time what to do, where to carry out the work or when and how to do it?
- Can they work a set amount of hours?
- Can someone move them from task to task?
- Are they paid by the hour, week, or month?
- Can they get overtime pay or bonus payment?

If the answer is 'Yes' to all of the following questions, it will usually mean that the worker is self-employed:

- Can they hire someone to do the work or engage helpers at their own expense?
- Do they risk their own money?
- Do they provide the main items of equipment they need to do their job, not just the small tools that many employees provide for themselves?
- Do they agree to do a job for a fixed price regardless of how long the job may take?
- Can they decide what work to do, how and when to do the work and where to provide the services?
- Do they regularly work for a number of different people?
- Do they have to correct unsatisfactory work in their own time and at their own expense?'

(www.hmrc.gov.uk – Employment status).

5 The terms of the contract

The essence of the contract of employment is in the rights and obligations it confers on the parties. The terms of a contract indicate what the parties **intend**. The terms of a contract of employment may derive from a variety of documents and sources.

5.1 Express terms

These are terms which are agreed (either in writing or orally) between the parties (for example, hours to be worked, level of remuneration, number of days' holiday, etc). Some of the main express terms are considered below in detail.

5.2 Common law implied terms

These are terms which are implied by the courts into the contract to **fill the gaps** left by the absence of express terms (for example, a duty of co-operation between employer and employee). These terms may be implied into all contracts of employment or in an individual contract and are discussed below in detail.

5.3 Works rules

Employers may lay down works or company rules in a handbook. In the public sector they may be called the *Staff Code*. Works rules can either be terms of the contract or merely unilaterally imposed management instructions which have no contractual effect. If a works rule is found not to be a contractual term, the employer is free to change the rules unilaterally at any time. If the employee refuses to operate the initial or changed rule s/he may be in a position where s/he is refusing to obey a *reasonable management order* and may be fairly dismissed. An example might be the organisation's equal opportunities policy which has not been incorporated into individual's contracts of employment.

These rules are sometimes described as being **'collateral'** to the contract. The courts recognise the employer's right to manage and to enforce these rules. This is known as the management prerogative.

5.4 Codes of practice

These provide guidelines to the employer and the employee. They are important, but as stated above are not legally binding upon the parties. However, the codes may be used in evidence in proceedings before a tribunal and if an employer has not followed a code that fact may be taken into consideration by a tribunal when deciding on the outcome of a case.

5.5 Custom and practice

Terms of a contract of employment may sometimes be found in those practices or customs which are applied in a particular industry or organisation. For a custom or practice to become a contractual term it must be:

(a)   Reasonable

(b)   Notorious (ie, well-known)

(c)   Definite (ie, been applied consistently), and

(d)   Have a history (ie, be applied over a period of time – probably years rather than months).

5.6 Statutorily imposed terms

Statutes are a primary source of employment terms, imposing obligations and duties on the parties to the employment contract and placing constraints upon the type and nature of the terms and conditions of employment. The **Employment Rights Act 1996 (s 1)**, for example imposes a duty on the employer to provide a written statement of terms to the employee within two months of the commencement of employment. An example of where statute law **imposed** a term in the contract of every employee was the **Equal Pay Act 1970** (as amended) which has imposed an equality clause so that no employee should be paid less because of their gender.

Unfair Contract Terms Act (UCTA), 1977. For years there has been argument and doubt over the implementation of the UCTA to contracts of employment. By virtue of section 3(1), section 3(2) only applies where one contracting party 'deals as consumer or on the others written standard terms of business'. Section 3(2) prohibits a contracting party from excluding or restricting his or her liability for breach of contract, or from rendering a contractual performance substantially different from that which was reasonably expected of him or her, or rendering no performance at all. However, such a term may be exercisable if it is *'reasonable'*. For reasons of interpretation it has been reasonable to assume contracts of employment do not fall within this ambit of protection.

5.7 Collective agreements

Collective agreements are the product of joint negotiations between unions and employers' associations. They include many terms which will be of importance to the employment relationship such as those relating to pay, hours of work, and so on. A problem can arise however, where an individual employee is not an initial party to the agreement. The **law of privity of contract** will prevent them from enforcing the relevant provisions of the agreement on their own behalf.

An example would be where the employee attempts to force the employer to award a pay rise which has been negotiated under a collective agreement. Unless the relevant provisions of the collective agreement have been **incorporated** into the individual's contract of employment they will be unenforceable. The contract of employment remains a **private** legal agreement between the individual employee and employer.

The provision of a collective agreement may be incorporated into an individual contract either expressly or by implication.

6 Express terms of the contract

6.1 Limited restrictions

The parties have the freedom to negotiate and agree the terms of the contract of employment subject to a number of limited restrictions.

- The employer **cannot restrict** their liability for death or injury caused to their employees by their negligence or the negligence of another of their employees

- Express terms of the contract must **not** infringe the discrimination legislation or other legislation such as the National Minimum Wage Act 1998 and

- No contractual term may attempt to exclude judicial proceedings or the jurisdiction of the courts.

Finally, there are a number of statutes which cannot be contracted-out of by an express term, such as the Public Interest Disclosure Act 1998 or certain parts of the Working Time Regulations 1998.

6.2 Written statement of the financial terms of employment

It is desirable that as many terms as possible are agreed between the parties before entering into the contract and that the terms should be set down clearly in writing. This will ensure certainty and minimise future disputes over the nature and scope of the contract. The **Employment Rights Act 1996** (ERA 1996) provides that a **written statement** of the **principal terms of employment** must be supplied to persons who are employed for at least one month or more within two months of commencement of employment. (This is often referred to as the 'section 1 statement.') This right exists after one month of employment but must be completed by the end of the second month, even if the person's employment has finished by then. This applies to new employees. Existing employees who meet the qualifying criteria will be entitled to receive notification of any **changes** to these specified terms and conditions in the same way, within one month.

The information can be given in instalments in the two month period, provided certain details are included in the 'principal statement'. This information could be placed in one document such as the offer letter. Many employers will attach the principal statement to the offer letter.

For most of the terms, full information must be provided and there is little scope for reference to other sources, eg, work rules. For certain terms – that must be fully stipulated – the ERA 1996 allows reference to another document but only if it is reasonably accessible at the workplace.

For those terms which must be included in the 'principal statement' there is nothing preventing an employer referring to other documentation such as a staff handbook or a summary of the relevant work rules/collective agreements for the details to be set out. Where this information is particularly compendious a summary handbook may be the best option for the employer.

6.3 Statement of terms

Generally, the statement of main terms and conditions is **not** legally binding (the essence of the binding contract usually being the offer letter). However, an employer can choose to make the statement legally binding by clearly indicating this in the offer letter.

The written statement **must** contain the following information.

(a) The **identity** of the parties (ie, their respective names and titles and preferably their addresses).

(b) The **date** on which the employee's continuous **employment began**. This clause is designed to protect the position of employees who have been involved in the takeover of a business. If the continuity of such an employee is not preserved s/he will be able to claim a redundancy; the actual date on which the contract of employment commenced must be included.

(c) The scale or rate of **remuneration** provided to the employee, the method of calculating the remuneration **and** the intervals at which payment is made. (Remuneration should for this purpose include **all** financial-based rewards and incentives).

(d) **Hours of work and normal working hours:** this is of particular importance when calculating redundancy payments and the basic award for unfair dismissal. For the sake of clarity an employer should specify whether overtime is mandatory and thereby part of the normal working hours or whether it is voluntary. (Note that the Working Time Regulations 1998 places restrictions upon the number of hours which can be worked.)

(e) Entitlement to **holiday and holiday pay**. The impact of the Working Time Regulations on this matter is considerable because all employees and workers other than the genuinely self-employed will be entitled to four weeks' paid leave.

(f) Any terms and conditions relating to **incapacity for work** owing to sickness or injury, including any provision for sick pay.

(g) Terms and conditions relating to **pensions** and pension schemes. Where there is a contractual right to benefits under a pension scheme, employers must discharge their duties under the scheme in good faith, and as far as possible ensure that the benefits to which the employee is entitled are forthcoming. In addition, most of the employees' rights under such pension schemes will be protected where the Transfer of Undertakings Regulations apply.

(h) Notification as to whether a **contracting out certificate** is in force. Normally any contractual term which attempts to exclude or limit any part of the Employment Rights Act 1996 or the presentation of a complaint to Employment Tribunal will be void. The exceptions are where there is a waiver clause in a fixed-term contract or where there is a contracting-out certificate in force. The latter will be issued by an ACAS conciliation offer to record a conciliated agreement between two individual parties which excludes further legal action in the Employment Tribunal and only under the statutory provisions under which this was brought or could have been brought. The terms of the agreement are recorded on form COT3.

(i) The **length of notice** to which the employee is entitled (such notice must be at least equal to the statutory requirement).

(j) The employee's **job title or a brief description** of the employee's duties. This is of particular importance in relation to unfair dismissal and redundancy claims. **Note:** For the employer clearly it may be preferable not to make the job description contractually binding.

(k) Where the employment is **temporary**, the period for which it is expected to continue or, if it is for a fixed term, the date when it is to end.

(l) The **place of work** and whether the employee may be expected to work at various places. Again, this may be of importance in relation to unfair dismissal or redundancy claims. Sensible employers will include a mobility clause, but this is subject to limitations.

(m) Any **collective agreements** which may affect the terms of the contract. To avoid having to detail every incorporated collective agreement an employer should:

   (i) Provide a summary

   (ii) Indicate new agreements will be included, eg, 'such as may be agreed from time to time .....'

   (iii) Specify the union negotiation rights/topics and

   (iv) Have those agreements clearly accessible at work

(n) Any procedure applicable to the taking of disciplinary decisions relating to the employee, or to a decision to dismiss the employee. The employee can be referred to an accessible document specifying such a procedure. This is intended to ensure that employees are aware of their right to at least the minimum disciplinary and dismissal procedures. However, the **ACAS Code of Practice on Disciplinary and Grievance Procedures** makes it clear that rules on disciplinary and dismissal procedures are desirable. A tribunal which is dealing with a claim in which disciplinary rules may be relevant may take the absence of such rules into consideration when reaching its decision as to reasonableness of the employer's action.

(o) The name or description of a person to whom employees may apply if they have a **grievance** or are dissatisfied with any disciplinary decision and the manner in which such an application should be made.

(p) Information relating to the terms of employment where the employee is required to **work outside the UK** for longer than one month. Where employees work outside the UK for over one month, they must be provided with the statement before they go; and it must contain details of:

   (i) The period for which they are to work outside the UK
   (ii) The currency in which they are to be paid
   (iii) Any additional pay or benefits
   (iv) Terms relating to their return to the UK

6.4 Information given in instalments

It should be noted that parts of the above information may be given in instalments, in particular, information relating to:

- The contracting-out certificate
- Information on **temporary employment**
- **Collective agreement** details
- Information in relation to employees **working outside the UK**, and
- The person to whom a **grievance** may be addressed and the method of application.

Finally, if there are **no relevant particulars** relating to the above matters then that fact should be stated in the Section 1 statement.

It is important to remember that the statement given does not constitute a contract or even conclusive evidence of the terms of a contract. If the employer does not give the employee a Section 1 statement, or the statement given is incomplete, the employee may complain to the Employment Tribunal. The tribunal may determine what the particulars are, but generally may not invent a term which has not been agreed upon by the parties. The employer must give the employee notice of changes in the terms at the earliest opportunity and, in any event, within **one month** of the change. In practice, many if not all of the terms listed in the Section 1 statement are part of the express terms of the contract of employment. Where the employer is clear that the content of the statement constitutes the express terms, s/he may append the statement to the offer letter sent to the successful job candidate. The statement and the offer letter will then be read in conjunction with one another so that the former will constitute the express terms of the contract.

6.5 Summary

To summarise, the principal statement is evidence that key terms have been agreed by the parties. It is for this reason that employers will ask any new employee to sign two copies of the statement and return one to the employer as proof of acceptance and agreement of the contract terms. Unless it was the clear intention of the parties to be contractually bound by them, the tribunals and courts will look to other evidence of what contractual terms do actually exist.

7 Specific express clauses

When drawing-up a contract of employment a number of specific clauses and their implications are worth consideration.

7.1 Indefinite contracts

The clause should specify the notice period to be given by the employer and the employee.

Notice periods should be reasonable at common law. In the case of senior employees the notice period may be fairly long to ensure that the employer is not deprived of a key employee at short notice, although it may be worth considering providing for reduced notice in the early stages of employment. In the case of non-senior employees shorter notice may be required but the period stated must comply with the statutory minimum period to be given by the employer to the employee.

Person employed from between one month and two years	1 week's notice
Person employed continuously for two years	2 weeks' notice plus 1 week's additional notice for each complete year of service up to a maximum of 12 weeks

7.2 Fixed-term contracts

Where the employee is engaged under a fixed-term contract the contract will bind both the employer and the employee for the stated period. An employer employing a person under a fixed-term contract should consider the following matters.

- It is possible to insert a '**break clause**' under which the parties may terminate the contract at any time without penalty by giving notice.

- A clause allowing the employer to terminate, without notice, on the happening of certain events such as long-term sickness or bankruptcy should be included in the contract.

- If the fixed-term contract is for more than one year the employer may **not** insert a term under which the employee waives or **contracts out** of their right to present a claim for unfair dismissal. In a contract of at least two years in duration a waiver clause may be inserted so the employee waives their right to a redundancy payment.

7.3 Flexibility and mobility clauses

An employee's duties and place of work should be set out in the contract of employment. It is in the interest of the employer to draw up these clauses as widely as possible. A flexibility clause in the contract is designed to cover all duties which the employer may wish the employee to undertake: such a clause may, for example, provide that the employee shall carry out 'such duties as the employer may from time-to-time direct'.

However, even if the clause is widely drawn it may still be limited by the scope of the job title.

A **mobility clause** defines the geographical area in which an employee may be required to work. Such clauses often provide that the employee may be required to work anywhere in the UK. However, three points should be noted in regard to mobility clauses.

(a) They may be subject to the **test of reasonableness**.

(b) In deciding the place of work for the purposes of redundancy the relevant place of work is where the employee **actually worked** and **not** where they could be asked to work under the contract.

(c) An employee who fails to obey a reasonable order to work at another site may be in breach of the duty to obey a reasonable order.

7.4 Clauses imposing a probationary period

An employer may wish to impose a probationary period on a new employee. If they do so, such a period will, nevertheless count towards the employee's period of continuity for the purposes of unfair dismissal and any claim for a redundancy payment. Furthermore, an employer who includes a probationary period in the contract should ensure that the contractual notice period does not exclude that period.

7.5 Clauses which reserve the right to make pay in lieu of notice

Generally, there is no problem with making a payment to an employee in lieu of notice, provided that it is at least equal to the sum which the employee would have received had they been given the required notice. The employer may, however wish to insert a clause specifically giving the right to pay in lieu of notice for the avoidance of any future dispute. If such a clause is incorporated into the contract it would appear that it will be treated as an emolument provided by the contract and is thus taxable as such.

In Chapter 4 the possibility of paying compensation on termination of employment up to the sum of £30,000 tax-free is considered. This can only occur if pay in lieu of notice is not a contractual term. Whilst termination is popular with employees as it provides the opportunity for the tax-free element, to make such a payment is in compensation for breach of contract. For the employer the consequence of the breach is to make the other contractual clauses unenforceable. Therefore the employer has the choice of making pay in-lieu of notice a contractual clause with the tax and National Insurance implications for both the employee and employer but be able to rely on the rest of the contract, or, exclude the clause and utilise a compromise agreement to enforce certain conditions on the employee. Compromise agreements are discussed in Chapter 8.

7.6 Clauses relating to the ownership of inventions, copyright and discoveries

In cases where the employee is likely to produce material which might be copyrighted by the employee or make discoveries or inventions in the course of employment, it is desirable to include a clause in the contract stating to whom ownership belongs. The general rule is that inventions made in the course of employment belong to the employer but the employee may be entitled to an award of compensation if the invention is of outstanding benefit to the employer.

7.7 Clauses to prevent use of confidential sensitive information

Both during and after the period of employment an employer may wish to restrict the employee (or former employee) from revealing or using information which was acquired while working for the employer. While the common law does imply a **term of confidentiality** into the employment contract this *may* not be sufficient. The sensible employer may, therefore, include one or more express terms to protect confidential information or trade secrets.

As noted above, these clauses are *prima facie* void under common law as being clauses in restraint of trade. In addition, the **Public Interest Disclosure Act 1998** (now Part IVA of the Employment Rights Act 1996) does, in very limited circumstances, give protection to so-called '**whistleblowers**' who reveal confidential information. The person revealing the information must, however, 'act in good faith'.

7.8 Collective agreements

The best way of ensuring that relevant terms of a collective agreement are incorporated into an employee's contract is by express provision to this effect. A clause may be inserted into the contract, for example stating that 'the worker is employed on the basis of the national agreements which are for the time being in force'. Often collective agreements will be incorporated by express statement in the Section 1 statement. Once the provisions have become part of an individual's contract they will be **binding** on **both parties**.

7.9 Other documents

In addition to collective agreements the employers may have other documents to which they wish the employee to adhere. Two of the most common documents fulfilling this use will be the employer's **Works Rules** and the employer's **disciplinary and grievance procedures**.

The employer may choose not to incorporate **Works Rules** into the contract. If they are not incorporated the employer may change them without consultation with the employee. However, since the Works Rules provide instructions as to how an employee should carry out the work, an employee who fails to comply with the instructions contained in the Works Rules is in breach of the duty to obey reasonable management orders and may be dismissed on grounds of misconduct. On the other hand, if they are incorporated the employer may have to seek agreement with the employee for such a change.

The employer must provide details of the disciplinary procedures for those employees, but apart from this requirement it may be to the employer's advantage to ensure that disciplinary and grievance procedures are contractual. Where the employer incorporates the rules and procedures into the contract it may be easier to defend a claim of unfair dismissal if the employer is able to show that the employee was in breach of the contract by virtue of breaking these rules. Also, the **Employment Rights (Dispute Resolution) Act 1998** includes a provision to allow the tribunal, when determining the amount of compensation to be awarded to an applicant, to take into account whether the applicant followed the in-house disciplinary procedures before making the claim to the tribunal.

8 Duties of the employer

8.1 Introduction

Since the beginning of the 19th century the courts have developed a series of implied terms which place duties and obligations on employers and employees alike.

8.2 To pay wages

The employer has a duty to pay **contractually agreed** wages to the employee. If no wage has been agreed the court will assess what the employee's work is reasonably worth by way of an action for *quantum meruit* (for as much as the work is worth).

8.3 To provide work

This is not a general duty, provided that the employer **pays** the employee. There is no breach of an implied term not to provide work. However, a number of exceptions to the rule do exist, in which an employee may expect to be given work:

- Where an employee's earnings depend solely on the provision of work such as where they undertake piecework, (eg, a machine operator or salesperson)

- Where the employee is employed on skilled work they have the right to have the opportunity to exercise the skill, (eg, a professional such as solicitor or doctor)

- Where it may be understood that part of the consideration is the opportunity to gain publicity, (eg, when a person is engaged as an actor)

8.4 To indemnify the employee

The employer must indemnify the employee for expenses and liabilities incurred by the employee in the course of the employment.

8.5 Mutual trust and confidence

This is arguably the **most important implied term** as far as the employee is concerned, since breach of this term is often used as grounds for claiming constructive unfair dismissal. Moreover, it is one of the implied terms which the courts have developed in recent times. It is the closest any of the implied terms comes to 'reasonableness' or 'fair dealing'.

The employer must behave with necessary courtesy and consideration towards the employee so that the contract may be effectively carried-out. As stated in the case of *Coutaulds Northern Textiles Ltd v Andrew [1979] IRLR 84* the employer should not: 'without reasonable and proper cause, conduct themselves in a manner calculated or likely to destroy or seriously damage the relationship of mutual confidence and trust between the employer and the employee'.

A breach of this duty by the employer may lead to the employee claiming that there has been a **constructive dismissal** and bringing an action for **unfair dismissal**.

8.6 Provision of references

Generally speaking, unless an express term is included in the contract, there is no legal duty to provide a reference for a former employee. There is **probably an implied duty to provide a reference** for a current employee. Where the employer does provide a reference it must be an honest and truthful one, otherwise a person who suffers damage as a result of the false statement may have an action in negligence or defamation against the person who made the statement.

9 Employer's obligations at common law

9.1 To ensure the employee's safety

All employers have a common law duty to take reasonable care of their employees. In addition to the common law duty, there are a number of relevant statutory provisions in the area of safety at work, in particular found in the **Health and Safety at Work Act 1974** and associated Regulations. Any discussion of an employer's liability in relation to the safety of the employees without consideration of the statutory provisions would be both incomplete, and unwise. An examination of the statutory provisions has, therefore been included below. It is important to remember that the common law duty is one which will give rise to a **civil action** while the statutory provisions are generally based upon **criminal liability**.

9.2 The health and safety duty under common law

At common law the employer is under an obligation to take 'reasonable practical steps to ensure the health and safety of his employees'. This doctrine requires everyone to ensure that activities do not cause injury or damage to another through some careless act or omission. It should be stressed that the employer is not expected to guard against all eventualities, but to take **reasonable care** in the circumstances. The duty is a personal one so that the employer cannot delegate the responsibility to a manager or safety specialist.

The employer will only be held liable for injuries to the employees if s/he fails to safeguard against something which is **reasonably foreseeable**. If an employer is aware, or ought to be aware of a source of potential danger they must **assess** the **risk** to the employee and take reasonable steps to eliminate or minimise the risk.

9.3 The common law and statutory duty to ensure reasonable safety

The duty to ensure reasonable safety can be subdivided into four categories.

(a) Duty to provide safe premises
(b) Duty to provide safe plant and appliances
(c) Duty to provide a safe system of work
(d) Duty to provide competent fellow employees.

(a) **Duty to provide safe premises**

The **Occupiers Liability Acts 1957 (Lawful Visitors) and 1984 (Trespassers)** place a statutory duty of care on the employer to ensure that the employees and others who come on to the premises are safe. Thus, they must ensure that any dangers are clearly indicated or cordoned off. A notice simply excluding or denying liability is not sufficient, but the employer is only under a duty to take reasonable care.

(b) **Duty to provide safe plant and appliances**

All tools, equipment, machinery and plant which the employee uses or comes into contact with must be reasonably safe for work. If the employer provides inadequate or defective equipment there will be a breach of this duty and potential liability under the Construction (Health, Safety and Welfare) Regulations 1996 and the Provision and Use of Work Equipment Regulations 1998. Furthermore, the employer should ensure that there is a proper system of inspection and testing in place so that any defects can be discovered and measures to remedy the problem may be taken.

An employee who is injured as a consequence of a manufacturing defect in a piece of equipment would, under the law of negligence, have to sue the person at fault, ie, the manufacturer. This may be difficult if not impossible for the employee to do.

The Employer's Liability (Defective Equipment) Act 1969 recognises this problem and provides that where an employee is injured as the result of a defect in equipment provided by his/her employer for the purpose of the business, and where the defect is the fault of the manufacturer, nevertheless that defect will be deemed to be attributable to the employer. The employee will, therefore, be able to sue the employer for damages. Should this happen, the employer or his/her insurers can attempt to recover the damages from the manufacturer.

(c) **Duty to provide a safe system of work**

The duty to provide a safe system of work covers a wide range of matters including systems of working, training and provision of protective equipment. The steps which the employer must take to ensure that the employee implements the training and advice given, or uses the protective equipment provided, depends upon the nature of the risk involved, the experience of the employees and the likelihood of serious injury.

In practice, if the employer wants to ensure that the employee implements training and advice given and uses the protective equipment provided they should make it a condition of the contract of employment, indicating disciplinary measures which will be taken against the employee in the event of breach.

(d) **Duty to provide competent fellow employees**

The employee can expect that the employer will engage competent fellow workers in the workplace. This duty extends to employees who may be a danger because of inexperience or ineptitude or who are 'practical jokers'. In addition, the principle of vicarious liability applies where the employer will be liable for the negligent acts of his/her employees **during the course of employment**.

9.4 Duty to take reasonable care in respect of the employee's financial well-being

There is an implied contractual obligation on employers to take reasonable steps to inform employees of a term of the contract so that employees may enjoy the benefits of that term – in circumstances where the employee could not reasonably be expected to be aware of the term unless it was drawn to their attention (particularly in the case of the contractual terms not being individually negotiated but collectively agreed).

10 Duties of the employee

10.1 Implied duties

The implied duties placed on the employee by the common law include:

(a) Duty to give personal service
(b) Duty to obey reasonable and lawful orders
(c) To be ready and willing to work
(d) Co-operation and adaptability
(e) Duty of fidelity
(f) Duty of skill and care

This is not a definitive list.

(a) **Duty to give personal service**

The relationship of employer and employee is a personal one and the employee may not delegate to others the performance of his/her duties.

(b) **Duty to obey reasonable and lawful orders**

This is the most fundamental duty of the employee. The employee must not wilfully disobey a lawful order. The duty only extends to lawful and reasonable orders. Thus, s/he is not under a duty to obey an order which would require her/him to break the law, for example to obey an order which results in unlawful discrimination. Note: this is different from disobeying a reasonable and lawful order which falls outside the scope of the contract (although in this case the employer may be able to fairly dismiss the employee).

(c) **To be ready and willing to work**

Where the employee is not prepared to work for the employer in accordance with (a) and (b) above the employee will be in breach of contract. This has been developed by (d) below.

(d) **Co-operation and adaptability**

Recently the courts have expanded the duty to obey reasonable orders and created a wider duty of co-operation and adaptability.

The duty of co-operation means the employee has a duty not to impede the employer's business. It is clear that industrial (strike) action will breach the contract, but the employee may be in breach of the duty to co-operate if s/he engages in industrial action which falls short of a strike.

(e) **Duty of fidelity – to give faithful and honest service**

The employee has a duty of fidelity towards the employer. This means the employee is required to act in good faith towards the employer. The duty includes a number of aspects principally relating to confidentiality and non-competition, some of which apply after employment has ceased.

(i) The employee must not make a secret profit nor take a bribe and will be required to account to the employer for any secret profit made or bribe taken.

(ii) The employee must not place themselves in a position whereby their **own interests conflict** with those of the employer. Clearly, this will cover situations where the employee agrees to do work personally for existing customers who might otherwise get the work done through the employer.

(iii) An employee who works for a **competitor** during the currency of the employment may be breaching the duty of fidelity. However, the courts have been reluctant to accept that what a worker does in their own spare time should be of any concern to the employer and will seldom grant the employer an injunction to prevent the employee from working for the competitor unless it can be shown that the employer's business is being seriously damaged.

(iv) The employee must not disclose confidential information or trade secrets either during employment or afterwards since to do so may harm the employer's business.

(f) **Duty of skill and care**

The employee is under a duty to exercise reasonable skill and care in the performance of the duties. There are two aspects to this duty.

First an employee who performs duties **negligently** will be in breach of the duty and will be liable to indemnify the employer for any loss suffered as a result of the breach. If the negligent act is a serious one it may warrant dismissal but minor acts will not constitute dismissal unless there is a series of such acts.

Second an employee who professes to hold a particular skill or level of expertise must exercise that skill to the standard expected of a person in that position. Failure to do so will be a breach of the duty and may entitle the employer to dismiss instantly.

11 Confidentiality

11.1 Introduction

The implied terms of the contract place a duty of 'good faith' on the employee. This implied duty places a number of obligations on the employee during the employment period including duties not to divulge or otherwise misuse confidential information, and not to work for competitors where to do so would cause their employer's business serious harm. However, these common law duties may not provide sufficient protection for the employer's business after the employee has left employment. It is advisable for employers to insert an express contractual restrictive covenant if they wish to protect confidential information after the employment relationship has finished.

11.2 Reasons for drafting accurate enforceable contract terms

The reasons for drafting accurate, enforceable contract terms are summarised below.

(a) The duty restricting the divulgence of confidential information is limited when applying to former employees, and will only extend to the disclosure of trade secrets or any other information of a sufficiently high degree of confidentiality that should not be used for anyone's benefit other than the employer in question. This includes possible customer connections, but not general information acquired by the employee during their employment.

In order to determine whether particular information falls into the category of information which should not be disclosed after employment has ceased, all of the following issues must be considered:

(i) The nature of the employment and whether confidential information was being regularly handled (this would impose a higher degree of confidentiality)

(ii) The nature of the information (only that which is in the nature of a trade secret or material of highly confidential nature will be capable of being protected)

(iii) Whether the information can be easily isolated from other information which the employee is free to use or disclose, and

(iv) How far the employer impressed upon the employee the need for confidentiality.

In cases where the court finds that there has been a breach of this duty by a former employee it may grant an injunction to restrain them from disclosing the information or preventing them from carrying out a contract with a third party.

(b) The implied duty of fidelity will not prevent a former employee from working in any capacity for a competitor, or indeed from setting up their own business in direct competition.

In order to prevent unfair competition after the employment ends, an employer must insert into the employee's contract one or more express terms covering both confidentiality and non-solicitation. Contracts should be drafted carefully to restrain employees both during employment (including on garden leave) as well as post-employment.

11.3 Restraint of trade

A restraint of trade in a contract of employment is a clause by which the employee undertakes that they will accept certain restraints on their future employment and activities.

The main types of restraint clauses may cover

- Restraining a former employee from using information obtained while in the service of the employer (a confidentiality clause)

- Soliciting of former customers and (possibly) the soliciting of former employees (a non-solicitation clause), and

- Placing a restriction preventing the employee from working for a competitor or setting-up business in competition (a non-competition clause). Some restrictive covenants are based on geographical areas. It should be noted that the area in question should be no larger than is necessary to protect the legitimate interests of the employer. Restrictive covenants must be specifically tailored to the circumstances and matters to be protected, and wherever possible with the particular individual's skills, information, or abilities in mind. Because of increasing sensitivity of commercial information employers are using these types of restraint clauses more frequently.

12 Restraint of trade

12.1 The rules

An employer who believes that these clauses might be used to protect their business against any future competition would be wrong. The courts have long been reluctant to enforce provisions which may prevent a person from legitimately earning a living and will only grant a remedy to an employer subject to the clause complying with strict rules.

First the clause will be subject to the normal rules of contract. If the court finds that there has been no consideration given for the employee's promise to restrict future employment the clause will not be enforceable. This is likely to be the case if the covenant was only agreed at the end of the relationship. Likewise, if the employer causes a fundamental breach of the contract, the clause becomes unenforceable.

Second, any restraint of trade covenant contained in a contract of employment is contrary to public policy and void *unless* it can be shown that it is reasonable in all the circumstances. In order for the clause to be valid and enforceable the employer wishing to rely on it must prove that:

(a) They have a legitimate interest to protect. The interest which requires protection may be a trade secret or other information (eg, trade connections) which 'if disclosed to a competitor would be liable to cause real or significant damage to the owner of the secret'. A clause inserted solely to protect competition will not be enforceable.

(b) The restraint must go no further than is reasonable for the protection of the employer's business interests or secrets taking into account the nature of the activities which are to be restrained. Whether the clause is reasonable in itself will depend upon a number of further factors:

  (i) **The nature of the employee's work**

  The business from which the employee is barred must be no wider than the business in which s/he was employed. In addition, there must be a real possibility that the employee has some intimate knowledge about the affairs or requirements of customers or access to some confidential information or secrets which if used by that employee when s/he leaves may have a damaging effect on the employer's business.

  For example, an employer would not be justified in placing a restriction on an employee who had no contact with clients or access to confidential information.

  (ii) **The time and area covered by the clause**

  The time restraint must not be excessive. A restraint in a non-competition clause in excess of two years, for example, will only be justified in very exceptional circumstances, while the time restraint in a non-solicitation clause should be no more than a few months. The area in which the restraint is to operate must also be reasonable; generally, it must not be wider than the area in which the employer carried-out their business. On the other hand, if the employee has connections or responsibilities for a specified area only then should the clause seek to cover the relevant area.

  (iii) **Harm caused to the employer**

  The employer must show that actual or potential harm will be caused to their business as a result of a breach of the restrictive covenant.

12.2 Enforceability of the clause

If the restraint does not protect a property interest or is drafted too widely and is, therefore, unreasonable in time or area, it is void and hence unenforceable. The court will not rewrite the clause so as to make it reasonable. However, in some cases the court may use the 'blue pencil rule' to sever that part of the clause which is too wide and leave the rest as an enforceable clause, providing that the severed parts are independent of one another and can be separated without affecting the meaning of the part which is to be enforced.

If the clause is found to be valid and enforceable the employer will usually want an injunction to restrain the employee from committing the breach, and may also be entitled to damages if they have suffered any loss.

As a final point, a restrictive covenant may be unenforceable no matter how reasonable if the employer has wrongfully terminated the employee's contract. An employer who wishes to dismiss an employee without giving the full notice may, provided the relevant term is included in the contract, give pay in lieu of notice. They would then be able to enforce a reasonable restraint clause against the employee.

13 Garden leave

It might be possible to achieve the same effect as a restraint of trade clause by providing in the contract of employment for a long period of notice to be given. If the employee wishes to resign and move to an actual or potential competitor the current employer may hold the employee to the notice period, but not require them to work during the period. Similarly, the employer may, provided the contract includes the relevant term, give pay in lieu of notice (PILON). The employee has, in effect, to take **garden leave**. This permits the employee's contacts and knowledge of the business to become out-of-date, or certainly not as valuable to the competitor as they would have been without the long notice period. Also, once the employee knows they are leaving to join a new employer they may positively seek out valuable information to the new employer. Although these type of provisions are not strictly speaking, restrictive covenants, they clearly do restrict the employee's activities and may adversely affect an employee's ability to carry on their trade or profession. The courts have, therefore, indicated that such clauses will be subject to the same type of tests which are applied to restraint covenants and an employer should bear this in mind when drafting the contract. Of particular importance is the need to include a contract clause to the effect that the employer has no obligation to provide work during the notice period.

Recent cases have seen the courts requiring the former employer to show that the ex-employee has:

- Customer connections
- Confidential information or trade secrets not in the public domain or
- Some form of customer goodwill before an injunction will be granted to restrain the employee from working for the new employer during the garden leave period.

14 Atypical contracts

Within the last twenty years, there has been a substantial growth in the use of so-called atypical contracts of employment by employers; that is, contracts which are not the norm.

There has always been a need for short-term and fixed-term contracts due to variations in the seasons, consumer demands and production cycles which lead to fluctuations in the demand for workers.

The effect of recession and global competition in product markets as well as customer preferences for quality and choice has stimulated many employers to operate more flexibly.

Both organisational restructuring and workers' requirements for variable working hours have accelerated this process. Many employers have taken the opportunities presented by the deregulated labour market of the 1980s and 1990s to increase the variety of flexible contracts of employment, as have self-employed contract workers and small- and medium-sized enterprises.

All of this has meant that continuous and full-time employment contracts have declined, giving way to a more diverse range of contractual arrangements.

14.1 Main types of atypical contracts

Examples of the main types of atypical contracts which will be examined are:

- **Fixed-term**. These contracts specify a termination date.
- **Temporary-casual**. These contracts are based on a variation in the duration of the contract
- **Annual hours**. The employee is hired to work a certain number of hours, but will only know on a short period of notice, when the hours will be performed.
- **Zero-hours (or variable hours)**. These contracts are based on a variation on the time spent engaged on work. (They may also be fixed-term or casual.)

14.2 Fixed-term contracts

These contracts have grown, particularly in the education, leisure and agricultural sectors and in central and local government. Over a half of temporary contracts in the UK at the end of the twentieth century constituted some form of fixed-term contract.

14.3 Key differences between fixed-term and continuous contract

The key difference between a fixed-term contract and a 'continuous' (or 'open-ended') contract is that from the formation of the contract a specified termination date or period of existence will be stated. Contracts which do not contain these details **expressly indicated** will **not** be **treated** as fixed-term contracts.

Fixed-term contracts may contain reference to a period of notice which can permit the employer (or the employee) to terminate it earlier than specified.

Should the employer terminate the contract without proper notice they will be obliged to pay the employee damages representing the pay due in the notice period. Where there is no notice period and the employer terminates it early, the employee will be entitled to damages representing the outstanding pay for the rest of the term of the contract (ie, wrongful dismissal).

A fixed-term contract of at least one month (or less where the employee has been continuously employed for at least three months) entitles the employee to be given a period of statutory notice, ie, one week. Where the contract **exceeds one month but is no more than one year in duration** the employee is entitled to the same period of statutory notice. Beyond two years' service the employee is entitled to the standard statutory notice periods.

The reason for the special protection for those on fixed-term contracts is to prevent an unscrupulous employer hiring (and dismissing) and re-hiring employees on fixed-term contracts of just under one month on each occasion over a long period of time without the employees building-up employment protection rights. Employees engaged on a series of fixed-term contracts **will accrue** continuous service for the purposes of employment protection. Where the gap between contracts is of a week or less, the continuity will be automatically preserved.

14.4 Sick pay

An employee working under a fixed-term contract of not more than three months is **not entitled** to Statutory Sick Pay (SSP). Where the employee is working under a contract which is preceded by another contract with the same employer which provides continuous employment for at least thirteen weeks, then the employee will be entitled to claim SSP.

15 Dismissal and waiver clauses in fixed-term contracts

The increase in the use by employers of fixed-term contracts led to the growth of waiver clauses. These commit the employee to a waiving of his or her rights to claim unfair dismissal and/or a redundancy payment. The law has evolved to slowly decrease the use of these waivers.

Termination of a limited term contract (with or without proper notice) is a dismissal in law. This will include circumstances where the employer decides simply not to renew the contract.

Unfair dismissal rights are where:

- The contract is terminated by the employer before the end of the fixed term; or
- The employee terminates the contract in circumstances where s/he is claiming constructive dismissal.

A fixed term contract will automatically be converted into a contract of indefinite duration once the employee has completed four years continuous employment under it (or renewals of it) unless there is objective justification for it being a fixed term contract.

15.1 Fixed-term employees (Prevention of Less Favourable Treatment) Regulations

The Fixed-Term Employees (Prevention of Less Favourable Treatment) Regulations 2002, came into force on 1st October 2002. The Regulations were prompted by the need to ensure that British law complies with the EC Fixed Term Work Directive 1999/70/EC. The basic idea is that it becomes unlawful to treat a fixed-term employee less favourably than a comparable permanent employee engaged in similar work, but subject to a defence of objective justification.

An employer can objectively justify individual terms which are less favourable if a fixed-term employee's contract taken as a whole is as favourable as contracts of permanent employees.

Other points to note include:

- Fixed term contracts are automatically converted to contracts of indefinite length after four years
- Removal of the ability of a fixed term employee to waive the right to statutory redundancy pay on expiry of the fixed term
- Making the completion of a task contract count as dismissal for unfair dismissal purposes

- A fixed term employee who considers they are being treated unfairly can require the employer to provide a written statement setting out the nature of the complaint.

16 Temporary and casual contracts of employment

16.1 Temporary contracts to cover other employees on maternity leave

If a person is engaged to temporarily cover the work of an employee on maternity leave and that person is notified in writing that the temporary contract will be terminated on the return to work of the employee the subsequent dismissal will be a dismissal for some other substantial reason (SOSR). The dismissal will only be automatically unfair where the test of reasonableness in all the circumstances is not satisfied. The fact that the employer fails to notify the temporary employee in writing of the reasons for the dismissal does not automatically render the dismissal unfair. This will be for the tribunal to decide.

Two practical factors favour the employer:

(a) Most temporary employees covering maternity leave posts will not have accrued one year's service to claim unfair dismissal. (The situation may be different where the temporary employee has been used to cover a succession of absences), and

(b) Tribunals will seldom override the returning employee's automatic statutory right to return to her previous job.

Contracts used to employ temporary staff to cover maternity absences cannot be referred to as fixed-term, unless the termination date is specified in some way. Many contracts will stipulate that they are **temporary** and will terminate upon the return of the employee on maternity leave. It is possible that an employer may decide to issue a fixed-term contract because they are unsure about the date on which the employee will return. However, given the nullity of any unfair dismissal waiver this may be unwise. Better for the employer to rely on fairly dismissing the temporary replacement to make way for the returning employee from maternity leave.

Nevertheless, to ensure fairness the employer must notify the replacement at the time of recruitment in writing that he or she will be dismissed when the woman on maternity leave does return to work.

These provisions also cover statutory suspension on health and safety grounds related to pregnancy/maternity, but do **not** cover absences on **parental leave**.

16.2 Global contracts of employment

The 1990s witnessed a growing trend for engaging workers on a casual basis. These workers are often keen to demonstrate that they have been working under a so-called **global contract**.

This will provide them with continuity for the purposes of employment protection. A global contract may **be implied** where there is a **series of specific employment contracts** which, when viewed as an overall employment relationship constitute one contract.

During the periods of inactivity those weeks when the employee is inactive would be counted. To operate this requires an obligation to offer work on an ongoing and continuous basis by the employer, and for the employee to have held themselves ready to accept it and performed those duties.

17 Annual hours and zero-hours contracts of employment

17.1 Introduction

This type of contract has increased with the demands of employers to provide 24-hour and 7-day week working arrangements which bring about substantial fluctuations in the usage of employees.

The main examples are annual hours and zero hours contracts.

- **Annual hours.** There might be fluctuations in demand for workers due to seasonal fluctuations, say in the leisure, hotel and catering industry, administration (eg, where there is a peak of work due to forms or registrations returned), or production (eg, where a manufacturer increases production to meet sudden demand or seasonal demands such as the goods associated with different periods of the year: lawnmowers in spring, special goods in the run-up to Christmas). The employee will probably be hired to work a certain number of hours in the year, but will not know when or how many they will work during which operating periods. Hours will be notified to employees, usually with one week's notice.

- **Zero hours contracts.** This type of contract, unlike annual hours contracts, does not have the benefit of a guaranteed number of hours. It is a way of maintaining an ongoing contractual relationship with employees while not guaranteeing any specified hours of work or pay in any period specified by the employer. This could range from one day to one year, although the latter is very unusual.

Given the growing trend for a 24/7 culture, the EU Commission has put forward proposals to tighten up the provision in the parent Directive for individual opt-outs from the 48 hour week. However, the EU Council of Ministers are unable to agree on this point.

17.2 Legal implications

Legal implications to the above are as follows.

- **Annual hours contracts**

    Until recently UK employers and employees have been generally able to negotiate whichever hours are required. This has, of course, been subject to the implied terms of the contract. The full implementation of the Working Time Regulations 1998 (EU Directive 2003/88) means that the employee must be given adequate rest periods. Because many annualised hours systems operate on cycles of four weeks or twelve weeks employers will have to take account of the effects of these rules in planning operations.

- **Zero hours contracts**

    The same principles and practical issues will apply here as they will to annual hours contracts in respect of working time rules. In both types of contracts individual employees should be treated in accordance with their status as an 'employee'. The problem for many employees is the uncertainty of when work may be available, the unsocial or inconvenient hours involved and the reduced income when few hours are offered by the employer.

18 Rights of part-time workers

18.1 Overview

The EC Part-Time Work Directive 97/81/EC gives effect to the 'framework agreement' on part-time work. Part-time workers now have the same rights as full time employees. The Part-time Workers (Prevention of Less Favourable Treatment) Regulations 2000 state that: 'a part-time worker has the right not to be treated by his employer less favourably than the employer treats a comparable full-time worker:

(a) As regards the terms of his contract, or

(b) By being subjected to any other detriment by any act, or deliberate failure to act, of his employer'.

This is subject to the important qualification that this right applies only if the treatment is on the grounds that the worker is a part-time worker, and the treatment is not justified on objective grounds.

The basic rationale behind the Regulations is that part-time workers should be entitled to the same treatment pro rata as full timers doing similar work unless different (ie less favourable) treatment can be objectively justified.

Part-time workers must:

- Receive the same hourly rate of pay
- Receive the same hourly rate of over-time pay once they have worked more than the normal full-time hours
- Not be excluded from training simply because they work part-time
- Have the same entitlements to annual leave and maternity/parental leave on a pro-rata basis as full-time colleagues, and
- Have the same right to membership of an occupational pension scheme as comparable full-time workers.

A part-time worker has the right to require the employer to give written reasons for any difference in treatment in comparison with a full time worker. If the employer fails to provide the statement within 21 days a tribunal 'may draw any inference which it considers it just and equitable to draw, including an inference that the employer has infringed the right in question'. If a worker believes that they have received less favourable treatment then they have the right to complain to an Employment Tribunal.

Information

3

1 Information

1.1 Introduction

Since the introduction of the Data Protection Act in 1984 employees have been gaining increased rights to information and consultation through a variety of legislative sources. These rights and employers' obligations have been strengthened considerably by the introduction of the **Data Protection Act 1998** (DPA). This chapter examines the rights of employees in respect of personal information and in situations such as whistleblowing.

The chapter also looks at what the employer needs to be aware of when recruiting and employing people with particular respect to references, employment of offenders, medical information and the increasing requirements associated with employing non-UK nationals.

2 The Data Protection Act 1998

The Act distinguishes between **personal data** and **sensitive personal data**.

Individuals can access their **personal data** and prevent it from being used for direct marketing and prevent it from being transferred outside the European Economic Area unless adequate levels of protection are ensured.

Sensitive data can be processed in the employment field only if the individual consents and it is necessary for the purposes of exercising or performing any obligation which is conferred or imposed by law on the data controller in connection with employment.

2.1 Personal data

Whether data constitutes personal data is a complex issue. To constitute personal data a living individual must be capable of being identified from the data.

Personal data is information that affects a person's privacy either in his or her personal or family life, business or professional capacity. The information may be biographical which goes beyond the recording of a person's involvement in a matter and the information may have the individual as its focus. Examples of information which is likely to count as 'personal data' are details of salary, medical history and tax liabilities. However, information which will not normally count as 'personal data' is a mere reference to a person's name, for example as recipient of an e-mail.

Sensitive personal data can be defined broadly to include data relating to:

- Ethnic or racial origin
- Political opinions and affiliations
- Religious beliefs
- Trade union membership or activities
- Physical or mental health
- Sex life (including sexual orientation) of the data subject
- The commission, or alleged commission of any criminal offence, any proceedings, or the sentence of a court in relation to the data subject.

Before proceeding any further it is necessary to define a number of terms used in the Act.

Term	Definition
Data	Data can take many forms: manual files, held on computer disk, video, audio system, microfiche, tape or data monitored and/or collected from telephone or e-mail systems.

Specifically it is information which is '*....processed by means of equipment operating automatically*', and data that is '*...recorded as part of a relevant filing system*'. The latter is defined as '*a set of non-automated information relating to one or more individuals which is recorded as part of a relevant filing system, and....is structured, either by reference to individuals or by reference to one or more criterion relating to individuals in such a way that specific information relating to particular individuals is readily accessible*'. [DPA 1998].

A file that is identified as belonging to an individual by name or by title will fall into this definition, even where the collation of the documents is not kept in chronological or other systemic order. However, day-to-day notes, for example kept by a supervisor or manager on an employee's performance is unlikely to fall within the definition. |
| **Automated data** | **Automated data** has special rules that apply to decision-making solely by automated means that relate to the data subject, eg, scanning of application forms, CVs, test results or productivity/performance monitoring. The exceptions are similar to those under s 10, but the data subject is empowered to seek prohibition of such a process and to have any results of the process reviewed by a human being. Also, the data subject is entitled to be informed of the '*logic*' of the automated decision. |

> **'Relevant filing systems'**
>
> Information which is held in manual form can constitute a 'relevant filing system' and be personal data for the purposes of the DPA. As this can be a difficult issue the Information Commissioner's office has issued technical guidance notes to clarify when the DPA has an impact on manual records.
>
>> 'The 'temp test' assumes that the temp in question is reasonably competent, requiring only a short induction, explanation and/or operating manual on the particular filing system in question for them to be able to use it.
>>
>> The temp test would not apply if any in-depth knowledge of your custom and practice is required, whether of your type of work, of the documents you hold or of any unusual features of your system, before a temp is, as a matter of practice, capable of operating the system. In such cases the system would not be a relevant filing system.'
>
> For example a file containing alphabetical dividers and/or sub-divided into categories which means it is easy to locate information about an individual is likely to constitute a relevant filing system. By contrast a file with documents dropped into it randomly or with sub-dividers that classify the contents of the file in a vague or ambiguous way is unlikely to be a relevant filing system.

Rights to withhold and prevent data processing enables the data subject to prevent the data controller from processing personal data where:

(a)   'The processing is causing or is likely to cause substantial damage or distress to the data subject or someone else', and

(b)   'That damage or distress is or would be unwarranted'.

Example

False health record, reference or disciplinary record

Any request must be in writing, the data controller must give a written response within 21 days and a 'reasonable period' be allowed for compliance. There are, however, a series of exemptions to the enforcement right, including:

- Processing is necessary for the entering into or the performance of a contract to which the data subject is a party (eg, necessary criminal record checks or reference-checking)

- To protect the data subject's interests

- To enable the data controller to fulfil legal obligations

- For the purpose of or in connection with any existing or prospective legal proceedings or

- Defence of legal rights.

Term	Comments
Data controller	Is a person who determines the purposes for which data will be processed under the law, and so includes employers as well as local and central government.
Data processor	Is a person who will process the data on behalf of the data controller, but who is not an employee of the data controller. So, any agency or contractor that collects or processes the data is defined in law. Employers may be both a data controller and a data processor.
Data processing	This means obtaining, recording or holding the data: the definition is very wide in practice covering such activities as disclosing, publishing, word processing, erasing or withholding personal data, using e-mail and other electronic means. Disclosure of certain data remains subject to exemption (see: **'Data exempted from access request'** below). Under the DPA 1984 the definition of 'processing' was narrower in meaning specifically 'by reference to the data subject'. The 1984 Act referred to '…any data relating to the data subject.'
Data subject	A living individual on whom there is personal data in existence. At work this will include employees, workers, un/successful job applicants and former employees, workers or volunteers.
Personal data	This can take many forms: information about a living person: the data subject, or data from which a living person can be identified that is in possession of, or likely to come into possession of the data controller. It includes any expression of opinion and anybody's intentions towards the data subject. [See the definition of **data** above.]

Specific types of personal data

Term	Comments
Eligible data	Personal data which is being processed. Employers should not process personal data unless (at least) the first of the data principles is satisfied (see Section 3).
Sensitive personal data	This is data that can be defined broadly to include data relating to: • Ethnic or racial origin • Political opinions and affiliations • Religious beliefs • Trade Union membership/activities • Physical or mental health • Sex life (including sexual orientation) of the data subject, and/or • The commission or alleged commission of any criminal offence, any proceedings for any offence or alleged offence, the disposal of such proceedings or the sentence of any court in such proceedings relating to the data subject.

2.2 Other conditions relating to sensitive personal data

As well as being subject to all **eight data protection principles** (see section 3), there are other conditions relating to sensitive personal data.

These include:

(a) The employee must give his/her explicit consent to the processing of this data.

(b) The processing is necessary for the purposes of exercising or performing any right or obligation placed on the employer by law in connection with employment.

Examples

An employer may record an employee's absences for the purposes of SSP entitlement, a criminal record check may be made for certain exempted occupations, and a record taken of the evidence produced by a job applicant for the employer to comply with asylum and immigration requirements.

(c) The processing is necessary in connection with any legal proceedings or for the purposes of obtaining legal advice (should the employer wish to defend a tribunal claim it may make use of personal data), including under legal qualified privilege.

(d) The processing is necessary for the administration of justice or for compliance with any statute. The employer could process data relating to an employee's criminal conviction for the purposes of complying with an 'attachment of earnings order'.

(e) For the purposes of ethnic monitoring with a view to the promotion of equality, provided proper safeguards are in place.

In practice, this means that those conducting employment interviews should not ask questions on a range of matters to which the data protection principles apply.

2.3 Access to and information about the processing of data

The data subject is entitled to be informed in full whether any personal data are being processed and, if so, be provided with certain details, such as:

- A description of the data
- The purposes for which it is being processed and
- The recipients of the data

The information must be conveyed to the data subject in an 'intelligible form'. Any entitlements must be pursued by the data subject in writing to the data controller and provide the access fee (currently £10 maximum) unless waived. Access requests must be responded to 'promptly' and in any event before the end of 40 days beginning with the day on which the request was received.

These rights are substantially strengthened in the 1998 statute, not least because they give the individual a right to prevent processing of personal data in certain circumstances.

A request concerning manual data will normally result in the individual being given a paper copy. With computerised data, other means, eg, e-mail will be acceptable. (A former employee can access information from their employer for the purposes of pursuing a statutory claim for unfair dismissal and unlawful discrimination in the Employment Tribunal.)

2.4 Data exempted from access requests

The data controller will have no duty to comply with an access request in respect of **data where a breach of confidence may arise**.

Example

For example, if where by releasing data, the identity of another individual could not be kept confidential. Job references, internal disciplinary reports and appraisals cannot be disclosed unless the individual concerned has consented or it is reasonable in all the circumstances to comply with the access request notwithstanding lack of consent. The latter will depend on:

- Any duty of confidentiality owed to the individual
- The steps taken to obtain his/her consent and
- Whether s/he is capable of giving consent.

However the data controller is required to disclose as much information as practicable without disclosing the identity of the individual(s).

References

The DPA exempts subject access rights where the reference is supplied by the data controller for prospective or continuing employment, training or education purposes, the prospective or actual appointment of the data subject or the provision of any service to the data subject. The exemption does not cover references given by a third party (eg, former employer).

However, if the third party is identified in the information, the data controller must obtain the third party's consent to the disclosure, unless it is reasonable, in all the circumstances, to comply with the request without obtaining consent. What does this mean in practice? The exemption is interpreted very narrowly so whereas the employee cannot make a subject access request to the employer (or former employer) providing the reference, he or she will be able to make that request to the employer receiving the reference. Thereafter, normal subject access rules apply. However, suppose the reference was originally provided on a strictly confidential basis? Consent of the provider of the reference may therefore be necessary for disclosure to be made to the (former) employee (ie, the data subject), *unless* it is reasonable in all the circumstances to dispense with obtaining consent. (See also References section 8.4)

Management data for forecasting and business or human resource planning

Exempted, but only where the disclosure 'would be likely to prejudice the conduct of that business or other activity', eg, proposed redundancies or long-term career planning. Also included is 'corporate finance'; the basic prerequisite for this exemption (other than for pricing) is where non-disclosure is to *safeguard* 'an important economic or financial interest of the United Kingdom'. However, the exemption only applies on a case-by-case basis and could be challenged.

Management negotiations

This covers such matters as records of the employer's proposals/plans in respect of pay increases, promotion or severance of employees, or reorganisations; in other words, matters where disclosure could prejudice their outcome.

Payroll data

Unless the data is exempt for some reason the data subject should be given access.

All payroll data can be deemed confidential and potentially falling within the ambit of the Act, but compliance with PAYE requirements is exempt. In order to comply with the Third Data Protection Principle all out-dated manual payroll data should be shredded and discs/tapes 'scratched'.

All queries by telephone should not be addressed until proof of identity is satisfied. This definitely is includes third party callers, no matter how convincing.

Crime and taxation

It seems there must be a '**substantial chance**' (rather than mere risk) that disclosure would be '**likely to prejudice**' any measure in respect of the detection and prevention of crime and lawful assessment/collection of any tax/duty. The exemption only applies where the data controller is the relevant authority.

3 Data protection principles

There are eight data protection principles which are explained below.

1. Personal data must be processed fairly and lawfully.

Practical meaning

The data subject must have consented to the processing of the data, which must be necessary for the performance of a contract of employment, or for taking steps at the employee's request for entering into such a contract. Consent cannot be inferred from the data subject's failure to respond to a communication from the data controller.

Example

Obtaining a job reference, compliance with a non-contractual obligation such as personal data relative to PAYE contributions. The data subject must have been given the identity of the data controller, the purpose(s) for which the data is to be processed and any '**further information**' such as in a questionnaire whether answers are voluntary or obligatory, rights of access and rectification of errors. This information must be provided (if requested) unless the data controller believes that to do so would involve a '**disproportionate effort**'.

2. Personal data must be obtained only for one or more specified and lawful purpose(s), and must not be processed in any manner incompatible with that or those purposes.

3. Personal data must be adequate, relevant and not excessive in relation to the purpose(s) for which they are processed.

Practical meaning

The data controller may be required to justify the processing or holding of data. The employer should, therefore regularly review the content of personal files and other files which contain personal data to verify the necessity of retaining the data that may have become outdated. As a general rule the data controller should hold and process only the required minimum amount of personal data.

4. Personal data must be accurate and, where necessary, kept up-to-date.

Practical meaning

Reasonable care must be taken by the data controller where the data subject notifies him/her of an inaccuracy. Good practice will mean employers establish a system whereby employees can inspect the content of personal files and update and correct information.

5. Personal data processed for any purpose(s) must not be kept any longer than is necessary for that purpose or for those purposes.

Practical meaning

This is partly covered under the fourth principle – for example, how long should the employer retain the file of a former employee? This should be determined by reference to the time-scale in which any legal action may be brought by the former employee against the employer. In personal injury claims this will be three years, but in some civil claims the period is six years.

6. Personal data must be processed in accordance with the data subject's rights under the Act.

Practical meaning

The employer should comply with notices given by the data subject in exercise of his/her rights to prevent processing likely to cause damage or distress or in breach of rights in relation to the data subject.

7. Appropriate technical and organisational measures must be taken against unauthorised or unlawful processing of personal data, and against accidental loss or destruction of, or damage to personal data

Practical meaning

Effective security must be maintained by the data controller and employees or others processing data must be trained, selected and authorised appropriately.

Computerised systems should have a back-up and data should not be removed from its normal place of storage without authorisation and good reason.

8. Personal data must not be transferred to a country or territory outside the European Economic Area unless that country or territory ensures an 'adequate level of protection' for the rights and freedoms of data subjects in relation to processing of personal data.

Practical meaning

Protection must be 'adequate in all the circumstances'. This principle does not apply if a number of conditions are met, including where the data subject has given consent for the data transfer to take place without sureties being in place. Otherwise, the data controller must take into account the nature of the data and the in(adequacy) of protective laws in the country or territory in question.

3.1 Health records

Any data covering an individual's physical or psychological health are likely to be classed as '**sensitive personal data**'. Data made by or on behalf of a health professional in 'connection with the care of that individual' will be included, but the data must be in the form of an 'accessible record', irrespective of whether it is held on manual file or electronically. Case records held by occupational health practitioners could be relevant, although arguably 'care for that individual' is likely to be the prerequisite for such a duty to exist.

3.2 The Information Commissioner

(a) The **Freedom of Information Act 2000** changed the title of the Data Protection Commissioner to that of Information Commissioner. The Commissioner has various powers including those of enforcement where a data controller has contravened any part of the Data Protection Act 1998. A data subject may ask the Commissioner to make an 'assessment' of whether the data processing is un/likely to conform with the Act. In so doing, the Commissioner may decide whether or not the data subject could be entitled to make an application. This may lead to enforcement action by the Commissioner where there is not full compliance.

(b) The Commissioner has the powers to instigate a criminal prosecution of a data controller because of a range of breaches of the Act, eg, processing personal data without notification, failure to conform with an enforcement notice, making a false statement in response to a request for information from a data subject or a failure to notify the Commissioner of changes to the notification register entry. An employer may appeal against an enforcement notice (and other action taken by the Commissioner) by applying to the Information Tribunal (formally known as the Data Protection Tribunal).

(c) In the event of a successful complaint by a data subject, the maximum compensation the employer can be awarded to pay is subject to the discretion of the court. This will be affected by the damage suffered by the individual including the seriousness of the breach and the distress caused.

(d) Failure to comply with any notice issued by the Commissioner or a breach of the DPA is a criminal offence and may lead to the imposition of a fine or even a prison sentence.

(e) As well as those indicated above, the Information Commissioner has a duty to:

   (i) Promote good practice by data controllers, in particular the observance of the Data Protection Principles

   (ii) Publish information about the Data Protection Act 1998

   (iii) Maintain a register of data controllers who are required to notify their processing; and developing/publishing Codes of Practice and Guidance

The Employment Practices Data Protection Code

The Commissioner publishes the *Employment Practices Data Protection Code*. The Code is in four parts and designed to help employers navigate the legislation.

- Recruitment and selection (i)
- Employment records (ii)
- Monitoring at work (iii)
- Workers' health (iv)

3.3 Retention periods for personal records

Employers are advised not to retain any personal data for a period of time other than for which it is necessary to do so. The Information Commissioner has advised that personal data for HR purposes be retained for no longer than the times shown below, but with the critical proviso that there may be circumstances under which it will be perfectly reasonable for the employer to hold data for a longer period (eg, because of legal proceedings, the nature of the business, to protect employees, etc). The time-scales shown also incorporate some of the other statutory retention periods.

Type of personal data	Duration of retention – Years
Application form	Six months to a year
References received	One
Payroll and tax information	Six (but pension records may be kept up to 12 years)

Type of personal data	Duration of retention – Years
Sickness records	Three
Annual leave records, including time cards	Two
Parental leave	5 years or 18 (if child receives disability allowance)
Maternity records	Three
Annual appraisal/assessment records	Five
Records relating to promotion, transfer, training, discipline and grievance	Six years from end of employment
References given/information to enable reference to be provided	Five years from reference/end of Employment
Summary of record of service, eg, name, position held, dates of employment	Ten years from end of employment
Records relating to accident or injury at work, but other Health & Safety records will have different retention periods based on Regulations made under the Health & Safety at Work Act 1974, eg, COSHH medical records must be kept for 40 years whereas test results under the Regulations must be retained for five years	Three years after the date of last entry

4 Regulation of Investigatory Powers Act 2000

4.1 Introduction

The statute is to ensure that a legislative framework is in place so that investigatory powers are in accordance with human rights. For that reason many of its provisions have been aimed at state bodies.

The Regulation of Investigatory Powers Act 2000 (RIPA) creates certain criminal offences and 'unlawful interception of communications on a private telecommunications system by the operator of that system, without the consent of the parties' (sender and recipient). Specifically, it is unlawful, without authority, to intentionally intercept private or public telecommunications. The *defence* is that both parties have *consented* to the interception, or that the employer made reasonable efforts to obtain consent *or* that the employer had reasonable grounds for believing both parties had given their consent.

4.2 Summary of the Act

The scope of the legislation is wide: communications in the public or private sectors, including postal services, telephone, facsimile and e-mail.

- Employers will have to **obtain the permission** of the sender and the receiver of any telecommunication in order to '*oversee*' the message, (ie, to monitor, and/or record it). The employer can intercept communications if he has reasonable grounds to believe both the sender and recipient have consented. In order to make such a claim the employer will have to show that he had made '**reasonable efforts**' to inform the parties of his intention to intercept and monitor.

- The obligations for employers contained in the Act raise the possibility that employers will have to **consult** with employee representatives in order to fulfil the requirement to obtain permission.

- In accordance with the Data Protection Act 1998 employers should obtain the consent of employees before **tracking** (ie, monitoring) communications.

4.3 Section 1(3) of the RIPA 2000 explored in detail

The section states:

'Any interception of a communication...by, or with the express or implied consent of, a person having the right to control the operation or the use of a private telecommunication system shall be actionable at the suit or instance of the sender or recipient, or intended recipient, of the communication if it is without lawful authority and is either:

(a) An interception of that communication in the course of its transmission by means of that private system; or

(b) An interception of that communication in the course of its transmission, by means of a public telecommunication system, to or from apparatus comprised in that private telecommunication system.'

Term	Comment
Communication	Means virtually any type of communication
Private telecommunication system	Means any internal system, including internal mobile 'phones
Interception in the course of transmission	Includes storage and further access to the communication at a later date, so covers e-mail in-boxes, web address pages, computer caches and back-up systems

Lawful authority	Means the person who controls the private telecommunication system will be liable unless consent to the interception has taken place by both parties. An express clause inserted into contracts of employment in pursuance of a *Computer Use Policy* is, therefore vital. This remains best advice, notwithstanding the effect of the **Lawful Business Practice Regulations 2000**.

5 Telecommunications (Lawful Business Practice) (Interception of Communications) Regulations 2000 (SI 2000/2699) (Regulation 3 amended by Regulation 34 of The Privacy and Electronic Communications (EC Directive) Regulation 2003)

5.1 Introduction

The Regulations, which are designed to regulate the interception of employees' telephone calls and e-mails by employers aim to ensure that the monitoring of communications is carried out in compliance with the **EC Telecommunications Data Protection Directive (No. 97/66) (adapted by the UK in December 1997)**. These Regulations authorise certain interceptions of telecommunication communications which would otherwise be prohibited by section 1 of the Regulation of Investigatory Powers Act 2000. The central theme is that the Secretary of State is empowered to make regulations to define the capability of employers to intercept and monitor employees' communications (facsimile, e-mail, telephone, Internet). Indeed, provided the employer acts in certain ways monitoring/recording of communications will not be unlawful under the RIPA 2000.

5.2 Specific ramifications for employers

There are three main elements to the Regulations:

(a) 'The interception of communications at work must be effected solely for the purpose of monitoring or keeping a record of communications relevant to the business'. This means that the employer can monitor private calls, but only with the consent of the parties. This can be obtained by warning the parties that this is a likelihood, eg, by placing warnings on outgoing e-mails; and

(b) The interception must take place on a telecommunications system provided for use wholly or partly in connection with that business; and

(c) All reasonable efforts must be made by the employer to inform every person who may use the telecommunications system that communications may be intercepted.

5.3 Exceptions

Essentially, these Regulations provide for a number of exceptions to the need to gain consent before lawful interception takes place. Reg. 3(1) (a) allows monitoring and recording contents of messages without consent where *any* of the following applies:

(a) The employer wishes to establish the existence of facts, eg, to provide evidence of commercial transactions/business communications

(b) Compliance with regulatory or self-regulatory practices or procedures relevant to the business

(c) To enforce standards by persons in the course of their duties (eg, customer-call monitoring, quality control, staff training)

(d) In preventing or detecting crime, fraud or corruption

(e) To investigate and detect unauthorised use of the system (eg, monitoring to ensure compliance with employer's Internet and e-mail policies) and/or

(f) To protect the system against viruses, load distribution or hackers.

Additionally the employer is able to monitor (but not record) messages where:

- The communications received by the employee (irrespective of whether they relate to the business) in order to establish whether they relate to the business (this can include opening employees' voice-mail or e-mail), and/or

- To monitor staff help lines or counselling services to support the providers of advice/counselling (where anonymity is guaranteed to callers).

5.4 Limitations on the exceptions

Before these exceptions may be made use of it is important the employer recognises some **limitations** placed on them as follows:

- The interception must relate to the business or take place during the course of that business; and

- The system intercepted must be wholly or partly in connection with the business; or/and

- The employer must have 'made all reasonable efforts' to 'inform' all users and they have not objected to it. The employer can deal with this problem simply by inserting relevant clauses in contracts of employment, service contracts and by informing customers in writing.

5.5 Implications of the Regulations

Critically, '**sensitive personal data**' (eg, medical records, criminal records, ethnic data or data related to political or trade union membership) are not covered by the above provisions. Under the Human Rights Convention individuals have the right to a '**reasonable expectation of privacy**'. However, even the Convention and the DPA make the point that all rights of privacy must be balanced against the human rights of others and matters such as national security.

The exceptions contained in the Regulations provide **statutory definitions** of what is proportional where consent may not be granted and the individual has not objected. The issue of objections and consent can be overcome by ensuring the employer has expressed (or where relevant, implied) consent.

Once appropriate employment contract clauses are in place and policies have been laid down the employer may discipline or dismiss employees who are caught breaching e-mail or other relevant policies. The monitoring and recording will have taken place in accordance with the above exceptions.

6 Data protection related matters

6.1 E-mail – broad coverage of legal liability

The wide use of e-mail and the downloading of data from websites etc, creates situations where employers can find themselves **vicariously liable** for the acts of their employees. For example:

Harassment. This can be sexual, sex-related or racial, religious in nature, age or disability-based or non-specific. For harassment to take place it is not necessary for anyone to have been actively or directly targeted.

Bullying. This could arise from the receipt of so-called '*flame-mail*' – abusive, aggressive or deliberately anti-social e-mail. These messages could be rude, upsetting, unduly sarcastic or sexually or racially unacceptable or derogatory in respect of the recipient's disability.

Trust and confidence. The two matters indicated above could also give rise to a breach of the implied contractual term of trust and confidence, permitting the employee to resign and begin proceedings for unfair constructive dismissal.

Libel. Comments made during the course of an e-mail exchange.

Defamation. This can occur where material is posted on a website.

Negligence. Employers will be vicariously liable for a person acting as their 'agent'.

In the case of harassment and bullying of employees it will be relatively easy for the victim to show that the act in question was perpetrated during 'the course of employment'.

Examples

- Sending pornographic material to someone of the opposite sex; or
- Sending cartoons or language (eg, 'jokes') to someone of the opposite sex or of another racial group.

It will be no defence to argue that the communication was sent without meaning harm. Even where the communication is sent between two persons, of which neither are the victim, a third person may be able to successfully argue that such an activity contributes towards an atmosphere or culture of harassment resulting in discrimination.

6.2 Policy implementation

As part of a data protection policy the following could be considered.

Introduce a strict 'no personal use' policy, but possibly:

- Permit reasonable personal use of e-mail and Internet (eg, for essential purposes), or
- Permit personal use during employee's own time, eg, lunch periods, or
- Permit employees unrestricted use, although this has risks.

6.3 Unacceptable use of e-mail/Internet

Examples

- Use of unauthorised or pirated software
- Downloading pornographic or sexually explicit material
- Infringement of copyright by copying or forwarding material
- Sending attachments to messages that contain statements or pictures that could be interpreted as being sexually or racially unlawful
- Similarly, sending defamatory or derogatory material
- Sending confidential or sensitive material outside the organisation
- Sending/forwarding chain-mail
- Excessive personal use

7 Recommended course of action for employers

The following represents some of the basic steps that could be taken by employers who wish to establish clear conformity with the Data Protection Act 1998 and other relevant legislation.

7.1 Employer's actions

Because of the alleged weaknesses in recent legislation from the perspective of employers seeking to protect their vital interests, it is critical that all employees are committed in contract to strictly prescribed behaviours.

- The employer should set up a data protection compliance programme so that all data management practices comply with law. They should assess all data collection, processing, monitoring and recording processes, and measure each part of the established system for compliance.

- The employer should draw up a policy that is specifically designed to meet organisational needs and specification. This must include the range and type of technology and communications systems used, and future developments. Clear business purpose(s) must be identified and documented to justify measures taken.

- The policy should be implemented consistently throughout the organisation.

- The policy should be regularly updated, monitored and re-distributed to employees. It should be a vital part of induction.

- The policy should be clearly referenced in the contract of employment as part of management's instructions (attention should be given to the requirements of the **Regulation of Investigatory Powers Act 2000** – in particular s 3).

- A clear policy on systems use must be prepared and disseminated to all employees. This would include examples of the type of communications or surveillance that is prohibited. Other matters could be house style, etiquette and terminology. Specific policies can be drawn-up for 'e-mail and Internet Use', 'Surveillance', 'Data Protection', and so on (the **Telecommunications (Lawful Business Practice) Regulations 2000 SI 2000/1337 Reg 3(1)(a)(iv)** allows monitoring to investigate or detect the unauthorised use of a private telecommunications system, provided the system controller has taken all reasonable steps to inform persons who may use the system of the monitoring).

- The employer should apply the Data Protection Principles included in the **Data Protection Act 1998**.

- All employees should be given clear instructions on the rules, parameters and limitations of the use of communications, surveillance and technology-based systems. This must include clear instructions on the receipt and use of any personal communications, including the use of the employer's facilities and systems for personal use.

- Confidentiality should be maintained in all systems. Appropriate encryption and codes should be used. Passwords should be reset regularly. A non-disclosure policy must be routinely enforced through contracts of employment. Consequences of hacking and unauthorised sharing of employer's data should be a disciplinary offence.

- Surveillance should be proportional to the need for its use. Full account of the **Human Rights Act 1998** and the **Data Protection Act 1998** must be made in this respect. Reasonable surveillance could be for purposes of monitoring volume and nature of communications, to enhance quality of customer services, to tailor staff training and to dissuade employees and public from committing criminal acts. As emphasised above, it is important to get initial agreement ('consent') from the employee by inserting relevant clauses in the contract of employment. But, note that in respect of personal data the Data Protection Act 1998 does not enable the employer to apply a blanket forced compliance consent in respect of data subjects. Insertion of relevant clauses into documentation collateral to the contract (eg, management rules) may not be sufficient to satisfy the requirements of the Information Commissioner.

- The employer should ban personal use of software or unofficial use of pin numbers or codes. They should also ban personal use of games, videos or clip art.

- The non-receipt and eradication of any computer virus must be paramount. This means that the receipt of any non-solicited or suspect electronic communication must be deleted.

- Breaches of the above rules must be made a disciplinary offence. Clear references should be included in a disciplinary procedure, which also takes account of the **ACAS Code of Practice on Disciplinary and Grievance Procedures**, the Employment Act 2002 and the Employment Act 2002 (Dispute Resolution) Regulations 2004 SI no.752. Examples of both breaches of discipline and the likely penalties (such as dismissal) must be included in employer's procedures. (NB: Even without a policy it is probably the case that excessive use of the employer's system for personal reasons or serious misuse of a computer would be a breach of contract (implied terms) that could render the individual liable for disciplinary action or dismissal.) As with any sound disciplinary policy it must clearly set out the standards of behaviour that will not be tolerated.

- The employer should provide for a grievance and complaints machinery for matters arising out of any of the above. Also, a clear contact point/person should be identified for advice.

- The employer should take into account other relevant legislation such as **the Public Interest Disclosure Act 1998**.

8 Employee information in relation to recruitment and selection

8.1 The right of foreign persons to work in the UK

Foreign nationals who wish to work in the UK fall into three main categories:

(a) **Nationals of the European Economic Area (EEA)**

> **The European Economic Area**
>
> Austria, Belgium, Bulgaria, Cyprus, Czech Republic, Denmark, Estonia, Finland, France, Germany, Greece, Hungary, Iceland, Irish Republic, Italy, Latvia, Liechtenstein, Lithuania, Luxembourg, Malta, Netherlands, Norway, Poland, Portugal, Romania, Slovakia, Slovenia, Spain, Sweden, United Kingdom.
>
> Iceland, Liechtenstein and Norway are not members of the European Union (EU) but citizens of these countries have the same rights to enter, live in and work in the United Kingdom as EU citizens.

All EEA and Swiss nationals can enter and live in the UK without needing to apply for permission.

Certain EEA nationals do not automaticaly have the right to work in the UK:

- Nationals of a country that joined the European Union (EU) in 2004, may need to register with the Borders Agency when starting work.

- Bulgarian and Romanian nationals may need to apply for permission before they can start work.

- All other EEA and Swiss nationals are free to take work in the UK without needing to apply for permission.

Some states such as Turkey have Association status with limited rights.

(b) **Non-EEA nationals for whom a work visa is not necessary**

Some categories of non-EEA persons do not require work permits, the two main examples are:

1. A business visitor. The visitor must be able to show that they:
   - Only want to visit the UK for up to six months
   - Plan to leave the UK at the end of the visit
   - Have enough money to support and accommodate themselves without working, help from public funds or that they will be supported and accommodated by relatives or friends

- Do not intend to charge members of the public for services provided or goods received
- Do not intend to study
- Can meet the cost of the return or onward journey
- Are based abroad and have no intention of transferring their base to the UK even temporarily
- Are receiving salary from abroad

2. A citizen of a Commonwealth country and one grandparent was born in the UK (including the Channel Islands and the Isle of Man), they have UK ancestry.

Eligibility:

- A Commonwealth citizen
- Aged 17 or over
- Have a grandparent who was born in the UK (including the Channel Islands and the Isle of Man), or a grandparent who was born before 31 March 1922 in what is now the Republic of Ireland
- Are able to work and plan to work in the UK and
- Can adequately support and accommodate themselves and their dependants without help from public funds

(c) **Non-EEA nationals requiring a work visa**

To update the immigration issues facing the UK, the Labour government revised the previous systems and over time introduced a five-tier points-based system. However reflecting the political sensitivity of immigration the tiers are already subject to suspension and modification having only been fully implemented for a number of months.

The points-based system

- The points-based system only covers migrants from outside the European Economic Area (EEA) and Switzerland.
- Migrants will need to pass a points-based assessment before they are given permission to enter or remain in the United Kingdom.
- The system consists of five tiers. Each tier has different points requirements.

The five tiers comprise:

- **Tier 1:** For highly skilled migrants, entrepreneurs, investors, and graduate students.
- **Tier 2:** This is for skilled workers who have a job offer, most importantly for the employer, General (recruitment) and Intra Company Transfers.
- **Tier 3:** For a limited numbers of lower skilled workers to fill temporary shortages in the labour market.
- **Tier 4:** Students.
- **Tier 5:** For youth mobility and temporary workers, such as those entering the country under Working Holiday agreements with other countries.

The role of the sponsor

Migrants applying under any tier except Tier 1 need to be sponsored in order for their application to be successful. If an employer wishes to recruit a migrant they will have to apply for a sponsor licence.

Employer sponsor licence

An employer is required to have a licence before they can sponsor skilled or temporary workers under the points-based system. To get a licence, they are required to have good human resources systems and compliance in place. This means:

- Monitoring immigration status and preventing illegal employment
- Maintaining migrant contact details
- Recordkeeping
- Migrant tracking and monitoring
- Professional registrations and accreditations

The successful employer will be given an A or B rating and added to the UK Border Agency's published register of sponsors. The B rating is for sponsors who the Border Agency thinks could be a risk to immigration control or who do not have all the correct systems in place. They must follow a sponsorship action plan designed to help them become A-rated, or they risk losing their licence.

Certificates of sponsorship

Sponsors are responsible for assigning certificates of sponsorship to migrant workers in Tiers 2 and 5.

Once accredited as a sponsor the employer will have an allocated number of certificates of sponsorship which empower them to bring sponsored workers into the country. The number will be first agreed with the Border Agency and based on the anticipated number required. Once these are allocated the employer is able to apply for a further allocation, however this will need to be justified.

The worker will need the certificate of sponsorship when they apply for a visa to come to or stay in the UK. They will also need to pass a points-based assessment before they can come to or stay in the UK.

Sponsorship duties

As a licensed sponsor, the employer is responsible for ensuring that migrants comply with their immigration conditions, by keeping records on them and reporting any changes (such as a failure to turn up for work) to the Border Agency. Failure to comply can result in a licence being downgraded or withdrawn.

Tier 2

General and Intra Company Transfers

Key elements of the points-based system

1. The employer must obtain a sponsor licence before they can employ skilled workers under Tiers 2 and 5.
2. The employer must comply with their sponsorship duties.
3. The employer must issue a certificate of sponsorship to each non-EEA worker who they want to sponsor, so that they can apply for a new visa or extension of their stay.
4. They must use the sponsorship management system to issue and pay for each certificate of sponsorship, and to fulfil their reporting duties.

General

This is for people coming to the UK with a skilled job offer to fill a gap in the workforce that cannot be filled by a settled worker.

Intra Company Transfer (ICT)

There are three sub-categories in the ICT category:

- Established staff. This route is for established, skilled employees to be transferred to the UK branch of their organisation to fill a post that cannot be filled by a settled worker.

- Graduate trainee. This route allows the transfer of recent graduate recruits to a UK branch of the organisation, for training purposes.

- Skills transfer. This route allows the transfer of new recruits to a UK branch of the organisation to acquire the skills and knowledge that they will need overseas, or to impart their specialist skills or knowledge to the UK workforce.

Points scoring

Points are awarded under the points based system for the following:

- Qualifications (this ranges from GCSE A-Level equivalents to PhDs)
- Future Expected Earnings (the salary that is received by the applicant)
- Sponsorship (the type of sponsorship being applied for)
- English language skills
- Available maintenance (funds available to support the applicant).

In order for a worker to apply they require a valid certificate of sponsor. This can only be issued by a sponsor who is registered with the UK Border Agency.

As an indication of the evolving position regarding the immigration requirements it is interesting to note:

- In 2010 the government reduced the number of people eligible to enter the UK on a Tier 1 visa and proposed to revise the criteria for entry under this Tier.

- In 2011 the government is proposing to permanently limit the number of Tier 2 General entries.

- Tiers 3 and 5 were introduced as temporary migration schemes without the ability to switch to other tiers. However during 2010 the government suspended Tier 3, reflecting the employment issues in the UK.

Posting of Workers Directive 1996 (96/71)

This came into effect in 1999 and covers EU states only. Most UK legislation incorporates the principles in the Directive, but a number of regulations were introduced in 1999 to ensure full compliance.

The Directive applies to undertakings which:

(i) Post workers to another state on their account and under their direction under a contract concluded between the undertaking and a party in the other state for whom the services are intended

(ii) Make intra-company postings or

(iii) Are temporary employment undertakings or agencies which hire out workers to undertakings established or operating in an EU member state.

Protection is provided for those posted workers in an employment relationship in respect of:

(i) Maximum work periods and minimum rest periods

(ii) Minimum paid holidays

(iii) Minimum rates of pay

(iv) Conditions on the hiring of workers

(v) Health, safety and hygiene at work

(vi) Measures to protect pregnant women, new mothers, children and young people, and

(vii) Equality of treatment between men and women.

The objective of this legislation is that no posted worker should enjoy a lower rate or standard of protection or reward in respect of the above compared to the nationally or sectorally applied terms and conditions applicable in the country to which s/he has been posted.

8.2 Employer's obligations under the Immigration, Asylum and Nationality Act 2006

The Act makes it a civil and criminal offence to

' employ an adult (defined as someone having attained 16 years of age) subject to immigration control if.........he has not been granted leave to enter or remain in the UK. Or his leave to enter or remain is invalid...or has ceased to have effect.....is subject to a condition preventing him from accepting the employment...'

The penalties are:

- An unlimited fine and/or a prison sentence of up to two years for employers who employ an adult who they know is not legally entitled to work in the UK; or

- A civil penalty of up to £10,000 per employee if the employer did not make appropriate checks and did not know that the worker was not legally entitled to work in the UK. An employer who has been served with a civil penalty is entitled to object to the Secretary of State.

The offence can only be committed in respect of an **employee**, not a self-employed worker. The former category may include agency workers but any liability will be with the employing agency.

Although a person with no right to work in the UK might be discovered working for an employer, that employer *may* be excused from paying a penalty if he shows that he complied with any of the prescribed requirements in relation to the employment. Clearly, sensible employers will put in place proper checks to avoid such a situation occurring in the first place.

8.3 How should an employer establish a defence under the Immigration, Asylum and Nationality Act 2006?

An employer is excused from paying a penalty under the Act if:

(a) The employee or prospective employee produces to the employer any of the documents or combinations of documents described in Lists A or B in the Schedule to the order (a person producing documents from List B will have a time limit on their legal liability to stay and work in the UK), and

(b) The employer complies with the requirements set out in Article 6 of the order.

(c) For the duration of the employment, if the document or combination of documents is produced prior to the commencement of employment; or

(d) Subject to Article 5, for the remainder of the employment, if the document or combination of documents is produced after the employment has commenced.

The documents which can verify the holder's right to work in the UK include the following:

> **LIST A DOCUMENTS**
>
> 1. An ID Card (issued to the holder under the Identity Cards Act 2006) or a passport showing that the holder, or a person named in the passport as the child of the holder, is a British citizen or a citizen of the United Kingdom and Colonies having the right of abode in the United Kingdom; **or**
>
> 2. An ID card (issued to the holder under the Identity Cards Act 2006), a national identity card or a passport which has the effect of identifying the holder, or a person named in the passport as the child of the holder, as a national of the European Economic Area or Switzerland; **or**
>
> 3. A residence permit, registration certificate or document certifying or indicating permanent residence issued by the Home Office or the Border and Immigration Agency to a national of a European Economic Area country or Switzerland; **or**
>
> 4. A permanent residence card issued by the Home Office or the Border and Immigration Agency to the family member of a national of a European Economic Area country or Switzerland; **or**
>
> 5. A Biometric Immigration Document issued by the Border and Immigration Agency to the holder which indicates that the person named in it is allowed to stay indefinitely in the United Kingdom, or has no time limit on their stay in the United Kingdom; **or**
>
> 6. A passport or other travel document endorsed to show that the holder is exempt from immigration control, is allowed to stay indefinitely in the United Kingdom, has the right of abode in the United Kingdom, or has no time limit on their stay in the United Kingdom; **or**
>
> 7. An Immigration Status Document issued by the Home Office or the Border and Immigration Agency to the holder with an endorsement indicating that the person named in it is allowed to stay indefinitely in the United Kingdom, or has no time limit on their stay in the United Kingdom, **when produced in combination with** an official document giving the person's permanent National Insurance Number and their name issued by a Government agency or a previous employer (eg P45, P60, National Insurance Card); **or**
>
> 8. A full birth certificate issued in the United Kingdom which includes the name(s) of at least one of the holder's parents, **when produced in combination with** an official document giving the person's permanent National Insurance Number and their name issued by a Government agency or a previous employer (eg P45, P60, National Insurance Card); **or**

9. A full adoption certificate issued in the United Kingdom which includes the name(s) of at least one of the holder's adoptive parents, **when produced in combination with** an official document giving the person's permanent National Insurance Number and their name issued by a Government agency or a previous employer (eg P45, P60, National Insurance Card); **or**

10. A birth certificate issued in the Channel Islands, the Isle of Man, or Ireland, **when produced in combination with** an official document giving the person's permanent National Insurance Number and their name issued by a Government agency or a previous employer (eg P45, P60, National Insurance Card); **or**

11. An adoption certificate issued in the Channel Islands, the Isle of Man, or Ireland, **when produced in combination with** an official document giving the person's permanent National Insurance Number and their name issued by a Government agency or a previous employer (eg P45, P60, National Insurance Card); **or**

12. A certificate of registration or naturalisation as a British citizen, **when produced in** combination with an official document giving the person's permanent National Insurance Number and their name issued by a Government agency or a previous employer (eg P45, P60, National Insurance Card); **or**

13. A letter issued by the Home Office or the Border and Immigration Agency to the holder which indicates that the person named in it is allowed to stay indefinitely in the United Kingdom, or has no time limit on their stay, **when produced in combination with** an official document giving the person's permanent National Insurance Number and their name issued by a Government agency or a previous employer (eg P45, P60, National Insurance Card).

LIST B DOCUMENTS

1. A passport or other travel document endorsed to show that the holder is allowed to stay in the United Kingdom and is allowed to do the work in question, provided that it does not require the issue of a work permit; **or**

2. A Biometric Immigration Document, issued by the Border and Immigration Agency to the holder which indicates that the person named in it can stay in the United Kingdom and is allowed to do the work in question; **or**

3. A work permit or other approval to take employment issued by the Home Office or the Border and Immigration Agency, **when produced in combination with** either a passport or another travel document endorsed to show that the holder is allowed to stay in the United Kingdom and is allowed to do the work in question, or a letter issued by the Home Office or the Border and Immigration Agency to the holder, or the employer or prospective employer confirming the same; **or**

4. A certificate of application issued by the Home Office or the Border and Immigration Agency to or for a family member of a national of a European Economic Area country or Switzerland, stating that the holder is permitted to take employment, which is less than six months old, when produced in combination with evidence of verification by the Border and Immigration Agency Employer Checking Service; **or**

5. A residence card or document issued by the Home Office or the Border and Immigration Agency to a family member of a national of a European Economic Area country or Switzerland; **or**

6. An Application Registration Card (ARC) issued by the Home Office or the Border and Immigration Agency stating that the holder is permitted to take employment, **when produced in combination with** evidence of verification by the Border and Immigration Agency Employer Checking Service; **or**

7. An Immigration Status Document issued by the Home Office or the Border and Immigration Agency to the holder with an endorsement indicating that the person named in it can stay in the United Kingdom, and is allowed to do the work in question, **when produced in combination with** an official document giving the person's permanent National Insurance Number and their name issued by a Government agency or previous employer (eg P45, P60, National Insurance Card); **or**

8. A letter issued by the Home Office or the Border and Immigration Agency to the holder or the employer or prospective employer, which indicates that the person named in it can stay in the United Kingdom and is allowed to do the work in question, **when produced in combination with** an official document giving the person's permanent National Insurance Number and their name issued by a Government agency or previous employer (e.g. P45, P60, National Insurance Card)

(Guidance For Employers on the avoidance of unlawful discrimination in employment practice while seeking to prevent illegal working – Code of Practice 2008; www.bia.homeoffice.gov.uk)

The Order also sets out the '*checking*' requirements, which the employer has to adhere to when s/he is checking the documents. The list is extensive and should be viewed in full. However, some of the requirements are:

(a) The employer takes all reasonable steps to check the validity

(b) Copy(ies) are retained securely for a period of not less than two years after the employment has come to an end

(c) The employer must be satisfied of the likeness of any photograph produced

(d) The birth certificate and visual birth date of the employee are the same

(e) The employee is the rightful owner of the document and

(f) If the document is a passport it has been copied in a specified way

Employers will be required to undertake repeat document checks at least once a year for those employees joining them after 29th February 2008 who have limited leave to enter or remain in the United Kingdom, if they wish to retain their statutory excuse. Employers who acquire employees following a transfer of undertakings (TUPE transfer) will be given 28 days' grace to undertake the appropriate document checks.

The biggest difficulty for employers is to avoid any complaints of race discrimination in respect of refusing work or dismissing the employee where there is suspicion about his or her right to work in the UK. The Code of Practice does contain some advice on this, namely:

- Have clear written procedures for the recruitment and selection of all staff, based on equal and fair treatment for all applicants. Copies of these procedures should be made available to all relevant staff.

- All job selections should be on the basis of suitability for the post. You should not make assumptions about a person's right to work or immigration status on the basis of their colour, race, nationality, or ethnic or national origins, or the length of time they have been resident in the UK.

- Treat all applicants in the same way at each stage of the recruitment process.

- Ask applicants to provide the specified document(s) to obtain a statutory excuse at any stage **before** they start work.

- Job applicants should not be treated less favourably if they produce a document or documents from **List B** rather than **List A**.

- Once a person who has limited leave to remain has established their initial and ongoing entitlement to work, they should not be treated less favourably during their employment.

- Only ask questions about an applicant's or employee's immigration status, where necessary, to determine whether their status imposes limitations on the number of hours they are entitled to work each week, or on the length of time they are permitted to work within their overall period or type of leave given.

- If a person is not able to produce the appropriate listed document(s), the employer should not assume that he or she is living or working in the UK illegally. The employer should instead refer the person to the Border Agency. **It is ultimately the decision of the employer whether or not to employ an individual.**

8.4 References

Despite long-standing doubts over the validity of evaluating prospective employees by obtaining references they continue to enjoy widespread use. Some of the basic steps which an employer should follow in seeking a reference are:

- A reference should only be sought with the prospective employee's consent.

- In making a conditional offer of employment subject to a 'satisfactory' reference it is important to ensure the prospective employee is informed that it should be 'satisfactory' to the employer.

- The role and timing of references should be clearly decided in advance. For instance, are they to be used for screening or the final offer of a job? Will the job be offered subject to a satisfactory reference or obtained before the offer of a job is made?

- Usually, only employment references are of use to a prospective employer. Personal references can be used for specific reasons, particularly for those applicants without a work history eg, social interests, school, college or university activities, and interest in team activities.

- A checklist should be drawn-up to help focus the prospective employer on particular aspects of the candidate linked to the person specification and job description.

8.5 Legal responsibilities of employer, providing references

There is usually no obligation on an employer to provide a worker with a reference on termination of the employment contract. An exception is where a reference is required by a regulatory body such as the Financial Services Authority (FSA). The **legal responsibilities** of those employers requesting and providing references can be summarised as follows.

(a) **Prospective employers requesting a reference**

Employers should ensure that references are kept confidential and not passed on to third parties with no direct interest in the selection of a candidate.

(b) **Previous or present employers providing a reference**

(i) Former or current employers **owe a duty of care** to the (former) employee in the preparation of his/her reference (that is the employer will be liable for damages for consequences arising out of a reasonably foreseeable negligent act. An example would be where the employer prepared a highly critical reference without bothering to properly check the facts). An employee is able to sue for negligent misstatement where the reference is not constructed with due care and attention.

(ii) Employers are not completely protected by the defence of 'qualified privilege', in expressing their honest (albeit prejudiced) beliefs freely and frankly. Where malice can be shown on the part of the employer providing the reference they lose the protection of 'qualified privilege'. To prove this is difficult, however, and because there is no legal aid for actions of defamation those claims submitted by (former) employees are rare.

(iii) Once negligence **has been established** on the part of the (former) employer, the employee, in order to obtain damages, does **not** have to prove that they **would have secured** the new job had it not been for the negligent reference. What must be proved, however, is that there **was a reasonable chance** of securing the new job.

(iv) In industries where it is the norm to provide job references there is probably an implied term in the contract of the **(current)** employee that an employer would provide an honest reference in good faith.

(v) A prospective employer (to whom the reference is given) can sue for damages (for the negligence of the reference-provider), if they rely on the information contained in the reference to their **disadvantage**. For instance, the information subsequently proves to be inaccurate and the employee in question is hired but through their incompetence or dishonesty causes loss to new the employer. Where the reference provider knowingly makes a false statement (but not necessarily intended damage) the new employer might be able to sue for **fraudulent mis-statement**. (However see point immediately below.)

References provided by a (former) employer to a prospective employer are not grounds for **libel** even if the information is inaccurate, if the former believes the information is correct and provides it **in good faith**.

The (former) employee may sue for damages because of the **slander** (spoken word) or **libel** (written word) of their (former) employer where that employer knows the information to be untrue. Alternatively they may also sue where the information falls into the hands of a third party not directly interested in the selection process. Sensible employers will mark references '**private and confidential**' and address them to named representatives of the employer requesting the reference. Both parties should be aware of the relevant sections of the Data Protection Act 1998.

A situation could arise where an employer hires an employee without properly checking the relevant references or *bona fides* of the employee. Should the new employee subsequently cause damage to a third party the latter could sue the employer for negligent hiring. An example would be where a person fraudulently alleging to be a medical practitioner was hired without any proper checks on their background, qualifications and other references. Any patient who suffered harm at the hands of such a person could sue the employer.

(c) **A true, accurate and fair reference**

A reference must be 'true, accurate and fair' and it must not give an unfair or misleading impression overall. Employers should confine unfavourable statements about the employee to those matters into which they had made reasonable investigation and had reasonable grounds for believing to be true.

Information to be provided in a reference. This should be in the form of a checklist. The questions should be printed in a letter sent to the referee-employer. The provider of the reference should be asked to give their name (signature and printed), their contact telephone number and address, their position in the company and their working relationship with the employee. The referee-employer should be informed in writing of the job in question and relevant details (such as a job description and person specification). Also, they should be informed that the information to be provided is private and confidential, and that should the candidate be unsuccessful the information in the reference will be destroyed.

Steps to avoid legal problems

- References should always be in writing *(telephone references should be followed-up in writing)*

- A pre-prepared checklist should be used for each job reference and the letter requesting the reference based on it

- Only specified authorised persons in an organisation should be permitted to prepare references. If necessary these should be authorised by a senior manager or the HR/personnel department or officer

- References should be prepared based on factual records (eg, personal file, disciplinary records and appraisal records), and

- Information should be kept private and confidential, and within the terms of Data Protection principles.

In practice, many employers only give a purely factual reference confirming dates of employment and job title, to avoid any possibility of action being taken against them. Obviously, such a reference is only of limited value to the worker. Due to the difficulties, it is usually advisable to obtain an agreed reference as part of any settlement negotiated on an unfair dismissal or discrimination case.

Disclaimer notices

Notices attached or written into references which disclaim legal liability (such as 'without prejudice') do not over-ride those principles laid out in the sections above. In addition these disclaimers are subject to the test of 'reasonableness' in the **Unfair Contract Terms Act 1978**.

8.6 Information relating to criminal convictions

The legislation: the **Rehabilitation of Offenders Act 1974 (RoOAct)**. The principles behind the legislation is that after a specified period of time a criminal conviction becomes 'spent' – that is, the conviction can no longer be taken into account by an employer when making decisions to hire employees. Section 1 of the Act provides that at the end of the '**spent**' period the individual becomes a '**rehabilitated person**'.

8.7 Rehabilitation period

The rehabilitation period commences with the date of the sentence. These are as follows.

Sentence	Becomes spent after
Imprisonment of between 6 months and 2 years and 6 months	10 years
Imprisonment of up to 6 months	7 years
Borstal training	7 years
A fine or other sentence not otherwise covered in this table	5 years
Conditional discharge	The period of the order, or a minimum of 12 months (whichever is longer)
Absolute discharge	6 months
Conditional Caution	3 months
Simple Caution, Reprimand, Final Warning	Spent immediately
Probation order, conditional discharge or bind over	1 year (or until order expires, whichever is the longer)
Detention Centre Order	3 years
Remand home, attendance centre or approved school order	The period of the order and a further year after the order expires
Hospital order under the Mental Health Act	Five years, or a period ending two years after the order expires (whichever is longer)
Discharge with ignominy or dismissal with disgrace from the Armed Forces	10 years
Dismissal from the Armed Forces	7 years
Detention in the Armed Forces	5 years

Important

(i) A sentence of more than 2 years and 6 months' imprisonment can never become spent.

(ii) Those aged under 18 years of age on the date of conviction enjoy rehabilitation periods of approximately half those in the right hand column.

Certain convictions can **never become spent**. These include:

- Imprisonment or custody for life
- Sentences of imprisonment, youth custody or corrective training for a term exceeding thirty months and
- Detention during Her Majesty's pleasure.

Once a conviction has become 'spent' the 'rehabilitated person' is not obliged to disclose to an employer or prospective employer:

- The spent conviction
- The offence for which s/he was sentenced or
- Any circumstances surrounding the conviction in any judicial proceedings – in answer to any questions relating to his/her past behaviour or by virtue of any agreement requiring him/her to disclose such information.

These questions could be asked on a job application form, during a selection interview or when requesting a reference. Similarly, any dismissal arising out of the discovery of a spent conviction may be unfair.

Where a further offence is committed during the rehabilitation period this will have the effect of **extending** the period accordingly.

Those engaged in certain occupations and professions are obliged to disclose any spent convictions and may be dismissed or excluded from that employment because of such a conviction. These occupations and professions include:

- Doctors, nurses, pharmacists, midwives, dentists
- Solicitors, barristers and accountants
- Teachers and police officers

The legislation has been further extended to employers in a number of sectors, but particularly those dealing with children and vulnerable persons.

Those concerned in the provision of accommodation, care, leisure and recreational facilities, schooling, social services, supervision or training to persons under eighteen years of age – where the job holder would have access to these minors in the normal course of duties – OR where the duties carried-out are wholly or mainly on the premises where such provision takes place. The latter would include caretakers, maintenance staff, administrative and bursarial staff.

They are now obliged to ascertain whether or not a job applicant does have a 'spent' or 'unspent' conviction which could disbar them from work in that sector.

8.8 Criminal Records Bureau

The Criminal Records Bureau (CRB) acts as a 'one-stop-shop' for organisations, checking police records and, in relevant cases, information held by the Independent Safeguarding Authority (ISA). The CRB is an executive agency of the Home Office.

The CRB offers two levels of criminal conviction disclosure:

Standard check

Is available for any position or licensing application listed in the Rehabilitation of Offenders Act 1974, (Exceptions) Order 1975 (ROA). Standard CRB checks show current and spent convictions, cautions, reprimands and warnings held on the Police National Computer.

A Standard check cannot reveal if a person is ISA-registered or barred from working with children or vulnerable adults.

Enhanced check

An Enhanced CRB check is available to anyone who works in what is known as a 'prescribed position'. These are the positions which are in the ROA and have also been named in Police Act Regulations. Regulated Activity with either Children or Vulnerable Adults, certain Judicial Appointments and Gambling Licence Applications are examples of prescribed positions.

Enhanced CRB checks contain the same information as the Standard CRB checks but with the addition of

- Any relevant and proportionate information held by the local police forces
- A check of the new Children and or Vulnerable Adults barred lists where requested

The CRB has issued a Code of Practice as a guide to the issuing of certificates.

8.9 Spent convictions and unfair dismissal

The Act provides that dismissal or exclusion from office of an individual for having or not revealing a 'spent' conviction shall be unlawful. The 'rehabilitated' person must have one year's continuous employment to bring a complaint of unfair dismissal to the Employment Tribunal.

8.10 Spent convictions and the right not to be excluded from office

Surprisingly, there is no specified statutory right for a 'rehabilitated' person to bring a complaint of 'Refusal to Employ' against the employer. There is no right of redress by way of a complaint to the Employment Tribunal. Although it could be argued by the 'rehabilitated' person that the prospective employer's actions in refusing him/her employment is a breach of the latter's statutory duty, the Employment Rights Act 1996 in listing breaches of statutory duty does not specify a breach of the Rehabilitation of Offenders Act 1974 as one of them. An application could be made to the High Court (QBD) that any failure to employ is a breach of statutory duty and for an injunction to be granted to restrain the employer's recruitment process. The use of this form of redress is very unlikely to be pursued and provides a poor remedy to the 'rehabilitated person' because the court cannot order the recruitment of a specific person.

8.11 Spent convictions – references

Prospective employers should not request information in regard to a person's 'spent' convictions. This does not prevent a referee (eg, an agency or former employer) giving details about 'spent' convictions provided the information is given without **malice.**

Where the information is given in good faith there will be no breach, but the employer who acts on such information to the detriment of the 'rehabilitated' person will be committing an unlawful act.

9 Medical information

9.1 Introduction

Many employers when hiring new employees rely on a self-completed questionnaire, or a brief examination by the organisation's doctor or nurse in order to verify the individual's state of health. There are strong commercial and legal reasons for having a suitable health screening process in place.

The Equality Act 2010 states:

> 'Except in the situations specified in this section, an employer must not ask about a job applicant's health until that person has been either offered a job (on a conditional or unconditional basis) or been included in a pool of successful candidates to be offered a job when a suitable position arises. The specified situations where health-related enquiries can be made are for the purposes of:

- Finding out whether a job applicant would be able to participate in an assessment to test his or her suitability for the work;
- Making reasonable adjustments to enable the disabled person to participate in the recruitment process;
- Finding out whether a job applicant would be able to undertake a function that is intrinsic to the job, with reasonable adjustments in place as required;
- Monitoring diversity in applications for jobs;
- Supporting positive action in employment for disabled people; and
- Enabling an employer to identify suitable candidates for a job where there is an occupational requirement for the person to be disabled.'

'Health screening' could be contrary to the Act if it does not limit itself to only those aspects 'intrinsic to the job'.

A second reason why employers wish to submit existing employees to medical examination is where the individual has been absent for a long period or has been absent for short but frequent periods. A validation process will not only help ascertain their fitness for future work, but help to make decisions in respect of transfer to less demanding work, to retire the employee on ill-health grounds (where often a pension entitlement is triggered), or where there are grounds for dismissal because of incapacity. Although it may be deemed reasonable for the employer to request the employee to undergo a medical examination, the prudent employer will include in the individual's contract of employment a clause which obliges the employee to submit to a medical examination at the employer's discretion.

It is important to emphasise, however, that whenever an employee is requested to attend a medical examination this should be carefully explained to the individual, who should be given the opportunity of discussing it with an appropriate manager. Any dismissal of an employee who refuses to attend a medical examination without being informed of the reason is likely to be unfair.

The medical examination where it is conducted by any doctor is governed by the principles of **confidentiality and informed consent**. Access to and the retrieval of information from the individual's health records are subject to two separate pieces of legislation:

- Access to Medical Reports Act 1988
- Access to Health Records Act 1990, parts of which are now incorporated into the Data Protection Act 1998.

9.2 Medical references – Access to Medical Reports Act 1988

- Individuals have a statutory right of access to their own medical reports prepared for employment and insurance purposes within **six months** of preparation.
- Individuals may comment on and ask the doctor to amend reports (for inaccuracies) before they are sent to a(n) (prospective) employer.
- Individuals may withhold consent for a report to be supplied or for an application to be made in the first place. (NB. the safety of others sometimes overrides this, for example in the case of an individual who has some disease or complaint which could put in jeopardy the health of others.)
- The Act covers data provided by medical practitioners who have 'clinical care' of the individual (these could include company doctors).
- The information covered by the Act is in respect of its use for all matters, eg, recruitment, promotion, early retirement.

9.3 Access to Health Records Act 1990

This statute applies to medical information compiled after November 1991. It applies to health records not falling within the scope of the Data Protection Act 1998. The principal purpose of this legislation is to enable the individual to have access to all medical information kept on them and to correct inaccuracies, whereas the 1988 legislation only applies to specified, and possibly very limited reports provided for a third party.

9.4 Interface between health and medical records and the Data Protection Act 1998

Any personal data covering an individual's physical or psychological health which is made by or on behalf of a health professional in 'connection with the care of that individual' will be deemed sensitive personal data. For the employer to obtain such data it is therefore essential for the data subject to give his or her prior consent. Where the individual grants permission s/he may additionally require access to the report before it is sent to the employer, and thereafter withhold consent. The individual may also bring to the attention of the medical practitioner any part of the record s/he believes is incorrect and ask for it to be corrected.

Part II of the Information Commissioner's **Employment Practices Data Protection Code of Practice** (Employment Records) states that:

'For the purposes of this Code it is necessary to distinguish between records that include "sensitive data" and those that do not.

The term 'sickness record' is therefore used to describe a record which contains details of the illness or condition responsible for a worker's absence. Similarly, an injury record is a record which contains details of the injury suffered. The term 'absence record' is used to describe a record that may give the reason for absence as 'sickness' or 'accident' but does not include any reference to specific medical conditions.

Many employers keep accident records. Such a record will only be an "injury record" if it includes details of the injury suffered by an identifiable worker.

Sickness and injury records include information about workers' physical or mental health. The holding of sickness or injury records will therefore involve the processing of sensitive personal data. This means one of the conditions for processing sensitive personal data must be satisfied.

Employers are advised as far as practicable to restrict their record keeping to absence records rather than sickness or injury records.'

The Code makes it clear that employees will need to give their consent for the employer to hold sickness records. Such records are bound to include sensitive personal data. Where data are held to satisfy statutory requirements (eg, SSP administration) consent will *not* be required.

10 Information relating to equality in the workplace

10.1 Monitoring

> The Equality and Human Rights Commission recommends the monitoring of the workforce.
>
> 'While there is currently no legal requirement on most organisations (including private sector businesses, smaller public bodies, voluntary and community sector organisations) to monitor and report on their staff profile, this can help an employer to assess whether, for example, they are:
>
> - Recruiting employees who are disadvantaged or under-represented
> - Promoting people fairly whatever their protected characteristic
> - Checking that women and men's pay is comparable in similar or equivalent jobs, or because the work they undertake is of equal value in relation to factors such as effort, skill and decision-making, and
> - Making progress towards the aims set out in their equality policy if they have one'
>
> 'It is important that you only collect information that you can use effectively. You need to be clear why you are asking applicants and workers for information and what you will use it for.'
>
> Recognising the introduction of the Equality Act the Commission states:
>
> 'In general, you must not ask a job applicant questions relating to health or disability. One of the exceptions to this rule applies to monitoring. You are allowed to ask questions about disability and health during recruitment if the point of this is to find out how many job applicants are disabled people and whether they are shortlisted or appointed.
>
> Answers to monitoring questions about health or disability should be dealt with in the same way as the answers to other monitoring questions, in other words, they should be kept separately from the main application form. The person or people shortlisting and appointing should not see the information before deciding who to interview or appoint.'

The monitoring should also apply to those seeking employment, promotion, training and further education.

Should an employer decide to go further by having a comprehensive monitoring system (as a part of human resource planning system) that tracks the progress of different categories of individuals it is imperative that it is done with the utmost confidentiality.

11 Occupational pension schemes

11.1 Information which should be made available

The trustees of any occupational pension scheme must make available to members (and prospective members), including beneficiaries and independent trade unions certain information about the scheme. This will include:

- The arrangements of the scheme covering its type, and the payments and contributions to be made
- The benefits payable under the scheme and
- Details of the audited accounts and annual report

12 Information which may or may not be lawfully protected under the Public Interest Disclosure Act 1998 (Whistleblowing)

12.1 Introduction

This Act came into force in 1999. It amended the **Employment Rights Act 1996** and inserts a number of new sections into the 1996 statute. The statute does *not* provide general protection to all those who disclose information about their employers, but is designed to protect those who disclose information to third parties about alleged wrong-doings in **prescribed circumstances**. A complex legal framework is required to make the Act work. **Protected persons** include employees, workers and contractors – although the term '*employee*' will be used for this section. Any contractual clause designed to prohibit a protected disclosure will be void. A sensible employer will produce specific procedures in the light of the Act so that key persons are identified to whom any disclosure should be made.

12.2 Key elements of the Act

The **subject matter** must be covered by the statute for the employee to receive protection. A qualifying disclosure means any disclosure of information which in the **reasonable belief** of the employee making the disclosure, tends to show one or more of the following.

- That a **criminal offence** has been committed, is being committed or is likely to be committed
- That a person has failed, is failing or is likely to fail to comply with the **legal obligation** to which s/he is subject

- That a **miscarriage of justice** has occurred, is occurring or is likely to occur
- That the **health of safety** of any individual has been, is being or is likely to be endangered
- That the **environment** has been, is being or is likely to be damaged, or
- That information tending to show any matter falling within any one of the preceding paragraphs has been, is being or is likely to be **deliberately concealed**.

Note that positive proof will not be necessary, only that a reasonable belief that one or more of the circumstances (above) is arising. Some grounds will have to be shown by the complainant for the belief to be reasonable.

The Minister of State provided anecdotal guidance on the meaning of the 'subject matter'.

'We would not want the full protection of the law to apply to, for example, a worker who discloses that his boss smokes, drives a car, or quite legitimately manufactures hazardous chemicals. If, however, his boss smokes in a munitions factory, that might be a different matter, as might the fact that the firm pollutes a river by discharging poisonous waste into it, or that the manufacturing process cuts corners on safety, or that the disposal of dangerous chemical by products is unregulated.'

12.3 Qualifications to the 'protected' disclosure of information

The person making the disclosure is not committing a legal offence, and it will not qualify if it is a disclosure in respect of which legal professional privilege would apply. It will be immaterial where the circumstances founding the disclosure occur – this means that they could occur anywhere in the world.

12.4 Procedures for a 'protected' disclosure

The purpose of these sections is to encourage an employee who is disclosing information to do so through the proper channels, not to the press and media.

- Disclosure to employer or other responsible person

    Where appropriate, the employee may make a disclosure in good faith to his/her employer. It is argued this should mean that the disclosure should be made to the person(s) who is legally responsible for the matter in contention.

- Disclosure to legal adviser

- Disclosure to Minister of the Crown

    This will apply only where an employee works directly or indirectly for the Government.

- Disclosure to a prescribed person

These persons are those prescribed by the Public Interest Disclosure (Prescribed Persons) Order 1999. **Examples**: statutory health and safety representatives, the Health & Safety Executive and the Financial Services Authority.

- Disclosure in other cases

    This provides a wide *catch-all* category, but there are a number of provisions to restrict unreasonable disclosure:

    - The employee must believe the information disclosed and any allegation is substantially true
    - The employee does not make the disclosure for personal gain
    - It is reasonable for the employee to make the disclosure, and
    - Any one of the following conditions is met:
        - That the employee reasonably believes that if they make the disclosure to their employee/a prescribed person they will suffer a detriment
        - That the employee reasonably believes that if they make the disclosure to the employer (where no person is prescribed) the relevant information/material will be destroyed, or
        - That the worker has previously made a disclosure of substantially the same information to his or her employer, or to a prescribed person.

    A number of further conditions will have to be considered, including:

    - The identity of the person to whom the disclosure is made
    - The seriousness of the failure which is the subject of the disclosure, and
    - Whether the relevant failure is continuing or is likely to continue.

- Disclosure of 'exceptionally serious' breaches:

    This enables the employee to by-pass other normal procedures and those provided for above. Specific regard will be made by a tribunal to the identity of the person to whom the information is disclosed, and the employee must make the disclosure in 'good faith'.

12.5 Enforcement

Where an employee has made a protected disclosure and is dismissed or subject to other detriment the dismissal will be **automatically unfair**. In this context dismissal also means **redundancy** or a dismissal connected with a **transfer of an undertaking**.

There is no **qualifying service** necessary to bring a claim, and those above normal retiring age are protected. Dismissal of all employees, irrespective of **age** or length of service must therefore be carefully documented.

12.6 Compensation

These are the same as those for normal unfair dismissal procedures, subject to further Regulations. Any action short of dismissal against a protected person will also be prohibited.

Pay and benefits 4

1 The meaning of pay

1.1 Introduction

This chapter considers 'wages' and 'pay' in the context of employment law, not tax law, with the single exception of the taxation of Payments in Lieu of Notice. The chapter looks at pay in terms of wages and other benefits, but also considers Statutory Sick Pay, the National Minimum Wage and the issue of Equal Pay.

In law the term 'wages' has more often been used when defining employees' remuneration, rather than the terms 'salary' or even 'pay'. Part of the reason for this is historical: employees were traditionally paid wages, the salary becoming more widespread only in the years following the Second World War. In fact, 'wages' and 'pay' may have different legal meanings depending upon the piece of legislation which uses the terminology.

1.2 The meaning of 'pay' in European law

Insofar as Article 141 of the Treaty of Rome 1957 (equal pay) is concerned, pay can be defined as:

> '...the ordinary basic or minimum wage or salary or any other consideration, whether in cash or in kind, which the worker receives, directly or indirectly in respect of his employment, from his employer...'

The European Court of Justice (ECJ) has consistently held that 'pay' within the meaning of Article 141 (second paragraph of the Article) comprises any consideration, whether cash or in kind, that arises from the individual employee's employment from the respective employer. Any 'benefits' paid to the individual after employment has terminated will still come within the definition of 'pay'. It is important to remember that Article 141 applies to equal pay, and the decisions of the ECJ are directly related to equal pay cases.

The scope of Article 141 does not extend to 'other working conditions' such as hours or holidays. These are covered by the EC Equal Treatment Directive.

1.3 Employment Rights Act 1996

Turning to UK statute, the Employment Rights Act 1996 defines 'wages' as being:

'...any sum payable to the worker by his employer in connection with his employment.'

The Act also provides details of the types of pay that come within this definition of wages:

- Any fee, bonus, commission, holiday pay, statutory sick pay or other emolument referable to the worker's employment, whether payable under the contract or otherwise (eg non-contractual payment)
- Any sum payable under a reinstatement or re-engagement order made in unfair dismissal proceedings
- Any sum payable where an employee, having alleged they have been unfairly dismissed on trade union grounds, obtains interim relief, allowing the contract of employment to be continued until the matter is determined at a full hearing
- Where, after an employer becomes insolvent, the Secretary of State becomes liable to pay out of the National Insurance Fund certain monies including statutory guarantee payments and other payments in lieu of wages to the employee
- Statutory Sick Pay, and
- Statutory paternity, maternity and adoption pay

A 'worker' is defined under the Act as 'anyone working under a contract of service, apprenticeship or who undertakes personally to do work or services'. The latter part of this definition would include 'self-employed' persons providing casual or contract work, but exclude those providing a service for a client or customer through a business carried on by the worker.

Other types of pay are expressly excluded from the definition of wages:

- Payments by way of an advance under a loan or agreement or by way of an advance of wages. (Deductions in respect of a repayment of a loan are covered)*
- Any payment for expenses incurred by the worker in carrying out their employment*
- Any payment by way of a pension in connection with the worker's retirement or as compensation for loss of office*

- Redundancy payments and
- Payments to the worker other than in their capacity as a worker.

Tax law has established that the following are not 'wages':

- Essential car users allowance
- Some tips
- Unsocial hours allowance
- Ex gratia bonus payments

(NB. Bonus payments may be wages if payable under a legal entitlement)

In addition, case law has established the term 'remuneration'; this includes:

- Gross wages and salary*
- Payment for travelling time
- Pensions*
- Expenses or allowances (if paid as additional wages or salary, such as London weighting)*
- Holiday pay*, and
- Compulsory service charges, and gratuities added voluntarily to cheques and credit card payments.

It will probably not include:

- Holiday pay that is paid in advance of the holiday
- State benefits
- Payments-in-kind (eg company car, free accommodation – although they will be taxable) and
- Guarantee payments.*

1.4 The meaning of a 'week's pay'

The Act specifies the maximum amount which can be used as a week's pay in the computation of compensation in respect of an unfair dismissal claim, a claim for a redundancy payment, and for a claim under the insolvency rules. The amount is reviewed annually. Those elements of remuneration above which can be included in the calculation for the purposes of a week's pay are marked*.

1.5 The Wages Act 1986

Prior to the Wages Act 1986 (now incorporated into the Employment Rights Act 1996), the law in respect of 'wages' was determined by common law or by reference to the Truck Acts 1831 – 1940.

Their purpose was to ensure that employers paid wages 'in coin of the realm' (ie in cash), not in tokens or in goods. The Acts also required employers to fairly operate fines and deductions from pay for bad workmanship and loss of stock.

1.6 Cashless pay

The biggest problem presented to employers by the Truck Acts was that they impeded attempts to introduce cashless pay. The latter includes payment by cheque, bank (or building society) credit transfer, and different types of monetary benefits.

The Wages Act repealed the right of workers to receive wages in cash, thus enabling employers to move to cashless pay. (The Wages Act 1986 is now incorporated into the Employment Rights Act 1996).

Although under common law a worker is entitled to a 'reasonable' level of pay, there is a statutory requirement to pay the National Minimum Wage. In addition, the Employment Rights Act 1996 requires the employer to supply every employee with a statement of principal terms and conditions, including the scale or rate of pay or the method of calculation and the intervals at which it is paid.

2 The employer's duty to pay wages

2.1 Common law duty

The implied terms of the contract of employment provide that should the employee be 'ready and willing to work' (the employee's consideration) and if they decline to work then the employer is not obliged to pay wages. Traditionally, the right to pay is in return for availability to work rather than work actually performed. A situation may arise where the employee is prevented from working (eg a picket which bars the entrance to the workplace or very severe weather conditions). Whether the employee is still entitled to be paid will depend on the express terms of the contract agreed between the parties. This has important implications for the employee in respect of sick pay, holiday pay and bonuses.

> **Itemised pay statement**
>
> Most employees have a statutory right to receive individually, from their employer, a detailed written pay statement at or before the time of each weekly or monthly payment.
>
> The statement must give the following particulars
>
> - Gross amount of wages/salary
> - Amounts of any fixed deductions and purposes (trade union subscriptions, saving scheme contributions)
> - Amounts of variable deductions and purposes
> - Net amount of wages/salary payable
> - Amount and method of each part payment when different parts of the net pay are paid in different ways, eg separate figures of a cash payment and the balance credited to a bank account.

2.2 Failure to pay wages

The employer's failure to pay wages will normally be a breach of contract, but not necessarily a repudiatory breach, although it may be. The latter will occur where:

- The parties regard the term as vital; and
- Its consequences are so serious as to deprive the party not in breach of what they contracted for; and
- It shows the party in breach no longer intends to be bound by (an) essential term(s) of the contract.

A repudiatory breach will give rise to a situation where the injured party (the employee) could resign and claim there has been a constructive dismissal which may be used as the basis of an unfair dismissal claim. Whether there has been a repudiatory breach is, however, a matter of degree. An employer who denies a clear obligation to pay wages or seeks to withdraw a significant part of the employee's wages, such as a bonus, is most likely to have committed a repudiatory breach.

3 Deductions in wages

3.1 What is covered by the Act?

Deductions cannot be made from an employee's wages without their express permission in writing (other than for statutory purposes or where there is in existence a relevant provision in the contract to allow any deduction. Note: the employer cannot unilaterally insert such a clause, but where contract terms can be altered to accord with a collective agreement, this is lawful). A deduction for which the worker has given advanced written consent is lawful.

A statutory deduction will be for the purposes of income tax and National Insurance under the employer's PAYE scheme. Another example is an 'Attachment of Earnings Order', commonly paid because of an outstanding court order, eg a fine because of a criminal conviction.

3.2 What is a deduction?

The Act defines a deduction as:

> 'Where the total amount of any wages that are paid on any occasion by an employer to any worker employed by him is less than the total amount of the wages that are properly payable by him to the worker on that occasion (after deductions), the amount of the deficiency shall be treated for the purposes of this Part (of the Act) as a deduction made by the employer from the worker's wages on that occasion.'

It is worth noting that non-payment of wages on termination can amount to a deduction from wages. An Employment Tribunal has the jurisdiction to rule on a case of deductions from wages and/or non-payment of wages.

Pay in lieu of notice cannot be wages where it relates to a period after the termination of the contract. The reason for this is that the contract has been terminated, so the payment relates to a period *after* employment has come to an end. Such a payment constitutes damages for wrongful dismissal in not providing the employee with the proper contractual notice period.

It should be noted that any pay in lieu of notice which is paid on termination will be damages and not covered by the statute. Payments to an employee while on 'garden leave' will be wages for the purposes of the statute because the contract of employment continues to subsist.

3.3 Errors of computation

The only exception is where the deduction of the wages of an employee is due to an 'error of computation'. Errors in computation do not count as deductions. The interpretation of the relevant section which permits this exclusion has been interpreted narrowly so that deductions made due to a mistake on the part of the employer, including those as to statutory or contractual provisions, will not fall within the scope of the section.

Case law has held that an 'error of computation' must be an error on the part of the employer which affects the 'computation' of gross wages. An error is something incorrectly done through ignorance or inadvertence. Because of this interpretation it seems errors of computation are limited to occasions where there has been a mistake in writing or incorrect data has been fed into a computer or the wrong button on a machine has been pressed.

3.4 Deductions in respect of industrial action

The Act prevents an employee from bringing a claim for unlawful deductions before a tribunal where the employer has made deductions from pay following industrial action or other industrial action respectively.

4 Pay in lieu of notice payments

4.1 Payment in lieu of notice

A payment in lieu of notice (PILON) is a payment made when an employee is dismissed instead of requiring them to work their notice.

4.2 Are payments in lieu of notice taxable?

One issue with PILONs is the tax liability which will arise when a former employee receives PILON. The basic position is that Income tax is payable 'in respect of any office or employment on emoluments there from....'. Emoluments can include, '....all salaries, fees, wages.....and profits.....'. Under the Income Tax (Earnings and Pensions) Act compensation paid on termination of employment up to the sum of £30,000 will normally be tax-free because it is deemed to be damages for the employer's breach of contract in terminating the contract without proper notice (a contractual debt).

However, when the contract of employment expressly entitles the employer to terminate the contract early by making a payment in lieu of notice then that payment will be taxable as an emolument and, therefore, the employer must deduct tax at source.

However in situations where the employee's contract states that the employer 'may' make a PILON or makes no reference to PILON, and the employer makes a PILON payment then the employee is entitled to damages for breach of contract. The payment of damages is not taxable and constitutes a payment in connection with termination of employment. While this has an appeal for both the employer and employee it should not be overlooked that any such breach invalidates any restrictive covenants and so the employer will no longer be able to rely upon these.

HM Revenue and Customs – guidelines on PILON

In Spring 2003, the HM Revenue and Customs issued guidelines (Inland Revenue Tax Bulletin (no.63) February 2003) (*) on the matter:

(a) In the absence of any clear breach of contract by the employer, the making of a PILON payment will be viewed by the Revenue as the exercise of a contractual discretion, even though the sum provided and the form of payment is not that precisely indicated in the contract.

(b) Any decision taken by the employer not to exercise his contractual discretion should be placed in writing for it to be used as evidence.

(c) The payment of damages (instead of an emolument) will normally have a number of characteristics. These are:

 (i) The payment is expressly reduced to allow for 'mitigation', or to reflect the difference in tax treatment between an emolument from employment and damages.

 (ii) A damages payment will normally take account of all benefits payable during the period of contractual notice.

(d) The Revenue re-states its view that a non-contractual PILON may be taxable as an emolument. Two examples are provided:

 (i) Whenever a redundancy situation occurs the employee automatically receives a PILON for unworked notice.

 (ii) Wherever a practice is established of the making of PILON payments on the termination of contracts.

The Revenue states that both examples are of payments being made that are part of the employee-employer relationship, although not contractually provided for.

This approach has given rise to litigation. Many employers may argue that although PILON payments have been made in the past there is no policy or established practice to do so.

(*) See: *www.hmrc.gov.uk/bulletins/*

5 Recovery of wages

5.1 Breach of contract on termination of employment

Former employees can obtain redress for the non-payment of monies on termination of contract in either the Employment Tribunal or the civil courts. Tribunals have jurisdiction to hear complaints of breach of contract in respect of claims for damages on termination. This jurisdiction includes failure to pay contractual pay in lieu of notice. In common law such a breach would be termed 'wrongful dismissal'.

5.2 Overpayments of wages and expenses

Sections 13 and 15 of the ERA 1996 do not apply to deductions in respect of overpayments.

Recovery of any overpayment (restitution) to the employee at common law is a question of whether or not the overpayment was made by a mistake of law or fact.

Mistake of law. These overpayments are not recoverable. For instance, they may be made if an employer misinterpreted a statute or the contract of employment.

Mistake of fact. These overpayments may be recoverable. For instance, they may be made due to oversight, inadvertence or ignorance.

There are circumstances, however, where recovery may be estopped (ie prevented) if **three** conditions are satisfied:

(a) The employer in some respect represented to the employee (the payee) that the money did, in fact, belong to the employee

(b) The employee (the payee) was led to believe, therefore, that the money did, indeed, belong to them, and

(c) That the employee (payee) because of the mistake, and in good faith, changed their position (eg spent all the money) in circumstances where it would be inequitable for them to repay the monies.

If the employer goes ahead and deducts overpayments made because of a mistake of fact which satisfies the three conditions above, any dispute about whether those monies are repayable would be heard in the civil courts.

6 Non-contractual and discretionary payments

6.1 Failure to pay discretionary bonuses

The issue of whether commission and bonuses will be 'wages' is complex. Non-contractual bonuses can be treated as wages except in some very specific circumstances.

The issue typically arises where the expectation of receiving a bonus had been built up over time and has eroded the intention of being discretionary.

6.2 Payment of bonuses on termination

What is the position if an employee claiming damages for wrongful dismissal seeks additional compensation for a discretionary bonus due during the notice period? The basic principle is that *contractual* entitlement will be compensated for.

Therefore, a genuinely discretionary bonus is not payable as wrongful dismissal damages provided the employer did not exercise their discretion capriciously or in bad faith. Prudent employers should ensure that bonus schemes are genuinely discretionary or they will have difficulty in showing that the payments are not contractual.

The employer should have clear express discretionary provision incorporated into the contract of employment in order to ensure discretion.

7 Other forms of 'pay'

7.1 Car allowances and other benefits

Despite the fact that in many circumstances car allowances are taxable, the case law has deemed them not to be 'wages'. This position also relates to other benefits-in-kind such as vouchers, travel concessions, goods or concessionary services.

7.2 Claims arising from retail employment

Although the same rules in respect of wages and deductions outlined above apply to these employees, there are special conditions which also apply to them.

Deductions in respect of cash or stock deficiencies must not be made **any later than twelve months** after the deficiency was established by the employer. There is a limit of **one-tenth of gross daily pay** that can be deducted. Employers should not build into the normal calculation of an employee's 'wages' a pre-determined deduction for such purposes.

7.3 Redress for unlawful deduction of wages

Employees have two separate remedies if an employer makes an unauthorised deduction.

1. The employee can make a breach of contract claim or a complaint that money has been deducted contrary to the ERA 1996.

2. An employee or former employee may bring a claim of unlawful deduction to the Employment Tribunal within three months from the date of payment of the wages from which the deduction was made. Should the employee's complaint be upheld, s/he will be eligible to receive the full amount owing to her/him.

7.4 Holiday pay

The Working Time Regulations 1998 provide a statutory right to obtain paid holiday. Most employers do, of course, provide for holiday entitlement as part of contractual terms, and many grant paid holidays including special leave. Any holiday entitlements must be set out in the employee's section 1 statement of principal terms and conditions.

7.5 Contractual sick pay

There is no statutory obligation for an employer to provide employees with a contractual sick pay scheme. The section 1 statement of principal terms and conditions must, however, specify any terms relating to contractual benefits payable due to incapacity caused by illness. If no terms exist then this must be made clear.

As shown above, sick pay, whether contractual or statutory, comes within the definition of 'wages'. Where a contractual entitlement does exist then employers must expect to honour that commitment.

8 Introduction guarantee payments

Guarantee payments do not often occur in practice because most employees get paid regardless of whether they are provided with work. The purpose of providing employees with the right to a guarantee payment is to safeguard employees in situations where, because of no fault of theirs, the employer decides to close the business for a short period of time. This is caused by irregularities in orders for work or supplies of raw materials, and, therefore, theoretically affects certain parts of the manufacturing industry, or employers whose business is subject to weather and seasonal conditions.

9 Statutory rights

An employee's right to receive a guarantee payment from the employer was introduced in 1975 and can now be found in the Employment Rights Act 1996. The right is to fall back pay in respect of any normal day for which the employer provides no work.

10 Contractual rights

An employee may have inserted into the contract of employment (expressly or by implication) a clause which entitles the employer to lay-off (due to a decline in work) the employee with or without paying normal pay and benefits. This is usually inserted by virtue of a collective agreement. Subject to certain conditions where the employee is not entitled to receive full normal pay, there may be an entitlement to receive a statutory guarantee payment.

11 Eligibility to receive a statutory guarantee payment

Situations where employees are eligible to receive statutory guarantee payments are listed below.

(a) The right only applies to employees.

(b) The employee must have been employed for at least a period of one month.

(c) The employee must be employed in Great Britain.

(d) Each day for which there exists a claim must be a 'whole day', ie the normal working day for the employee. This can include two actual days where the employee is a night worker.

(e) The lay-off must be occasioned by:

   (i) A reduction in the employer's business; or

   (ii) Any other occurrence affecting normal working (eg power cut, flood, but not voluntary closure for a holiday).

11.1 Exclusion from right to claim

The right to claim a statutory guarantee payment is excluded when the lay-off is **due to industrial action taken by the employee**. This would include 'participation in' the action or where the employee had an 'interest in' the dispute. Where this could not be shown, it is likely the employee would have a right to claim.

The right is excluded where the employee **refuses suitable alternative work**: the work should be offered (where practicable) at least on the day before the employee is due to be laid-off; and the right is excluded where the employee **refuses to comply with the employer's reasonable requirements**.

11.2 Calculation of a guarantee payment

This is based on the following:

- The amount is subject to a maximum **daily** limit
- The **claim period** is limited to five days in any rolling period of three months
- Any overlap with **contractual pay** will reduce the guarantee payments, and
- The number of normal working hours will be multiplied by the guaranteed hourly rate to determine the daily amount (subject to the maximum). Normal working hours will not include overtime. Where non-regular hours are worked, a pattern of working hours may nevertheless be established.

12 Redress for non-payment

Whole or partial non-payment by the employer will entitle the employee to bring a complaint to the Employment Tribunal within three months of the workless day on which the payment is due.

Alternatively the employee can request conciliation of the dispute through the services of an ACAS conciliation officer.

13 Statutory Sick Pay

13.1 Purpose

Statutory Sick Pay (SSP) was introduced to give employees who are incapacitated from working a right to a minimum payment from their employers. Many employers do provide contractual sick pay which operates to 'top-up' the SSP in order to provide a reasonable level of income during sickness absence. The **longevity** of a contractual sick pay scheme may be more generous than that for SSP. For instance, many employers provide six months' full pay and six months' half pay before the employee would exhaust their right to remuneration. Like SSP, entitlement may be limited over a number of years and subject to length of service with the employer. This is perfectly lawful provided there is no unlawful discrimination on the grounds of age, sex, race, disability or part-time status etc.

13.2 Eligibility for SSP

To qualify for SSP the person must be an 'employee', employed in Great Britain. Self-employed workers do **not** qualify. Those **not** entitled to SSP include:

(a) Employees who earn less than the Lower Earnings Limit for which National Insurance contributions are payable.

(b) Employees who have, in the eight weeks preceding the start of their incapacity, been entitled to receive for one or more days incapacity benefit, maternity allowance, or severe disablement allowance.

(c) Employees who have not commenced work under their contract of employment for their employer.

Eligible employees are entitled to SSP in situations as follows.

(a) Each day in respect of which SSP is claimed must be a **'day of incapacity for work'**. This is defined in as 'a day on which the employee is incapable of doing work which he or she can reasonably be expected to perform under his or her contract'. This must be due to some specific disease or bodily or mental disablement, or:

- The employee is under medical care in respect of some specific medical condition and is absent from work on the advice of a doctor, and
- Is a carrier of an infectious disease or has been in contact with such a disease where the Medical Officer for Environmental Health has advised the employee not to work.

(b) **In the absence of any special agreement**, every day is a qualifying day (except when there are days on which no **one** employee of the employer is required to work). (With the increasing trend towards six- and seven-day working this is becoming more common.)

(c) **Waiting days**: the first three days of a period of incapacity are called 'waiting days' during when no SSP is paid. An employee would be eligible for SSP if **'a day of incapacity'** is a part of a **'period of incapacity for work'** (ie four or more **consecutive** days).

13.3 Qualifying days

An employee is not necessarily entitled to receive SSP on every day that they are incapacitated. It will only arise in respect of **'qualifying days'**. This may be the subject of agreement between the parties (provided that there is at least one qualifying day in a week). Thus, an employee who works an irregular working week which averages three days a week may agree that the qualifying days will be Tuesday to Thursday, even though they may occasionally work on a Friday, Saturday, Sunday or Monday.

Subject to this agreement the employee may receive SSP if they are incapacitated on one of these days when they would not normally work.

Example

An employee's qualifying days are:

Monday – Friday: The employee falls ill and becomes incapacitated for work on a Sunday. The employer does not open for work on any Sunday.

SSP will not be due until:

Thursday (the three waiting days will be Monday – Wednesday).

13.4 Linked periods of incapacity

Any two periods of incapacity for work (ie periods of four or more consecutive days on which the employee cannot attend work) which are separated by no more than **eight weeks** (56 calendar days) shall be treated as a **single** period of incapacity. When two periods are linked in this way, waiting days occur only in the first period. In the second period, each qualifying day attracts SSP.

13.5 Calculation of SSP

SSP is calculated on a single daily basic rate. For the purpose of calculation the week always begins on a Sunday. The daily rate is calculated by dividing the weekly rate by the number of qualifying days in that particular week. Qualifying days are those on which the employee's contract requires them to be available for work.

Example

Employee Y is absent from work from Monday 20 May to Sunday 16 June. S/he returns to work on Monday 17 June. The employee does not normally work Fridays – Sundays inclusive. The 'waiting' days will be 20 May – 22 May inclusive. The qualifying days will be: Thursday 23 May, Monday 27 May (the employee works on the Bank Holiday) – Thursday 30 May, Monday 3 June – Thursday 6 June, Monday 10 June – Thursday 13 June. Total: 13 days.

There are odd days included in this example for which SSP will be paid (ie not straight weeks).

The SSP (General) Regulations provide a table to calculate odd qualifying days as a decimal fraction of each qualifying week:

To manually calculate the SSP liability for the employer you must:

(a) Identify and isolate each period, in *weeks* or *PIWs* (period of incapacity for work) (as appropriate) in which the number of 'qualifying days' remained the same number.

Qualifying days	Decimal fraction for one day
7	0.143
6	0.167
5	0.2
4	0.25
3	0.334
2	0.5
1	1.0

(b) For each separate period (see above) calculate the number of 'qualifying' days for SSP. This number should be divided by the total number of qualifying days in the week. 13 qualifying days ÷ 4 weeks (the total period of incapacity: 20 May – 16 June) = 3.25 weeks [You will note the 0.25 is one quarter of the total number of days in the qualifying week – See above table].

(c) Add the various totals together. For employee Y this is the only period of incapacity within a 28 week period. There are no 'linked' periods of incapacity.

(d) Subtract from 28 (the limit allowed for SSP). This will give you the number of remaining weeks in which SSP can be paid in the three-year eligibility period. 28 weeks – 3.25 weeks = 25.75 weeks. If the employee continues to have 4 qualifying days per week the balance of days is calculated as follows: 0.25 decimal fraction for one day (see table above) × 3 = 0.75. So, the remaining eligibility period will be: 25 weeks and three days.

(e) From the above calculation eligibility for SSP can be ascertained:

For employee Y: 3.25 · the weekly rate of SSP. Each qualifying day will be paid at one quarter of the weekly rate.

So, for employee Y:

		£
3 × £79.15	=	237.45
£79.15 ÷ 4	=	19.79
		257.24

will be paid as SSP for employee Y for the total period of incapacity.

13.6 Normal weekly earnings

Any sum which is treated as earnings for the purposes of National Insurance contributions must be included and calculated on **gross** earnings, but this will exclude pay such as tips, payment-in-kind, pensions, expenses and redundancy payments.

In other words, all those elements of 'pay' indicated as being wages for the statutory purpose will normally be included. The following should be considered as earnings:

- Overtime payments, bonuses and commission
- Pay rises which **should** have been awarded to the employee at any time up to the end of the pay period

13.7 Maximum entitlement to SSP

The **maximum** entitlement to SSP in any one period of incapacity for work is **28 weeks**. This applies across linked periods of incapacity for work. Thus, if an employee received three weeks' SSP, recovers and then falls ill again within eight weeks, the maximum entitlement to SSP in the new period of illness will be 25 weeks. To '*link*' these two periods, both should have been of a duration of no less than four days.

Where an employee leaves their job after being incapacitated the SSP that they have received may be deducted from the maximum SSP payable by a new employer. This will be the case if the employee enters into a period of incapacity for work with the employer within eight weeks of being paid SSP by a previous employer. In order to enjoy this continuation the employee must request a 'leaver's statement' from their first employer.

Where the employee suffers from a series of linked periods of incapacity within **three** years but does not receive the total of **twenty-eight** weeks' SSP the entitlement to SSP will nevertheless come to an end. Eligibility to receive SSP will commence when a new unlinked period of incapacity begins.

(The employee may, of course, be eligible to receive certain state benefits.)

13.8 Obligations on the employee to notify their employer

The employer is entitled to withhold SSP if they are not properly notified of the employee's incapacity. Notification cannot be required earlier than the first day on which the employee is due to work (ie the first 'qualifying day').

The employer may, however, stipulate a time limit on receiving notification, and in any case this must be no later than one month late (providing they can show good reason for the delay).

Notification should be in writing, unless otherwise agreed.

NB The employer may, of course, stipulate a more onerous notification procedure so the employee may enjoy contractual sick pay and leave benefits.

13.9 Self-certification

Initial operation of SSP rules depends on employees submitting a self-certificate of incapacity. This should be provided after three consecutive days' incapacity. The employer may not require medical evidence within the first seven days of incapacity. It is for the employer, therefore, to initially make a judgement about the genuine nature of the employee's incapacity.

13.10 Records

A complete record of all incapacity absences must be kept for **at least three years** after the year to which they relate has expired. However an employer is required to keep records of SSP where their contractual sick pay is equal to or is greater than SSP entitlement.

13.11 Employer's rebate for SSP

Where an employer can demonstrate that in any month they paid out SSP entitlement which exceeds 13 per cent of the amount of their National Insurance liability they may obtain a rebate on that amount.

14 Statutory Maternity Pay (SMP), Maternity Allowance, Paternity Pay (SPP) and Adoption Pay (SAP)

Information on these subjects can be found in Chapter 5, Statutory benefits.

15 The National Minimum Wage Act 1998

15.1 Introduction

The purpose of the Act has been to introduce a statutory minimum level of pay throughout the country. The rate of National Minimum Wage (NMW) is effective from 1 October each year. The Low Pay Commission monitors and evaluates the NMW, and advises the government. Their remit is to:

1. Monitor, evaluate and review the NMW and its impact, with particular reference to:

    - The effect on pay, employment and competitiveness in the low paying sectors, with particular reference to the competitiveness of small firms
    - The effect on the pay structures and employment of different groups of workers, including in particular different age groups, women, ethnic minorities, people with disabilities and migrant workers.

2. Review the labour market position of young people, including those in apprenticeships and internships.

3. Review the levels of each of the different minimum wage rates and make recommendations for the forthcoming year.

4. Review the arrangements for the apprentice minimum wage.

www.lowpay.gov.uk

15.2 Definition and composition of the NMW

An employee has the right to be remunerated by his/her employer at a rate not less than the NMW.

All workplaces are covered, and only a small number of workers are excepted from the provisions.

The NMW applies to actual working time – that is, hours spent working exclusive of rest or meal breaks.

Entitlement to the NMW

Most adult workers in the United Kingdom must be paid at least the National Minimum Wage. This includes, for example:

- Homeworkers
- Agency staff
- Casual labourers

- Part-time workers
- Piece workers
- Foreign workers working in the UK

Exemptions

There are limited exemptions for certain groups of workers, these include:

- The genuinely self-employed
- Voluntary workers
- Workers who are based permanently outside the UK or who are based in the Channel Islands or the Isle of Man
- Workers who are still of compulsory school age
- Students on a work placement of less than one year that forms part of a UK further education or higher education course
- Residential members of a charitable community, the purpose of which is to practice or promote a belief of a religious – or similar – nature
- Those employed in a Jobcentre Plus Work Trial – but only for the first six weeks of the trial – and those taking part in some government employment programmes

Eligibility

There are four categories of NMW:

1. The main rate applies to workers aged 21 and over. (The age threshold was reduced to 21 on 1 October 2010).
2. The 18 to 20-year-old rate
3. The 16 to 17-year-old rate
4. The apprentice rate, for apprentices under the age of 19 or 19 or over and in the first year of their apprenticeship

15.3 Payments covered by the NMW

The NMW covers the following:

(a) **Basic pay**

The NMW applies to actual working time. The worker's individual hourly rate of pay must be determined by reference to total remuneration over a 'relevant pay reference period' and the hours worked in that period. The pay reference period is usually one month or one week depending on how the worker is paid. The NMW is calculated on gross pay.

The lowest rate is one hour or the fraction of an hour. For those employees on **zero hours contracts**, the NMW applies when a worker is required to be at work and is available for work, even though no work is actually available. This also applies to those who sleep on the premises – when they are available to work they must be paid the NMW in accordance with the reference period.

(b) **Incentive payments**

Those based on productivity and performance (output) such as bonuses, commission or performance-related pay: the **reference period** (that is, the period in which the particular incentives are received by the employee) is the period in which the level of pay for the purposes of the NMW is computed.

(c) **Service charges and gratuities (tips)**

Those which are centrally organised so that they are pooled and then distributed to all eligible employees, must be distributed through the payroll system. Those gratuities received in the form of cash direct from customers are not included in the computation for the NMW.

(d) **Those working from home**

Despite being paid by reference to output (piece workers), they are covered by the legislation.

15.4 Payments not covered by the NMW

The NMW does not include the following.

- Premium payments for overtime and shifts. Only standard pay for overtime is included
- All other allowances and supplements
- Benefits

These include employer pension contributions, health insurance, car, subsidised meals or membership of clubs, share option schemes and health insurance.

NB. Accommodation is not included in the above, but an offset is allowed.

15.5 Calculating the NMW

The starting point for calculating NMW is gross pay, the pay received by the worker before deducting tax and National Insurance contributions.

Gross pay **includes** the following:

- Incentive pay
- Bonuses
- Tips paid through the payroll
- Income tax and employee NI contributions
- Deduction or payments of a penalty
- Deduction or payment to repay a loan
- Deduction or payment to repay an advance of wages
- Deduction or payment to pay for purchases of shares or securities
- Deduction or payment to refund accidental overpayment of wages
- Union subscriptions
- Workers' pension contributions
- Unforced payments by worker for goods and services from the employer
- Accommodation up to the limit (maximum amount that can be offset is £4.73 per day from October 2011 but this may be amended in the future).

The following payments are **excluded** from gross pay:

- A loan
- An advance of wages
- A pension payment
- A lump sum on retirement
- A redundancy payment
- An expenses payment

In addition to the payments above, there are other elements that do not count towards National Minimum Wage pay and must be **subtracted** from gross pay. These are:

- Premium elements of overtime and shift payments
- Allowances which are not consolidated into standard pay
- Refund of money spent on work
- Deductions or payment for tools, uniform, etc
- Deductions or payment for employer's own use or benefit
- Payments by the worker to another person connected with the job
- Benefits-in-kind (meals, fuel, luncheon vouchers, car, medical insurance etc), except accommodation

15.6 Enforcement

- Employees and workers may bring a complaint in respect of non-payment of the NMW. An employee may bring a claim in respect of any dismissal or action short of dismissal involving some detriment as a result of seeking to enforce their right to the NMW.

- The **burden of proof** is placed on the employer who must positively show that the NMW has been paid.

- Officers appointed by the government enforce the NMW by instigating legal action, gaining access to premises, inspecting records (which must be kept for all workers and employees), and obtaining an explanation of records from the employer. The officer may issue a compliance order to the employer. The officer may also issue a penalty notice to the employer for the non-payment of the NMW; the penalty rate is twice the standard rate of NMW applicable.

- It is a criminal offence to refuse or wilfully neglect to pay a worker a rate less than the NMW, to fail to keep records, to knowingly keep false records, and to intentionally delay or obstruct an officer.

16 Equal pay

16.1 Equality Act 2010

The provisions of the Equal Pay Act 1970 are to a large extent replicated in the Equality Act. However one important difference is that in choosing a comparator a claimant will be able to name a predecessor.

Consequently this section will examine the Equal Pay Act 1970 and its subsequent amendments and then look at the changes introduced by the Equality Act 2010.

16.2 The legal framework

The Equal Pay Act 1970 became effective from 1 January 1975.

- Implicit in all contracts of employment is an '**equality clause**' which should eradicate pay inequalities.

- The concept of **equal pay for work of equal value** was not included in the original legislation. Later, the **Equal Pay (Amendment) Regulations 1983** incorporated equal value provisions into equal pay legislation.

16.3 Equal pay

- The Equal Pay Act complements the Sex Discrimination Act 1975 and other related legislation such as the Part-Time Workers Regulations 2000.

- Virtually all employees are covered, including apprentices.

- There is no length of service requirement to make a claim to the tribunal.

- The provision of the Act applies **equally to women and men**. However, because claimants are mainly women we will use the feminine gender here.

- The legislation is not limited to pay; it includes terms and conditions of employment, fringe benefits, redundancy payments and pensions. Much of this coverage is due to decisions by the European Court of Justice, which have extended the scope of the Directive, and which the government have subsequently consolidated into legislation.

- Article 141 of the Treaty of Rome has direct effect in the UK (ie, individuals can claim directly under this Article of the Treaty).

- An individual cannot contract out of the Act.

- In the case 'where a pay system lacks transparency', ie, is unclear – and has resulted in lower average pay for female employees – then the burden of proof is on the employer to show it is not discriminatory.

However, where the difference in pay is not due to a difference in sex, there is no requirement to show that difference in pay was objectively justified.

- A Code of Practice on Equal Pay is available from the **Commission for Equality and Human Rights (CEHR)** website at *www.cehr.org.uk*.

17 Bringing an equal pay claim

17.1 The process – the three heads of claim

The Equal Pay Act provides that a woman may claim equal pay in respect of pay and contract terms with a man (or *vice-versa*) in any one of three ways.

a) Like work	Where she can show that she is employed on like work with a man, so that it covers work 'of the same or broadly similar nature'. Any differences between the things which the woman does and those which the man does which are not of any practical importance in relation to terms and conditions cannot be considered as genuine material factor (GMF) defence by the employer.
(b) Work rated equivalent under a job evaluation scheme	Where she can show that she is employed on work rated as equivalent with that of a man under a job evaluation scheme. The job evaluation scheme must be an analytical one and the scheme must have shown that her job and that of her male comparator was of 'equal value in terms of the demand made on a worker under various headings', eg, effort, skill, or decision-making.
(c) Work of equal value	Most cases now fall under this heading. Little or no guidance was provided in the amended legislation (1983) as to what might constitute 'equal pay for work of equal value' so the law has developed mainly through the decisions of the courts.

17.2 The Occupational Pension Schemes (Equal Treatment) Regulations 1995

All company pension schemes must contain an equal treatment rule which ensures that men and women are offered the same rights to join a scheme, and are provided with the same benefits within a scheme.

17.3 Fundamental conditions of making a claim

An employee may submit a claim at any time during employment or to the tribunal within six months of her employment ending.

The claimant must have identified at least one comparator of the opposite sex. Unlike other discrimination claims, the comparator must be a real person, and not a hypothetical one. There can be no comparison between persons of the same sex.

The woman's comparator must work for the same employer or an associated employer (working at different establishments) or for another body for which there is a 'single source' that can remedy any inequality in pay or other contract term. A comparator of the opposite sex can be a predecessor or successor in her own job. The pay and contract terms of the comparator do not have to be identical to those of the claimant provided they are working at establishments at which 'common terms and conditions of employment are observed'. They do *not* have to be nominally broadly similar for a valid claim to be made. The effect of the 'equality clause' can be seen in this context:

(a) The woman's claim will be based on the fact that:

   (i) If any term of her contract (whether concerned with pay or not) is less favourable to her than the corresponding term in the man's contract, then that term in her contract must be modified so that it ceases to be less favourable.

   (ii) If this contract includes a beneficial term which is not to be found in her contract, then the term must become part of her contract also.

(b) Once the woman's claim has established using one or more valid comparators the Tribunal will ask three sequential questions:

   (i) Have the two jobs been rated equivalent under a job evaluation scheme? If yes, the tribunal will go on to consider whether the scheme was analytical or not.

   (ii) If not, are they like work comparisons?

   (iii) If not, are they equal value?

18 How a claim is dealt with by the Employment Tribunal

18.1 Questionnaire procedure – standard forms are prescribed by the Equal Pay (Questions and Replies) Order 2003

Before submitting a claim to the tribunal a claimant can make use of a questionnaire. The right to do so (which brings equal pay claims into line with the questionnaire procedure for sex and race discrimination claims) was introduced in April 2003. Using the questionnaire enables individuals who believe they have not received equal 'pay' to put a number of questions to the employer to establish whether this is the case, and if so, the reasons why. If the individual decides to take the case to tribunal, the information gathered will help the complainant to make a more effective presentation of the evidence and permit the tribunal to deal with matters more expeditiously.

The questionnaire includes

- A statement of why the individual believes s/he is not receiving equal pay
- A statement identifying the comparator(s)
- Factual questions to determine whether s/he is receiving equal pay to that of the comparator(s) and if so, why
- A question on whether the employer agrees that the comparator(s) are doing equal work or work of equal value
- Space for the complainant's own questions

Questions must be served either before a complaint is made to a tribunal or within 21 days of the day when a complaint was made, unless the tribunal allows them to be served within a further period of time, upon application by the claimant. Replies must be served within 8 weeks of the service of the questions. Adverse inferences may be drawn by the tribunal if the employer fails to answer the questions or is evasive.

18.2 Time limits

The questionnaire must be responded to within eight weeks of receipt. Inferences may be drawn by the tribunal for late or non-return, although compliance with the questionnaire procedure is not compulsory. The questionnaire must be served within a specific time-period. If served before a tribunal complaint it must be served the day before the day when the claim is lodged. It is likely that the disclosure of any personal data belonging to a third party would be exempt from the disclosure request rules under the Data Protection Act 1998. This is because the employer is complying with a request in accordance with judicial proceedings or in pursuit of its legitimate interests, although the position is not absolutely clear and there *may* be a conflict between the two duties.

18.3 Group claims

It has always been the case that employees or former employees bringing claims must do so on an individual basis or individually at the same time as other claimants when the tribunals and courts may allow certain claims to be heard together. No 'class' actions are permissible within the tribunal system. However, the government is now considering the submission of group claims using one ET1 form.

18.4 Timescales for making a claim

Claims must be brought within employment tenure or no later than six months after termination of the contract to which the claim relates. However, it is possible to submit a claim where the employee had been in a stable employment relationship with the employer consisting of two or more consecutive contracts to bring a claim within six months' of the termination of the last contract.

In addition, the period of six months may be extended where:

(a) The employer 'deliberately concealed from the claimant any fact relevant to the contravention of a term modified or included by virtue of an equality clause to which the proceedings relate'; or

(b) Where the claimant was 'under a disability' at the time when she was first paid unequally. The six-month rule starts to run once the claimant ceases to be 'under a disability'.

18.5 Striking out of claims

A tribunal can strike out a claim, but only on grounds where the claimant's work has been rated as unequal to that of the comparator under a valid (ie, analytical) job evaluation scheme.

A claim may also be struck out simply on the grounds that it has no reasonable grounds of success.

18.6 Importance of analytical job evaluation

The best way in which an employer can block any further proceedings in an equal pay claim is to show that the job evaluation scheme used to determine the 'pay' of the claimant and her comparator is an analytical one void of sex bias. The tribunal may decide the scheme is 'otherwise unsuitable to be relied upon'.

18.7 Appointment of independent expert

Previously, the tribunal could not decide the outcome of a case until it had received the report of an independent expert (if appointed). Now, the tribunal may withdraw instructions to the expert and decide the outcome of the case itself. This change was brought about because some independent experts' reports were taking several months to prepare.

ACAS is required to hold a list of independent experts. The role of the expert is to assist the tribunal in establishing facts by enquiring into the details of the job evaluation scheme in question and to report on its effectiveness, objectivity, analytical status and whether it contained any sex bias. The expert must keep to the timetable set by the tribunal and keep them informed of progress.

Further expert evidence can be called if in the tribunal's opinion it will assist in deciding the outcome of the case. However, no other expert evidence can be submitted without the tribunal's permission and without it being disclosed to all parties at least 28 days before the full hearing.

The expert's report once submitted to the tribunal usually triggers a huge number of questions from the parties. However, questions may be asked only once, copied to all parties beforehand no later than 28 days after the report was copied to the parties. The expert must respond to each question within 28 days.

18.8 Specialist Tribunals

The President of the Employment Tribunals may establish specialist panels of tribunal chairmen and lay members to hear complex equal pay cases.

18.9 The three-stage equal value hearing

Generally, tribunal chairmen now have stronger powers to restrict the amount/time of evidence submitted. If an independent expert is appointed a hearing will normally have three stages, otherwise only two stages will be necessary.

Stage 1 hearing	A full tribunal must conduct the hearing. The tribunal may strike out the claim (see above). If not struck-out the tribunal will either appoint an independent expert (Stage 2) or move straight to a full hearing (Stage 3). Where certain necessary information is not ready at the Stage 1 hearing the tribunal will require the parties to provide that information within strict timescales: (i) Within 14 days of Stage 1 hearing the claimant must disclose in writing the name(s) of her comparator(s) or if not possible to give sufficient information for the comparator(s) to be identified. (ii) Within 28 days of Stage 1 hearing the respondent must disclose in writing the name(s) of the comparator(s) if the claimant was unable to do so, to exchange job descriptions and to disclose relevant facts. (iii) Within 56 days of Stage 1 hearing the parties must provide the tribunal with a joint statement setting out the descriptions of the claimant and the comparator; relevant facts with regard to the question of equal value; any facts on which they disagree; and a summary of reasons for disagreement. The respondent must grant access to his premises by the claimant and her representative. (iv) No later than 56 days prior to the full hearing all written evidence must be disclosed to all the parties. (v) No later than 28 days prior to the full hearing statements of facts and issues on which the parties dis/agree must be presented to the tribunal.
Stage 2 hearing	This hearing will resolve facts arising out of Stage 1 hearing so that the independent expert may commence work. A specified date will be given to the expert to submit his report.
Stage 3 hearing	This is the full hearing at which the tribunal will decide on the case. The independent expert's report will be submitted as evidence (if relevant). It is at this stage that the employer can raise the Genuine Material Factor (GMF) defence.

19 Discussions about pay

The Equality Act introduces a provision that makes clauses that aim to prevent employees receiving, making or seeking 'relevant pay disclosures' unenforceable. The employee is also allowed to ask questions and seek details from both current and former work colleagues about their pay.

In claiming protection under these provisions it would have to be shown that there has been a 'relevant pay disclosure'. This will be any pay discussion that has the purpose of enabling the employee either to find out whether or to what extent there is, in relation to the work in question, a connection between pay and having or not having a particular protected characteristic.

The employee or former employee is also protected against victimisation if they suffer a detriment because they have taken action:

- Seeking a disclosure that would be a relevant pay disclosure
- Making or seeking to make a relevant pay disclosure
- Receiving information disclosed in a relevant pay disclosure.

Pay discussions with advisers will also gain protection and as a result, if the employee approaches a trade union representative who is not also a colleague, any disclosures made in the context of that conversation will also be protected.

20 Gender pay gap information

The Equality Act includes a provision that employers with 250 or more employees will be required to publish information relating to the pay of employees for the purpose of showing whether there are differences in pay between men and women in their employment. The proposed commencement date was 2013.

However the government in 2010 has indicated that it will not utilise this provision and will encourage employers on a voluntary basis.

21 Individual rights for time off

21.1 Introduction

There are several specific statutory individual rights to take time off from work which exist. Some of these have already been examined in other sections of this book. In this chapter we will examine those individual rights for time off which do not easily fall within other areas of individual employment or collective law.

- **Time off for trade union officials and members** to undertake certain duties and activities.

    The Employment Act 2002 inserted a new s 168A into the TULR(C) Act 1992 that entitles an employee who is a member of an independent trade union recognised by the employer and who is a **learning representative** of the trade union to reasonable paid time off.

    Any relevant employee may take time off to access the services of a union learning representative.

- Time off for employees under notice of redundancy in order for them to:
    - Look for alternative employment, and
    - To undertake re-training

- **Time off for safety representatives** (and employee representatives)
- **Time off for pregnant employees** to receive ante-natal care

21.2 Time off for public duties

An employee is allowed reasonable time off to discharge certain public duties as a:

- Justice of the Peace (JP)
- Member of a Trust for local or regional public services, eg police authority, National Health Service Hospital Trust, school governing body, local authority or statutory tribunal
- Member of a national public service, eg government agency or HM prison governing board.

'Reasonable time off' will be based on:

(a) The amount of time required to undertake these specific duties
(b) How much time off is taken in respect of other duties, and
(c) The effect on the employer's business.

Local authorities may not permit their employees to take paid time off which exceeds 208 hours per annum for the purposes of performing duties as a local authority councillor.

There is **no statutory right** to take paid time off to perform duties as a member of a court jury or court witness. Preventing or obstructing an employee performing these duties would, however, be **contempt of court**. On these grounds it is probable that a term permitting the employee to undertake these duties is **implied** into the contract of employment.

21.3 Employee's remedies

An employee can bring a complaint to the Employment Tribunal that they have not been permitted to take reasonable time off or been paid for that time off. The period in which a complaint can be presented is **three months** from the date of the failure to grant permission or failure to make appropriate payment. The tribunal may make a declaration and order compensation to be paid to the employee, including making good any losses incurred by the employee. The tribunal does not, however, have the powers to **enforce** a period of time off.

21.4 Time off for education/training

Any employee aged 16 or 17 not in full-time secondary education and who has not achieved a prescribed 'standard of achievement' is entitled to take reasonable paid time-off from work to study or train towards a 'relevant qualification'. An employee aged 18 is also allowed to finish any qualification already started.

In 2010 the 'standard of achievement' was Level 2 qualifications at school. Level 2 qualifications include:

- GCSEs at grades A*-C
- An NVQ Level 2
- Certain other qualifications, such as a BTEC First Diploma

The employer should not expect the employee to make up lost work.

21.5 Time off for employee representatives in respect of consultation with their employer

Three sets of statutory rights exist within this category:

(a) Rights to paid time off to act as an employee representative in respect of redundancy consultation

(b) Rights to time off to act as an employee representative in respect of transfer of Undertakings

(c) Rights to paid time off to act as an employee representative in respect of attendance at a meeting of a European Works Council

In all three categories time off is extended to the performance of duties as a candidate or employee representative in respect of the election to this position.

21.6 Time off for employees who are trustees of occupational pension schemes to perform their duties under those schemes

Employees have the right to reasonable paid time off to perform duties as a trustee or to undergo training in that respect. The employee's remedy for non-compliance by the employer is very similar to time off for public duties.

Statutory benefits 5

1 Maternity rights

1.1 Introduction

This chapter will look at the various 'family friendly' legislation that has developed over the decades to provide statutory benefits in relation to:

- Maternity
- Paternity
- Parental leave
- Adoption
- Flexible Working

1.2 Maternity rights

Statutory maternity rights were established in 1975, but since that date women's rights in respect of pregnancy and maternity have been significantly strengthened. In the last fifteen years a number of important ambiguities have been cleared-up, notably the right of a woman to return to work at the end of her maternity leave. In addition, the UK government, as part of its domestic 'family-friendly' policy, has strengthened the statutory regime of maternity leave and pay.

1.3 Basic rights

Pregnant employees have five basic rights

- To paid time-off for antenatal care
- To Statutory Maternity Leave, (a maximum of 52 weeks in total)
- To Statutory Maternity Pay (SMP) (or maternity allowance)
- To return to work after absence due to the baby's birth and maternity leave

- Not to be unfairly dismissed or suffer detriment because of reasons related to pregnancy or maternity

1.4 Antenatal care

- There is no minimum qualifying period
- The employee has the right not to be unreasonably refused time-off during working hours for an ante-natal appointment, nor to be refused pay (normal pay) for the absence
- 'Parent craft' classes and medical appointments are included
- The employee may be asked to provide proof of appointment (except for the first appointment)
- Complaints must be submitted to an Employment Tribunal within three months if unreasonably refused. Where the complaint is justified the Tribunal must order the employer to pay the applicant the equivalent of the amount that she would have received during the time-off

Where a new or expectant mother is employed to carry out work which, by reason of her condition, places her health and safety at risk, her employer is obliged by the **Management of Health and Safety at Work Regulations 1999** to assess the risk and take steps to ensure that she is not exposed to it. The Regulations provide that the employer must alter the employee's working conditions or hours of work where it is reasonable to do so, if this would 'avoid' the risk identified.

2 Maternity leave provisions

The following provisions are the minimum statutory maternity leave entitlements, employers may always offer more favourable contractual terms.

The provisions relating to adoption are broadly similar to those given below (see section 7).

2.1 Statutory Maternity Leave

Regardless of length of service, hours worked or other service-related criteria all women are entitled to 52 weeks Statutory Maternity Leave:

- 26 weeks Ordinary Maternity Leave (OML), and
- 26 weeks Additional Maternity Leave (AML)

(i) **Ordinary Maternity Leave (OML)**

Ordinary Maternity Leave (OML)	This leave can only start any time from the eleventh week before 'expected week of childbirth' (EWC). Subject to medical approval a woman may opt to work right up to her EWC, thus maximising her 26 weeks OML or 52 weeks Statutory Maternity Leave. (Eligibility for Statutory Maternity Pay is however, dependent on 26 weeks' continuous service by the beginning of the 14th week before the Expected Week of Childbirth (EWC).)
Notification	The woman must notify her employer of her intention to take OML in or before the 15th week (or as soon as reasonably practicable) before the date on which she intends to commence OML (ie EWC). It cannot be earlier than the beginning of the 11th week before the EWC. Where the employer requests it, the notification should be in writing. In addition the employee must inform the employer of her pregnancy and the EWC. Any changes to maternity leave dates after notification has taken place must be no later than 28 days before the new start date.
Commencement	OML will commence on the earliest of: • Date employee notifies her employer • Day which follows the first day after the beginning of the fourth week before the EWC on which she is absent from work wholly or partly because of pregnancy, or • The day which follows the day on which childbirth occurs. OML automatically starts on the following day even when that day falls before the beginning of the 11th week before the EWC. **Pregnancy related absence** Normally, sick leave will apply, but where such an absence begins after the beginning of the fourth week before the EWC, the employee's OML will automatically start.

Terms and conditions during absence	All terms and conditions apply during OML, except remuneration (meaning wages or salary). Seniority and pension rights will continue to accrue, as well as benefits-in-kind (eg life insurance, company car, vouchers). Profit or performance-based payments may be continued. Annual leave continues to accrue. Contractual obligations placed on the employee (other than being 'ready and willing to work') will continue to apply. Service also continues to accrue.
Return to work	The employee is entitled to return to work in the job she was employed to do before commencement of OML. There is no need for the employee to inform her employer she is returning to work, unless she wishes to do so earlier, in which case 8 weeks' notice must be given. Please note that the employer must notify the employee of the date her maternity leave entitlement will end, eg, AML end-date within **28 days of receiving her notification.**

(ii) **Compulsory maternity leave**

All women	Must take two weeks' maternity leave following the birth of their child. A breach of this requirement will be a criminal offence and a prosecution taken against the employer. In practice this means that the employer should not contact the mother on any work-related matter during the two weeks. The two weeks' compulsory leave is counted in the 26 weeks ordinary leave period.

(iii) **Additional Maternity Leave (AML)**

Who is entitled?	All woman are entitled to Additional Maternity Leave (ie: an additional 26 weeks).
Length of leave	Commences at end of OML. The aim is to run leave periods concurrently with the SMP period. Notification: • The rules are those set-out under OML above. • Where the employee wishes to return earlier she must inform her employer no later than 28 days before the earlier date.

The contract of employment	Will continue throughout the period of absence. An employee on AML will be entitled to the terms and conditions of employment which would have applied had she not been absent on AML, for example the contract terms of mutual trust and confidence, good faith, notice of termination provision, grievance and disciplinary procedures, disclosure of confidential information and the acceptance of gifts, etc. Those taking AML accrue holiday leave (in accordance with the Working Time Regulations 1998). Service also continues to accrue. **Note,** the employer cannot pay an employee in lieu of any untaken **statutory annual leave** unless the contract is terminated.
End	The employee's maternity leave period finishes at the end of the 52nd week of absence. Absence from work after that date due to a pregnancy-related illness or any post-natal condition will be deemed to be absence from work and treated like any other absence (although any detriment subsequently suffered by the woman could give rise to a claim for sex discrimination).

2.2 Contact during maternity leave

The employer can make contact with the employee during their maternity leave by any means. The amount of reasonable contact is dependent upon the preference of the employee.

The employer must keep an employee informed of promotion opportunities and other information relating to her job that she would normally be made aware if attending the workplace, eg redundancy situations.

2.3 Keeping-in-touch (KIT) days during maternity leave

Employees may, in agreement with the employer, work for up to ten days – known as KIT days. Such work will be under their contract of employment without affecting their right to maternity leave or pay. Any amount of work regardless of duration, undertaken on a KIT day will count as one KIT day. Work can include normal duties or attending conference or receiving training.

Payment for KIT days

The amount of pay the employee will receive for working on a KIT day is to be agreed between the employer and employee. The payment can take account of SMP already being paid. The payment must be at least the National Minimum Wage.

If the employee is receiving statutory maternity pay (SMP) when working a KIT day, she will continue to receive SMP for that week. If the employee works more than ten KIT days in her SMP period, she is not entitled to SMP for any week in which she works.

Protection against detriment or dismissal in relation to KIT days

There is no obligation on an employee to work a KIT day, likewise any days worked need to be agreed with the employer. Neither party can insist upon the arrangement.

It is unlawful to treat an employee unfairly or dismiss her because she:

- Refused to work a KIT day
- Worked – or considered working – a KIT day

2.4 Return to work from OML and AML

(a) **OML**. The employee is entitled to return to work to the 'job in which she was employed before her absence', with her seniority, pension rights and similar rights as they would have been if she had not been absent, and on 'terms and conditions no less favourable than those which would have applied if she had not been absent'.

(b) **AML**. Basically, the same as with OML, but with an important exception:

Reinstatement to previous work not reasonably practicable: In these circumstances the employer can offer an alternative job which is both suitable for her and appropriate for her to do in the circumstances. Terms and conditions must be no less favourable than those applying before leave commenced. Special rules apply to redundancy during maternity leave.

Note: It is possible to take parental leave immediately after the end of SML. If the parental leave was for four weeks or less, and was not preceded by any AML, the employee is entitled to return to the same job as before.

If the parental leave period is for longer than four weeks, or is preceded by a period of AML, the employee is treated as though they were returning to work after AML.

2.5 Date of return to work

Notice is not required from the employee if returning at the end of her OML or AML.

Notice to return early

If the employee wishes to return early from OML or AML she must give her employer at least 8 weeks' notice of the date on which she intends to return. If the notice given is less than 8 weeks it is at the employer's discretion whether to allow the employee to return earlier. The notice does not have to be in writing. It is worth remembering that the employer should have informed the employee of the date their OML or AML is due to end.

Sickness

Where the employee is sick at the end of her OML or AML the employer's normal sick absence procedures should apply.

3 Statutory maternity pay and maternity allowance

3.1 Eligibility

Six conditions must be satisfied for the woman to receive SMP. She must have:

(a) At least 26 weeks' continuous service up to and including the 'qualifying week'. This is the 15th week before the EWC

(b) Become pregnant and been confined before reaching the start of the 11th week before the EWC

(c) Ceased working for the employer

(d) Average weekly earnings up to and including the qualifying week equal to the lower earnings limit for NIC

(e) Given 28 days' notice to her employer of the date on which she expects the liability for SMP to commence (unless this is not reasonably practicable)

(f) Produced a medical certificate re: pregnancy and EWC

3.2 Rates of pay

The rates of SMP are:

- For the first six weeks of the 'maternity pay period' the higher, earnings-related rate will remain at 90% of the employee's average weekly earnings

- For the remaining 33 weeks the woman will receive whichever is the lower of either the Standard Rate or 90% of the employee's average weekly earnings.

The Standard Rate is the amount stated by the government and typically referred to as 'Statutory Maternity Pay' eg £128.73 in 2011/2012.

In total, therefore a woman will receive:

- First six weeks: 90% of employee's normal weekly earnings
- Remaining 33 weeks: Standard Rate or 90% of her average weekly earnings, whichever is the lower

To calculate the normal weekly earnings it will be necessary to base it upon the eight weeks of earnings immediately preceding the 15th week before the EWC.

The rates of Statutory Maternity Pay and Maternity Allowance are subject to revision by the Department for Work and Pensions each April.

3.3 Restoration of entitlement to SMP after termination of contract

Should a woman's employment terminate (for whatever reason) after the beginning of the 15th week before the EWC, she will remain entitled to receive SMP.

3.4 Maternity Allowance

Maternity Allowance is available to women who may not have the eligibility to receive SMP because they do not have the requisite service or who have been earning less than the lower earnings limit for NI purposes.

The standard rate of MA and the payment period increases in line with the increases to SMP. The standard rate of MA is the currently published rate or 90% of the average weekly earnings, whichever is the lower. The pay period is a maximum of 39 weeks. The qualification period is 26 weeks' employment or self-employment within a 66-week period ending with the week before the EWC.

3.5 Dismissal and detriment

The Regulations provide that an employee has the right **not to be subjected to any detriment** by an act, or any deliberate failure to act, by her employer – in connection with any reason **related to her pregnancy**. This covers ante-natal care, the maternity leave period (OML or AML) and in relation to any detrimental action taken against the employee after maternity leave has finished.

For example, the employer takes into account the employee's absence on AML in calculating the 'absence period' for the purpose of dismissal for incapacity.

A woman has the right not to be subject to any detriment short of dismissal by any act, or any deliberate failure to act by her employer for any 'prescribed reason'.

The prescribed reasons are:

(a) Being or having been pregnant

(b) Having given birth to a child

(c) Being suspended from work on maternity grounds, ie, for health and safety reasons, or

(d) Taking, or seeking to take OML, or AML (*unless* she failed to comply with the notice requirements).

The Equality Act, provides legislation that protects women from discrimination during the period of the pregnancy and any statutory maternity leave to which she is entitled. However it emphasises during this period, these types of discrimination cannot be treated as sex discrimination. This is because pregnancy is recognised as a unique condition.

A complaint should be submitted to the tribunal in these circumstances citing detriment for a 'prescribed reason'. If the complaint is well founded the tribunal shall make a declaration to that effect and may make an award of compensation on the basis of what is just and equitable having regard to the infringement complained of and any loss attributable to the act which formed the basis of the complaint.

Dismissal. Where a woman is not entitled to return to work by virtue of dismissal (including redundancy) this will be an 'ordinary dismissal' and it will be for the employer to show it was fair and reasonable. Dismissal for pregnancy or taking maternity leave is automatically unfair.

Where the reason, or principal reason for any dismissal is that the employee was selected for redundancy and the dismissal ends the employee's OML or AML, that employee may regard herself as unfairly dismissed.

During the employee's OML or AML where the employer believes it is not reasonably practicable to continue to employ the woman because of redundancy, the employee concerned is entitled to be offered alternative employment with her employer (or successor or associated employer) under a new contract of employment. The work to be carried out should be of a kind which is both suitable, and the work capacity, location and other terms and conditions are not substantially less favourable than if the woman had continued to be employed under her previous contract.

4 Paternity leave

Ordinary Paternity Leave is either one week or two consecutive weeks which can be taken any time up to eight weeks after the date of birth or placement for adoption. The content of this section refers to births but can be equally applied to adoptions. The amount paid is the same as for Maternity Pay ie the lower of either the Standard Rate (£128.73 in 2011/2012) or 90% of the employee's average weekly earnings.

From April 2011 Additional Paternity Leave will be available this allows an extra 26 weeks' leave to be taken. The amount paid is the same as for Ordinary Paternity Leave. This however can only commence 20 weeks after the baby is born and the mother has returned to work.

4.1 Qualifying for Ordinary Paternity Leave

To qualify for Ordinary Paternity Leave the person taking the leave must be:

- An employee
- In continuous employment with their employer for 26 weeks before the end of the 15th week before the start of the week when the baby is due
- Be employed with their employer the week before the leave starts
- The father of the child (or be married to the mother or adopter of the child or be his or her partner including the female partner in a same sex relationship of a mother or female adopter)
- Expecting to have (or already have) responsibility for the upbringing of the child

Employees planning to take paternity leave must notify their employer in the 15th week before the week the baby is due, unless this is not reasonably practicable.

4.2 The leave

The provisions do not provide a legal right to time off to accompany their partners to antenatal appointments.

Paternity leave is either one week or two consecutive weeks which can be taken any time up to eight weeks after the date of birth or placement for adoption. The leave can only begin once the child is born, and must be taken within 56 days of the birth.

While absent on Statutory Paternity Leave an employee is:

- Entitled to all the benefits and obligations other than entitlement to wages or salary, to which he would be entitled if at work, and
- Entitled to have his job back at the end of the paternity leave
- The employee is bound by obligations arising under their terms and conditions of employment.

It is automatically unfair dismissal if an employee is dismissed because he took or sought to take paternity leave (or is selected for redundancy for that reason).

4.3 Qualifying for Additional Paternity Leave

From April 2011 Additional Paternity Leave is available allowing an extra 26 weeks' leave to be taken. Additional Paternity Leave has to be taken as a continuous block, with a minimum of two weeks. The employee must give eight weeks' written notice before taking paternity leave.

To qualify for APL the person must meet the following criteria

- An employee
- In continuous employment with their employer for 26 weeks before the end of the 15th week before the start of the week when the baby is due
- Be employed with their employer the week the before the leave starts
- Be the father of a child due on or after 3 April 2011
- The father of the child (or be married to the mother or adopter of the child or be his or her partner including the female partner in a same sex relationship of a mother or female adopter)
- Expecting to have(or already have) responsibility for the upbringing of the child

Additionally the employee must be taking the time off to care for the child and the child's mother must:

- Have been entitled to one or more of the following – Statutory Maternity Leave, Statutory Maternity Pay or Maternity Allowance
- Have returned to work and ceased claiming any relevant pay

If the employee's partner has returned to work, the leave can be taken between 20 weeks and one year after the child is born.

It is important to note that the mother and father cannot be absent at the same time.

4.4 Return to work from Additional Paternity Leave

(a) **OPL**. The employee is entitled to return to work to the same job in which he was employed before his absence, with his rights as they would have been if he had not been absent, and on no less favourable terms and conditions than those which would have applied if he had not been absent.

(b) **APL**. Basically, entitlements are the same as with OPL, but with an important exception:

Reinstatement to previous work not reasonably practicable: In these circumstances the employer can offer an alternative job which is both suitable for him and appropriate for him to do in the circumstances. Terms and conditions must be no less favourable than those applying before leave commenced.

5 Paternity pay

5.1 Ordinary Paternity Pay

The amount paid is the same as for Maternity Pay ie the lower of either the Standard Rate (£128.73 in 2011/2012) or 90% of the employee's average weekly earnings.

5.2 Additional Paternity Pay

These provisions are effective from April 2011. The amount paid is the same as for Ordinary Paternity Leave ie the lower of either the Standard Rate (£128.73 in 2011/2012) or 90% of the employee's average weekly earnings.

For Additional Statutory Paternity Pay the employee must meet the requirements to be entitled for Additional Paternity Leave and:

- Be taking Additional Paternity Leave
- Be not working for the purposes of caring for the child, during their partner's Statutory Maternity Pay or Maternity Allowance period

6 Parental leave and time off for dependants

6.1 Qualifying for parental leave

Parental leave is available to employees who have, or expect to have, parental responsibility for a child. The leave is **unpaid**. To be eligible, employees generally have to have one year's continuous service with their current employer.

Amount of leave	Every parent has a right to 13 weeks' leave (unpaid) before the child's fifth birthday (or 18 weeks' for a disabled child). They have, or expect to have, responsibility for the child, they do not however have to live with the child.
	The right applies to each child. Therefore, if an employee has twins they are entitled to 26 weeks' parental leave.
	Leave can only be taken in blocks of one week or in multiples of weeks. (Where the child is disabled the leave may be taken in blocks of one day or as multiples of one day).
	The leave cannot be transferred between parents.
	The entitlement (13 or 18 weeks) applies to each individual child, not to employment with an individual employer. Any outstanding amount is transferable to a new employer.
	Note:
	Employers are not required to keep formal records of parental leave taken by employees.
Leave for non-full time employees	For part-time employees 'a week' is deemed to be the normal working week (eg three-day week). For those working irregular hours the normal contractual hours should be totalled for the year and divided by 52 to determine the weekly, hourly or daily norm.
Notification	The employee is required to provide at least 21 days' notice before a period of parental leave begins, of both the intended start and end dates.
	Written notice does not have to be given unless requested by the employer.
	Providing the employee gives the right notice, their parental leave will commence on the day on which the child is:
	• Born – regardless of whether the child is born early or late • Placed for adoption
	If an employee has not given the requisite notice or the employer genuinely feels that the operation of the business would be unduly disrupted, the request for parental leave may be postponed. Any postponement may not exceed 6 months.
	There are two exceptions to the requirement to give 21 days' notice of any parental leave and in both cases if the requirements have been complied with the leave cannot be postponed.

	1. If the employee is the father of a child and intends to take a period of parental leave when the child is born, he must, at least 21 days before the beginning of the Expected Week of Childbirth: (a) Give notice to his employer of the Expected Week of Childbirth, and (b) The duration of the leave. 2. Where the leave relates to a child that is being adopted and the leave is due to begin on the date of the adoption, the employee must, at least 21 days before the beginning of the week of the adoption, or if this is not practicable, as soon as is reasonably practicable: (a) Give notice to the employer of the expected week of the adoption, and (b) The duration of the leave.
Employer can postpone leave	For business or organisational reasons, eg undue disruption, for example, where the work is of a seasonal nature. Maximum limit on postponement: six months, but this is where the employee was consulted and not more than seven days after receiving notice from the employee the employer gave counter notice specifying in writing the reasons for postponement, and the new leave dates (commencement and end dates).

A summary of the time off for dependants

There is no qualifying period for an employee to be entitled to time off that is 'necessary' to deal with the event.

There is no pre-determined statutory maximum period of leave. The leave is unpaid and the employee must give employer reasonable notice and inform them how long the absence is expected to last. There is no requirement for this to be in writing or with proof of evidence.

Examples of qualifying incidents:

- To provide assistance or make arrangements for the provision of care for the dependant who falls ill, or is injured or assaulted or who gives birth or who dies

- The unexpected disruption or termination of care arrangements for a dependant

- The unexpected incident involving the employee's child during school hours or on a school trip

The definition of a dependant: spouse, civil partner, child, parent or person who lives in the same household other than the employee, tenant, lodger or boarder.

7 Adoption leave

Work and Families Act 2006

Implemented by the Maternity and Parental Leave etc and the Paternity and Adoption Leave (Amendment) Regulations 2006 affecting children due to be placed on or after 1 April 2007. The basic idea is to mirror the rights to take maternity leave and harmonise entitlements. Both men and women are eligible. There are two types of adoption leave: Ordinary Adoption Leave (OAL) and Additional Adoption Leave (AAL).

- Eligible employees who are adopting are entitled to 52 weeks' adoption leave. This is made up of 26 weeks' ordinary adoption leave (OAL) and 26 weeks' additional adoption leave (AAL). Therefore, a total of 52 weeks' leave may be taken (but only 39 weeks will be paid).

- Employees who are adopting who meet qualifying conditions based on their length of service and average earnings are entitled to 39 weeks' Statutory Adoption Pay (SAP).

- If a couple is jointly adopting only one person is eligible for adoption leave and they must choose who takes the adoption leave; the other member of the couple may be eligible for Statutory Paternity Leave and pay (see sections 4 & 5). Where an individual is adopting, his or her partner may also be eligible for paternity leave and pay.

- Providing the child is newly placed for adoption, adoption leave is available to those adopting children up to 18 years of age.

- Adoption leave applies to those adopting children from overseas as well as from UK.

7.1 Rights of the employee during adoption leave

Ordinary Adoption Leave (OAL)

Ordinary adoption leave (OAL)	Eligibility for Ordinary Adoption Leave is dependent on 26 weeks' continuous service by the time: • The employee has received official notification or

	• Their adoption leave is due to begin, whichever is later, or • The employee has received official notification from the relevant UK authority of their eligibility to adopt a child from abroad.
Notification	Employees must give their employer notice, no more than seven days after they are notified of having been matched with the child, that they intend to take adoption leave and the date the child is expected to be placed with them for adoption. (To qualify for Adoption Pay, an employee must give their employer at least 28 days' notice of the start of adoption leave (unless this is not reasonably practicable)). Any changes to adoption leave dates after notification has taken place must be the earlier of: • 28 days before their original adoption leave date • 28 days before their new adoption leave date (unless this is not reasonably practicable)
Notification and confirmation of adoption leave – overseas adoptions	In cases where a child is being adopted from overseas, the employee is required to give notice in three stages. **First notification stage** The employee must inform the employer of the date: • On which they received official notification • The child is expected to enter the UK. **Second notification stage** In all cases, the employee must notify the employer with at least 28 days' notice of the actual date they intend adoption to start. This notice can be provided at the first stage if they know the date. Adoption leave cannot start before the child enters the UK. **Third notification stage (after the child has entered the UK)** Within 28 days of the child's date of entry the employees must tell the employer of the date the child entered the UK. If the adopter is going to claim adoption pay, they are required to give evidence of the date of entry.
Commencement	The ordinary adoption leave is 26 weeks commencing on either: (a) The date on which the child is placed with the adopter; or

	(b) A date which is no more than 14 days before the expected date of placement (EDP). **Overseas adoptions** Employees may choose to start their OAL from either the date the child enters the UK or a fixed date (as notified to their employer) no later than 28 days after the date the child enters the UK. Employees cannot use adoption leave for the purposes of travelling overseas to arrange the adoption or visit the child.
Terms and conditions during absence	All terms and conditions apply during OAL, except remuneration (meaning wages or salary). Seniority and pension rights will continue to accrue, as well as benefits-in-kind (eg life insurance, company car, vouchers). Profit or performance-based payments may be continued. Annual leave continues to accrue, it cannot however be taken during the adoption leave period; and so needs to be taken before or after the period. Service also continues to accrue. Contractual obligations placed on the employee (other than being 'ready and willing to work') will continue to apply. **Note,** the employer cannot pay an employee in lieu of any untaken **statutory annual leave** unless the contract is terminated.
Return to work	The employee is entitled to return to work in the job in which they were employed before commencement of OAL. There is no need for the employee to inform her employer she is returning to work, unless she wishes to do so earlier, in which case 8 weeks' notice must be given. Please note that the employer must notify the employee of the date their adoption leave entitlement will end within **28 days of receiving the notification** (stage 2 notification in the case of overseas adoptions). Employees who wish to return to work from adoption leave either earlier or later than agreed with the employer should provide 8 weeks' notice, unless the employer agrees to less notice being given.

Additional adoption leave (AAL)

The contract of employment	The contract of employment will continue throughout the period of absence. An employee on AOL will be entitled to the terms and conditions of employment which would have applied had they not been absent on AAL, for example the contract terms of mutual trust and confidence, good faith, notice of termination provision, grievance and disciplinary procedures, disclosure of confidential information and the acceptance of gifts, etc. Those taking AAL accrue holiday leave (in accordance with the Working Time Regulations 1998). Service also continues to accrue. **Note,** the employer cannot pay an employee in lieu of any untaken **statutory annual leave** unless the contract is terminated.
End	The employee's adoption leave period finishes at the end of the 52nd week of absence. Employees have a right to return to the same job after adoption leave. Where the employee takes AAL and if it is not reasonably practicable for the employer to hold the job open, the employee must still be offered a job that is suitable and appropriate, and the terms and conditions must be no less favourable.

7.2 Contact during adoption leave

The employer can make contact with the employee during their adoption leave by any means. The amount of reasonable contact is dependent upon the preference of the employee.

The employer must keep an employee informed of promotion opportunities and other information relating to his/her job that he/she would normally be made aware if attending the workplace, eg redundancy situations.

7.3 Keeping-in-touch (KIT) days during adoption leave

Employees may, in agreement with the employer, work for up to ten days' – known as KIT days. Such work will be under their contract of employment without affecting their right to maternity leave or pay. Any amount of work regardless of duration, undertaken on a KIT day will count as one KIT day. Work can include normal duties or attending conferences or receiving training.

Payment for KIT days

The amount of pay the employee will receive for working on a KIT day is to be agreed between the employer and employee. This may already be specified in the contract of employment or decided on a discretionary, case-by-case basis. The payment can take account of the Statutory Adoption Payment (SAP) payment already being received. The payment must be at least the National Minimum Wage.

If the employee is receiving SAP when working a KIT day, he/she will continue to receive SAP for that week. If the employee works more than ten KIT days in his/her SAP period, he/she is not entitled to SAP for any week in which he/she works.

Protection against detriment or dismissal in relation to KIT days

An employee only needs to work a KIT day if he/she wants to, likewise any days worked need to be with the employer's agreement. Neither party can insist upon the arrangement.

It is unlawful to treat an employee unfairly or dismiss him/her because he/she:

- Refused to work a KIT day
- Worked – or considered working – a KIT day

7.4 Dismissal and detriment

Adoptive parents will be protected from suffering a detriment or unfair dismissal for reasons connected with taking or seeking to take adoption leave or the benefits of adoption leave. The protection will begin when parents are approved for adoption.

8 Adoption Pay (SAP)

8.1 Statutory Adoption Pay

The Social Security and Contributions Act 1992 is amended by s 4 of the Act 2002. The effect is to provide for Statutory Adoption Pay (SAP) for the OAL period.

8.2 Entitlement to SAP

To qualify for SAP the employee must:

(a)   Be a person with whom a child is, or expected to be, placed for adoption

(b)   Given the required 28 days notice

(c)   Be an employee continuously employed for at least 26 weeks ending with the matching week

(d) Be absent from work on adoption leave

(e) Be in receipt of normal weekly earnings equal to or above the lower earnings limit [earnings under this limit may entitle the employee to income support], and

(f) Be a person who has elected to receive SAP (note: this is only possible if the employee has not elected to receive Statutory Paternity Pay).

Note, the notification procedures vary according to whether the child is adopted from the UK or overseas.

8.3 Payment details

- SAP is payable during the 'adoption pay period' which will be for a period not exceeding 39 weeks.
- Weekly rate: £128.73 per week or 90% of the employee's normal weekly earnings, whichever is lower (ie the same as 'Statutory Maternity Pay' eg £128.73 in 2011/2012).
- The normal weekly earnings is calculated in the same way as for SMP/SPP – based on the previous eight weeks.
- SAP commences on the first day of OAL.

8.4 Notification to employer

In order to be eligible to receive SAP the employee must notify their employer of the date on which liability of payment for SAP falls. The notification must be in writing if requested by the employer and provided no later than 28 days before the commencement date (or later if notice on that date is not reasonably practicable).

8.5 Miscellaneous provisions: SAP

- SAP is payable on the date when the adopted child is placed with the employee, or where termination of the placement takes place on or within 14 days before the EDP, on the day immediately following the last day of his or her employment. This has been included to reflect the same provisions in the amended SMP scheme.
- Any contractual provisions to over-ride any part of the relevant regulations will be void in law.

9 Right to request flexible working

9.1 Introduction

Employees have the legal right to apply to their employer for flexible working. In effect, this will mean an application to vary the contract of employment. Likewise, the employer will have a duty to consider the application and take various steps in order to deal with each application.

The application to work flexibly can apply to:

- Hours of work
- Times of working
- The location of work (including the home)

Any alteration to terms and conditions will be deemed permanent, and the employee cannot have any right to revert to their previous terms and conditions or to change them again.

9.2 Eligibility criteria

Parents who can make flexible working requests

A parent can request flexible working if they are either:

- The mother, father, adopter, guardian, special guardian, foster parent or private foster carer of the child or a person who has been granted a residence order in respect of a child

- Married to, or the partner or civil partner of, the child's mother, father, adopter, guardian, special guardian, foster parent or private foster carer or person who has been granted a residence order in respect of a child

Carers who can make flexible working requests

A carer can request flexible working if they care, or expect to be caring, for either:

- A spouse, partner, civil partner or relative
- Someone who lives at the carer's address

A relative is a mother, father, adopter, adoptee, guardian, special guardian, parent-in-law, son, son-in-law, daughter, daughter-in-law, brother, brother-in-law, sister, sister-in-law, uncle, aunt or grandparent. Step-relatives, adoptive relationships and half-blood relatives are also included.

9.3 How the application process works

The application should be made by the employee before the child reaches their eighteenth birthday and, if disabled, the age is also 18 years. A disabled child must be one who is entitled to receive disability living allowance.

The form of the application must contain a statement to the effect that:

- It is an application for flexible working
- The flexible working pattern requested is clear, and the effective date identified
- It explains the effect, if any, which the employee thinks might apply to the employer of him or her working flexibly, and how that effect may be dealt with satisfactorily
- The relationship between the applicant and the relevant child is explained
- The application must be in writing, stating whether a previous application has been submitted, and the date of any previous application; and be signed/dated. The employee does not have to explain *why* s/he wants to work flexibly
- No application can be accepted if it has been preceded by another application from the same employee within a period of the preceding 12 months.

9.4 Timescales

The application will be treated as having been received by the employer on the same day it is transmitted to the employer. An application sent by post will be treated as being received on the date it would have been received if it had been delivered in the ordinary course of being posted.

The employer must respond within 28 days of the application being made.

9.5 Procedure to be followed after receipt of application by the employer

A specific procedure must be followed:

- The employer must hold a meeting with the employee which is convenient to both parties and within 28 days of receipt of the application (ie, the date it was made).
- The employer must give its decision within 14 days of the meeting, including any compromise agreed between the parties. The notification must also include notice of the right of appeal.

- Where the application is refused, the reason(s) must be given in sufficiently clear terms and explaining the business grounds for refusal.

9.6 Interim arrangements

Recognising that many employers and employees alike find the formal commitment to the new working arrangements daunting, it can be best to initially manage the arrangements in a less binding manner. The Business Link website (*www.businesslink.gov.uk*) makes the following suggestions:

'Trial periods for flexible working arrangements

If you and/or the employee are not sure that the proposed flexible working pattern will work in practice, you could think about trying a different working arrangement or alternatively, you could consider a trial period.

Trial periods can potentially happen at two stages before a formal agreement is reached:

- Firstly, if you know that your employee will be applying, then you can agree to a trial period before they submit a formal written flexible working request. If you do this, the formal procedure will still be available to the employee in the future.

- Secondly, if the employee makes a formal written application, you could agree to an extension of time for you to make a decision and the trial period could happen before you reach a final agreement. In this case the rest of the formal procedure would still be available to the employee.

Informal temporary flexible working arrangements

If you and the employee think that a flexible working arrangement resulting in a permanent change to their contract of employment may not be the best solution, you could consider an informal temporary arrangement.

For example, this may be appropriate where the employee suddenly becomes the carer of an adult with a terminal illness or they have to care for someone with a fluctuating condition like Parkinson's disease.

You should put any such agreement in writing.'

9.7 Grounds on which employer may refuse an application

The employer may refuse an application only on one or more of the following grounds:

(a) Burden of additional costs

(b) Detrimental effect on ability to meet customer demand

(c) Inability to reorganise work among existing staff

(d) Inability to recruit additional staff

(e) Detrimental impact on quality

(f) Detrimental impact on performance

(g) Insufficiency of work during the periods in which the employee applies to work

(h) Planned structural changes militating against the proposed work arrangements, and

(i) Such other grounds as may be specified in regulations.

9.8 Appeal

The employee should be able to lodge his or her appeal within 14 days after the date on which the employer's decision was actually given. The appeal must be in writing and state the grounds of the appeal.

- Within 14 days of the receipt of the **appeal** the employer must arrange for an appeal meeting (unless, of course, the appeal is upheld before that date). Where possible, a manager of a grade senior to the manager who took the original rejection decision must decide the appeal.

- The employer must within 14 days of the **appeal meeting**, inform the employee of the decision. The reason for dismissing the appeal must be provided – that is, *a 'sufficient explanation'* for the refusal *or* details of when and how the changes will take effect if upheld.

- The employer must ensure that the employee is informed of his/her right to be accompanied at the first meeting and at the **appeal meeting**.

The person **accompanying** the employee may be:

(a) A fellow worker

(b) A full-time or part-time trade union official

(c) A lay trade union official experienced in, or trained appropriately in acting as the employee-companion, or

(d) Another member of staff from the workplace.

Forms: Flexible Working Application Acceptance Form (FW(B)) and Flexible Working Application Rejection Form (FW(C)). All communications between the parties that are specified in the Regulations should be in writing. The forms are available from the Department for Business, Innovation and Skills website.

9.9 Right to be accompanied by a companion

The right extends to both the original meeting and the appeal meeting. The companion must be a worker employed by the same employer as an employee. The applicant does *not* have the right to be accompanied by a trade union representative unless the employer already recognises that trade union for collective bargaining purposes *or* the employer voluntarily agrees to the request.

The companion will have the same rights as one exercising rights in respect of grievance and disciplinary hearings.

9.10 Extensions to the above time-limits

The above time-limits may be extended by mutual agreement. The extension agreement must be in a certain written and dated format. This should give both employer and employee the opportunity to reach a compromise.

9.11 Employer able to take application as withdrawn

Three situations allow the employer to take the application as being withdrawn:

(a) The employee notifies the employer orally or in writing of the withdrawal; or

(b) Without reasonable cause, the employee fails to attend the initial meeting or the appeal meeting on more than one occasion; or

(c) Without reasonable cause, the employee refuses to provide appropriate information to the employer to permit him or her to properly consider the application.

In situations (b) and (c) the employer must inform the employee in writing that s/he considers the application as withdrawn.

The employee will not be eligible to make another application for 12 months.

9.12 Changes to terms and conditions

Any changes in the employee's terms and conditions brought about as a result of the acceptance of the application will mean the employer has the right to reduce pay and benefits on an appropriate **pro rata basis**.

9.13 Redress provided by the Employment Tribunal

Where the employer has allegedly failed to comply with the statutory duties outlined above the employee may complain to the Employment Tribunal.

In addition, a complaint may be submitted where the employee believes the employer has based the decision to reject the application on incorrect facts.

However, in order to bring the complaint to tribunal the employee must have exhausted the employer's own internal appeals procedure and received the employer's decision. The complaint to tribunal must be made within three months of the date when the employee was informed of the appeal decision.

Ongoing employment 6

1 Introduction

This chapter considers the legislation that affects the day-to-day employment and engagement of workers. Once an employee has been recruited and placed on contract the contractual situation will normally be undisrupted for quite some time. However the business environment constantly changes and employers need to review their working practices. Such changes in working practices necessitate changes to the contracts of employment. This chapter looks at this process and the necessary steps. Additionally this chapter looks at the legislation associated with the Working Hours Directive and discrimination legislation that provided the foundation for the Equality Act.

Situations that occur during ongoing employment, specifically where disciplinary action occurs are covered in Chapter 8 – Termination of employment, although it is fully recognised that disciplinary action does not automatically result in dismissal.

2 Changing a contract

The contract of employment is **binding** on **both** parties. This means that it is unlawful for one party to vary the terms and conditions in the contract without the agreement of the other. Where one party attempts to change a contract term without the agreement of the other party this is known as a **unilateral** variation and may be a **breach** of contract.

2.1 Variation of contract

(a) **Flexible terms in contract**

The extent to which a worker or employee can vary terms without the employer's consent is extremely limited. A degree of flexibility may be built into the contract so that minor reasonable changes can be made by the employer – for example, requiring the employee to move to a different place of work. In the case of a change covered by a provision of this kind, the change in workplace location will be lawful.

(b) **Variation by agreement**

A **variation** may be made by **agreement** between the employer and employee. An employer may offer a financial incentive to secure the employee's agreement to a variation.

In some cases a contract may be varied over time by custom and practice, but this will not be legally enforceable if a contradictory express term already exists. Custom and practice will only imply a contractual term if it is necessary to make the contract work effectively. (Where a collective agreement with a recognised union is in place and the contract contains a relevant clause, the collective agreement may incorporate changed terms into individual contracts of employment.)

It should also be noted that if an employee finds a variation of contract unsatisfactory but nevertheless continues to work under the new terms and conditions **without** making his or her objections known, after a short time he or she could be deemed to have implicitly accepted the variation and it would become incorporated into the contract.

If an employer needs to vary the terms and conditions of employment and the employee, having been consulted, objects to the variation, then the employer may decide to terminate the contract by dismissing the employee with notice (or pay in lieu of notice). This is a risky approach for an employer to take. The employer would then be able to offer the job on the revised terms and conditions either to the dismissed employee or to another applicant. The dismissed employee (if they have the necessary qualifying service) could make a complaint of unfair dismissal. The tribunal would consider all the circumstances of the case, especially the business reasons for the variation of terms and conditions, whether there was reasonable consultation with the employee, and the employee's reasons for opposing the variation.

2.2 Breach of contract

If an employer attempts simply to impose a variation of contract on an employee without the employee's agreement, this will normally be a breach of contract.

An employee in response to a breach of contract could

(a) **Acquiesce** – do nothing and work to the new contract. After a short time they would be deemed to have implicitly accepted the breach.

(b) **Pursue breach** of contract claim for damages in county court if they suffer any financial loss as a result of the breach; alternatively they may pursue an unlawful deduction of wages claim in the tribunal.

(c) If they consider the breach a fundamental one they could **resign** and **claim unfair constructive dismissal** and/or a breach of contract on termination in the tribunal.

The best way to achieve change is by agreement as outlined in section 3.

3 Variation of the contract

There is no general power given to the employer or the employee to vary the terms of the contract even when it may be convenient to do so. Under the Employment Rights Act 1996 the employer must inform employees of any changes in contractual terms and conditions within **one month** of the change. A unilateral variation of the contract will usually constitute a breach of the contract, and such a variation made by the employer will, therefore, usually be a **constructive dismissal** which may entitle the employee to resign and claim unfair dismissal.

There is no law, however, that states that a unilateral variation of the terms will **automatically** bring the contract to an end. The other party to the contract, usually the employee, has a choice of whether to accept the breach or not.

3.1 General principles

There are general principles that apply to variations of a contract.

Statutory rights. The employee is entitled to be given minimum periods of notice of any changes.

Implied terms. Some terms may be broad or flexible enough to permit the employer to alter working practices, rather than principal contractual matters. Sensible employers will retain flexibility in job descriptions and job titles. Job descriptions should not be incorporated into contracts, but if they are they should contain a clear statement that they are flexible and subject to change.

General variations

These will only be acceptable where they apply to minor changes and non-fundamental matters eg, contained in works rules. An example of wording is shown below.

Example of general variation

'We are engaged in a business and it may be therefore necessary from time to time to vary your contractual terms and conditions of employment in respect of:............... (see paras of contract or staff handbook). The company reserves the right to make these changes which will be notified to you in writing within four weeks of the change. The company will endeavour to consult you about any changes, but retains the right to make such changes where a business need arises'.

3.2 Specific variation

These might include a mobility clause, flexibility clauses, variable levels of pay, and so on. Strictly speaking, these are not fundamental changes to the contractual terms, but instead making actual contractual terms flexible enough to meet different circumstances.

Compensatory schemes. It is common for public sector and large industrial concerns to have inserted into contracts clauses which allow the employer to 'buy-out' uneconomic working practices.

3.3 Reasonable notice

Normally reasonable notice should be given. Also, not exercising terms so as to make it impossible for the employees to perform the contract are prerequisites for the employer. In other words, the employer should exercise their discretion carefully. The employer is not obliged to act reasonably in exercising that discretion.

3.4 Contractual clause

Any contractual clauses which could benefit the employer by exercising them in a flexible way should be brought to the attention of the prospective employee before the contract is agreed.

This will follow the legal principle that an onerous or unusual term should not be exercised if it had not been brought to the other party's attention.

The employer will not act arbitrarily, capriciously or unreasonably in exercising terms which enable the employer to adapt an employee's contract subject to circumstances; and in so doing the duty of trust and confidence will not be breached.

3.5 Variation by consent – express consent

An important difference is where the old contract is varied, or where it is completely replaced.

Where there is doubt the courts will consider the intention of the parties and the significance of any changes in the employment relationship.

Where variations are to take effect this can be accomplished by a letter or memorandum of variation. This is not to overlook that when a salary review occurs this is a contractual change and should be treated as such.

3.6 Implied consent

This normally occurs where the employer has to impose new terms. It is a question of fact as to whether the employee acts in accordance with the new terms, and in which case the employee may be deemed to have accepted the new terms (or affirmed them) by virtue of conduct. But, for this to have credence, the employee must have knowledge of the new terms.

3.7 An employee may continue to work under protest

An employee who continues to work after the employer has made a unilateral change to the terms of the contract does not necessarily accept the change; particularly where the employee makes it clear that s/he is **working under protest**. Where the employee does not make an initial protest and works under the new terms s/he may be deemed to have accepted the change. Whether s/he has done so will depend on his/her conduct. Certain examples of conduct can show the employee has accepted (or **affirmed**) the new contract terms.

As time continues this may undermine statutory rights (eg to claim unfair constructive dismissal), but s/he will have five years in order to sue for a breach of contract in the civil courts.

3.8 Silence alone does not indicate acceptance

This particularly applies in matters of little or no immediate importance to the employee. For the employer to prove acceptance it is important for them to provide some form of consideration, particularly where the changes impact negatively on the workforce. It has been argued that simply allowing the employees to work is consideration, but this argument has its critics, and it is best assumed to be something financial.

Section 4 of the ERA 1996 requires that any **variation to principal terms and conditions** (laid-out in the s 1 statement) must be notified in writing to employees within one month of the change. The statement does not have contractual force, and notification is merely a record of the changes.

3.9 Termination and offer of new contract

This is a draconian step. Besides the employee relations issues, it involves dismissal and possible claims of unfair and wrongful dismissal. Full contractual notice must be given and simultaneously new contracts offered to commence immediately after the end of the notice period. Often the employer will argue dismissals were for *some other substantial reason*, but these must be shown to be fair and reasonable in all the circumstances and this will include a sound business reason.

3.10 Unilateral variation

This involves the employer changing terms without proper consent (irrespective of any prior notice or consultation). A unilateral variation is a breach of contract. Not all variations may constitute a repudiatory breach – some unilateral variations may be so minor as to fall within the management prerogative.

The employee has a number of options when faced with the employer's desire to change a contract:

- Accept (affirm) the change (expressly or by conduct); or
- Continue to work under protest and claim damages for breach of contract; or
- Accept the repudiation, leave and claim unfair constructive dismissal; or
- (If appropriate) claim an unlawful deduction of wages; or
- Continue to work and seek an injunction or declaration of parties' rights; or
- Commence industrial action.

3.11 Other reasons why a variation may not always constitute a breach

- What the employer proposes to change may not be a **term** of the contract but, in fact, a non-contractual management instruction or **custom**. In the circumstances no legal claims should arise.

- The contract may include **a term which allows for changes to be made** to various terms. Such a term should be clear and precise; for example, a term which allows for alterations to the working week will by implication not allow the employer to reduce hours or pay unless there is an express term to that effect, or agreement has been made with the employee.

  Nevertheless, an employer who intends to exercise a discretionary power to change the terms of a contract must not do so in such a way that they breach the duty of mutual trust and confidence.

- Where no agreement can be reached on the changes the employer may have no other option other than to give proper notice to the employee that the existing contract is being terminated with effect from a particular date, and that after that date the employer will offer a new contract on different terms. An employee given notice may be eligible to bring an action for unfair dismissal, but, even so, may not be successful if the employer can prove that the reason for the dismissal was for a sound business reason.

Step by step approach

A suggested step by step approach to change a contract of employment could be as follows.

Employers' actions

Employers' actions can be summarised as follows.

- Have a clear plan.

- Justify the changes by making a case for genuine organisational need for change. This must demonstrate the change will be

    - Beneficial to the organisation – a valid business need; and
    - A proper 'reasoned' decision

- Consult (as in redundancy procedures, if necessary with employee representatives/Trade Unions, and with individuals):

    - With a view to reaching agreement; and
    - Follow any procedures that are in place or stipulated

- Give timely notification of the new terms

- When making the offer give a reasonable period of time to the employee(s) in which to accept or refuse

For changes to be lawful and effective

The following must be in place.

(a) There must be a proper consultation

(b) There must be offer and acceptance

(c) Should the employee not accept 'positively and unequivocally', the terms remain the same; and

(d) Acceptance (or affirmation) can be written, by word of mouth or by conduct.

4 Continuity of employment

4.1 The importance of continuity of employment

To enjoy the protection of many statutory provisions the individual must have been **employed** (ie, as an employee) for the requisite periods of continuous service. This is particularly important when attempting to submit a complaint to the Employment Tribunal. Significant breaks can, but not always sever the required link between periods of employment.

4.2 Part-timers

Part-timers are eligible irrespective of hours worked, but one year's service is necessary to bring a claim to the tribunal.

4.3 Beginning of period of continuous employment (PCE)

This is the day that the employee starts work (ie, the date on which the contract commences). The period finishes on the date determined by statutory employment rights – eg, in dismissal. The effective date of dismissal (EDT) includes notice periods not (wrongfully) provided.

Computation

- Week by week (Sunday – Saturday)
- Calendar months
- Twelve months

The PCE of an employee is any week during the whole or part of which an employee's relations with an employer are governed by a contract of employment. A 'week' means one ending with a Saturday. This might include gaps of such a short duration, eg, a few days in the relevant week, that do not break continuity.

Continuity is also preserved during the whole or part of any week when the employee is 'absent from work (but) by arrangement or custom, the employee is regarded as continuing in' employment. Continuity is also preserved owing to a temporary cessation of work. To show continuity under these provisions it is not only necessary to show that there is some expectation of a return to work settled in advance, but that the employment relationship has continued during the break.

4.4 Weeks which count

- Week/part of week governed by contract of employment
- Periods of absence due to pregnancy/childbirth, illness or temporary cessation of work will count
- Following re-engagement/reinstatement after dismissal the PCE is unbroken (eg, tribunal order, or within a period of no more then four weeks following redundancy)
- Where an employee is re-engaged after receiving a redundancy payment and it is a term of re-engagement that s/he repays the redundancy pay then the PCE will be unbroken.

Receipt of redundancy payment – does it break continuity?

The question commonly arises where a redundancy payment is made but the individual is then re-employed by the same or another employer under the same contract. What is the employee's appropriate length of service if a second redundancy situation arises? In such circumstances, continuity is broken for the purposes of redundancy rights by virtue of the first payment. Where the Secretary of State has paid the redundancy payment as a result of the employer's insolvency this too will break continuity of employment for redundancy purposes. One of the criteria for the Secretary of State making the payment is that he or she is satisfied that the employee is 'entitled' to the payment.

4.5 Periods of no employment

- No contract in existence
- If the break or interval between contracts is short in relation to the overall period of employment their continuity is preserved. This is referred to as the Mathematical approach.
- Generally the cessation of work must be due to a reduction in the employer's overall *quantum* of work – not merely transferring it to someone else other than the employee concerned.

4.6 Weeks which do not count towards the PCE – but which do not break continuity

- Involvement in industrial action (unless employer dismisses)
- Absence due to a lock-out
- Employee not working within Great Britain and paying income tax or National Insurance contributions.

4.7 Other matters

- Receipt of a redundancy payment from the employer may not necessarily break continuity.

- Work with associated employers should maintain PCE.

- Gaps in employment due to a transfer (The TUPE) Regulations 1981 applying will not break PCE).

5 The Working Time Regulations 1998

5.1 Introduction

The Working Time Regulations 1998 first came into force in the UK on 1 October 1998. They implement the EC Working Time Directive (EC 93/104) introduced under Article 118A, now Article 138, of the Treaty of Rome. The Working Time Regulations have been amended by: The **Working Time Regulations 1999**; The **Working Time (Amendment) Regulations 2001**; The **Working Time (Amendment) Regulations 2002**; The **Working Time (Amendment) Regulations 2003**; The **Working Time (Amendment) Regulations 2006**; The **Working Time (Amendment) (No.2) Regulations 2006**; The **Serious Organised Crime and Police Act 2005 (Consequential and Supplementary Amendments to Secondary Legislation) Order 2006**; The **Working Time (Amendment) Regulations 2007** and The **Legislative Reform (Health and Safety Executive) Order 2008**.

The stated purpose of the Directive is to ensure the health and safety of workers in the community by enforcing 'minimum daily, weekly and annual periods of rest and adequate breaks' and 'placing a maximum limit on weekly working time'. 'Working time' under the Regulations means any period during which the worker is working at the employer's disposal and carrying out duties, plus any period during which s/he is receiving training. It includes, overtime, working lunches, travel on the job – but not to and from work. It also includes time while the worker is on call at or near a workplace, although not at home (unless agreed in advance with the employer). If the worker does not need to attend the workplace, but needs to be contactable at all times, then working time is only for the periods when the worker is actually doing work for the employer.

At present it stands that a worker can make a written agreement with the employer to 'opt out' of the 48-hour limit for a specified period or indefinitely.

5.2 The main provisions of the Regulations

Workers and employees are both covered by the Regulations.

The Regulations cover those classed as **workers**, and include:

- Those working under a contract of employment (employee)

- Those 'Working under any other contract where the individual undertakes to perform personally any work or services for another party (who) is not ...... a client or customer ......';

- Those who are paid a regular salary or wage and work for an organisation, business or individual. Their employer normally provides the worker with work, controls when and how the work is done, supplies them with tools and other equipment, and pays tax and National Insurance contributions. This includes part-time and temporary workers and the majority of agency workers and freelancers; and

- Someone doing in-house training or a trainee on work experience – for example doing National Traineeship – is also a worker. A young worker is someone who is above the minimum school leaving age but under 18.

The Regulations therefore apply to a wide range of individuals including agency workers, temporary employees, or those employed on a fixed-term or any type of casual hours contract.

5.3 Definition of worker

The Working Time Regulations 1998 states that a worker will be anyone who 'has entered into or works under (or, where the employment has ceased, worked under): (a) a contract of employment; or (b) any other contract, whether express or implied and (if it is express) whether oral or in writing, whereby the individual undertakes to do or perform personally any work or services for another party to the contract whose status is not by virtue of the contract that of client or customer of any profession or business undertaking carried on by the individual'.

It is worth noting that the Regulations have created a 'hybrid' category of worker that is so wide that it goes beyond those engaged on a contract of employment to include other forms of contract where the individual performs work or services personally. The only exception is where the individual is carrying on a profession or business where the other party is the client (ie a truly self-employed person). In other words, workers such as agency workers and freelance workers, including some self-employed persons, are covered, but not those genuinely pursuing a business activity on their own account.

5.4 The Regulations explained – extent of coverage

5.4.1 Basic coverage

The main provisions provide for:

- A limit of an average of 48 hours a week which a worker can be required to work (although workers can choose to work longer if they want to)

- Rest breaks while at work if the working day is longer than 6 hours. The rest break must be for at least 20 minutes, without any interruption and away from the work station

- Those aged 16 and above are covered, but 16-18 year-olds enjoy longer break/rest periods – a 30 minute rest break if they are expected to work for more than 4.5 hours at a stretch.

- Minimum daily rest period of 11 consecutive hours in every 24 and weekly rest period of 24 hours per seven days and 48 hours per 14 days – this is in addition to any daily rest periods. These breaks must be away from work

- A night worker is, broadly speaking, someone who works at least three hours between 11pm and 6am on most working days. Night workers must not, on average, work more than 8 hours in each 24-hour period, averaged over 17 weeks. If the work involves special hazards or heavy mental/physical strain there is an absolute limit of 8 hours in any 24-hour period. There is a duty to offer night workers free health assessments

An individual worker cannot opt out of the entitlement to rest periods and breaks. However, a collective or workforce agreement can modify or exclude these entitlements provided an equivalent period of compensatory rest is given.

These provisions apply to part-time as well as full-time employees and 'workers'. They also apply with additional safeguards to young workers, ie those between the ages of 16 and 18 and who are over school age.

The Working Time (Amendment) Regulations 2003 have extended the Regulations to apply to all public and private sectors of activity including:

- All non mobile workers in road (other than those subject to the Road Transport Directive), sea, inland waterways, lake transport, railway and offshore sectors

- Aviation workers (not covered by the Aviation Directive), and

- Junior doctors (wef: August 2004) had their annual working time fixed at 2,000 hours per annum. Rest entitlements are a minimum of seven monthly days off and 96 restdays.

The Regulations **do not apply** to:

- Individuals who are self-employed, running their own business and are free to work for different clients and customers
- The armed forces, the police and emergency services are outside the scope of the regulations in certain circumstances. However, **young workers** in the armed forces, the police and emergency services, the aviation sector and the road transport sector, **are** covered by the young workers provisions in the Working Time Regulations.

5.4.2 Flexibility in determining working hours

There are a number of ways in which the Regulations for the purposes of the length of the **working week** and other matters can be disallowed:

(a) **Collective agreement**

This is an agreement between an independent trade union and an employer or an employer's association.

(b) **Workforce agreement**

This is an agreement between an employer and employees and workers or their representatives, which:

(i) Is in writing

(ii) Is effective for a specified period not exceeding five years

(iii) Applies either to all the workers employed by a particular employer (except those covered by a collective agreement) or to such workers performing a particular function, working at a particular place or belonging to a particular department or unit

(iv) Is signed by the representatives of the workers (but excluding any representative who was not a worker when the agreement was first made available for signature), unless there are 20 or fewer workers of the employer, in which case it may be signed by a majority of the workforce; and

(v) Is circulated by the employer, before signature, with appropriate guidance on how it should be interpreted.

(c) **Relevant agreement**

This is:

(i) A workforce agreement which applies to the worker; or

(ii) Any provision in a collective agreement which is part of a contract between a worker and his or her employer; or

>   (iii)   Any other written agreement between a worker and his or her employer which is legally enforceable. This would include an agreement to disapply the maximum working week, so long as there is an individual written agreement with the worker that satisfies the conditions that are discussed below.

A record of such an 'opt-out' agreement should be kept by the employer (for no less than two years).

The advantages of all three types of agreement is that they will allow employers to:

- Define what periods count as working time and as night working time
- Specify the start date for the working week reference period, the weekly rest period and for averaging night work; and
- Specify the holiday year, any conditions for taking holiday and any adjustments for holiday pay on termination.

The individual agreement may be for a fixed time or for a continuous period. A three-month notice period can be inserted into the agreement by which it can be revoked by the individual. Where there is no notice period, the individual can withdraw consent giving no less than seven days' notice.

Both a collective and a workforce agreement will allow employers:

- To increase the working week reference period from 17 to 52 weeks where there are objective, technical or other organisational reasons; and
- To extend the definition of a night worker and to identify night work that the parties agree involves special hazards or heavy strain.

Having a workforce agreement will mean organising elections for employee representatives.

5.4.3 Unmeasured working time

Almost all the protections in the Working Time Regulations 1998 (WTR) 1998, except for annual leave, do not apply where the worker works on 'unmeasured working time'. It is unclear exactly what 'unmeasured time' means. The exception is intended to apply where, due to the specific nature of the work done, the duration of the worker's working time is not measured or predetermined, or it can be determined by the worker himself. The regulations give examples as managing executives or other persons with autonomous decision-making powers; family workers; or workers officiating in religious ceremonies.

The WTR 1998 imposes a contractual obligation on the employer not to require a worker to work more than an average of 48 hours per week, including overtime. The employer also has a duty, subject to criminal sanctions, to take all reasonable steps to ensure no more than 48 hours per week are worked unless the worker has opted out.

If an employee is 18 or over (not in an excluded sector of employment) and wishes to work more than 48 hours a week, they can choose to **opt out** of the 48 hour limit. This must be voluntary and in writing. It cannot be an agreement with the whole workforce and the employee should not be dismissed or subjected to a detriment (for example, refused promotion or overtime) for refusing to sign an opt-out.

Under the Road Transport (Working Time) Regulations mobile workers cannot 'opt-out' of the weekly working time limits. Mobile workers include drivers (including employed drivers, own-account drivers, and agency drivers), members of the vehicle crew, eg a second driver on a coach; anyone else who is part of the travelling staff, eg a bus conductor, a drayman, or a security guard aboard a vehicle carrying high-value goods.

If the employee signs an opt-out, they have the right to cancel this agreement at any time by giving between one week and three months' notice. The employee can agree this notice period with their employer when they sign the opt-out. They can also cancel an opt-out, even if it is part of a contract they have signed. If an employee who has been working more than 48 hours decides to exercise the opt-out and reduce his/her hours to 48, an employer can probably reduce the employee's pay proportionally, especially if pay is explicitly linked to hours worked.

5.5 Annual leave – basic entitlement

5.5.1 Basic entitlement

The WTR 1998 give workers the right to four weeks' paid annual leave. If there is no collective or workforce agreement setting the dates of the holiday year and no written agreement between the employer and worker on this point, the leave year starts, for workers employed before 1st October 1998, on 1st October; and for other workers, on the anniversary of the start of their employment. In the worker's first year they can only take holiday which they have accrued, rounded up to the nearest half day.

The Working Time (Amendment) Regulations 2007 increased the statutory entitlement to paid annual leave for all workers.

(a) From 1st April 2009, the basic entitlement was increased by additional leave entitlement of 1.6 weeks. The 1.6 weeks equates to 8 working days for a 5 day a week worker, giving a total entitlement of 28 working days. For those working fewer days a week the entitlement is scaled down, but for anyone working more than 5 days a week the limit is still 28 days.

(b) The same rules apply to extra leave as to ordinary leave regarding what is the leave year, when leave may be taken, and how pay is calculated.

However the additional leave may be treated differently. First, there is a relaxation of the normal provision that untaken leave may not be carried over to the next year, thus requiring the minimum of 20 days (for a full time worker) to be taken in the year. This requirement may be removed – but only for the additional leave – by a 'relevant agreement' (a collective agreement, a workforce agreement or a written contractual agreement with the individual worker). It should be noted that there is a facility to agree such a provision, but no obligation on employers to do so. Second, the facility to **pay in lieu ceases** to apply altogether, **except** on termination of employment.

5.5.2 Additional points

The following points are relevant to annual leave:

- Workers must give the employer notice that they want to take leave.
- Employers can set the times that workers take their leave, for example for a Christmas shutdown.

The pay due can be worked out using the formula:

$(A \times B) - C$ where: A is the period of leave the worker is entitled to. B is how much of the worker's leave year has elapsed before they left their job. C is the amount of leave taken by the worker between the start of the leave year and the date they are leaving.

Daily rate of accrued holiday pay: in the absence of an express contract term the Apportionment Act 1870 applies. The calculation should be based on a calendar day: 1/365th of annual salary (not a working day basis, eg 1/260th).

The leave entitlement under the regulations is not additional to bank holidays. There is no statutory right to take bank holidays off. Therefore a worker who is not otherwise paid in respect of bank holidays may take bank holidays as part of the annual leave entitlement in order to receive payment for these holidays.

> **'Bank Holidays'**
> - Schedule 1 of the Banking and Financial Dealings Act 1971 provides that Easter Monday, the last Monday in May and in August, 26 December (unless it is a Sunday) and 27 December in a year in which 25th or 26th December is a Sunday, each constitute a 'bank holiday'.
> - Christmas Day and Good Friday have been established historically as public holidays by custom.
> - New Year's Day and the first Monday in May have been designed as public holidays by royal proclamation at the behest of government.

5.5.3 Notice periods for taking annual leave

Employers and workers can agree how and when to give notice of when leave is to be taken. In the absence of an agreement, the basic requirement is that the worker must give notice which amounts to double the quantity of leave to be taken.

An employer may refuse the worker permission to take leave requested within a time period equivalent to the period of the leave. For example, if a worker wants to take a day's leave, they would have to give their employer at least two days' notice. If a worker has given the employer two days' notice that they want to take one day's leave, the employer can come back within one day to refuse the leave. This provides employers with flexibility where, for example, a number of other workers have also applied to take the same day off.

In effect, the worker may take leave whenever they wish, but the employer is empowered under the Regulations to give both positive notice and negative notice:

Positive notice. The employer may inform the worker that they should take leave on the '*relevant dates*'. The positive notice must be twice as many days in advance of the leave required as that leave (eg the employee wants 10 days' leave, so the employer must give notice no less than 20 days in advance).

Negative notice. The employer in giving **negative notice** (ie refusing the application) must give the same number of days requested as leave as notice that the desired leave cannot be taken (it is preferable not to give less than five days' notice).

5.6 The Regulations – specific provisions

5.6.1 The 'working week'

Working time is defined as:

(a) Any time spent when a worker is working, at the employer's disposal and carrying out the activity or duties, or

(b) Any period during which the worker is receiving relevant training (this is work experience provided by a training course or programme or training for employment, but not a course provided by an educational institution or by someone whose main business is to provide training)

(c) Any additional period which is to be treated as working time under a relevant agreement.

As all three elements of (a) must be satisfied, a number of practical issues arise from the definition:

Workers on call

If they are free to pursue their own activities, this would not be working time.

Lunch/tea/coffee/smoking breaks

As it is leisure time, it would not be working time. If, however, a lunch or other break is for business purposes or work is done during those breaks, it will be deemed working time.

Travelling to and from a place of work

Commuting to and from work would not count as working time, but travelling to a business meeting would if it is required by the job. However, lengthy journeys involving overnight travelling would probably not be working time, although time spent working while travelling would be covered. When a worker has to travel as part of their work, for example a 24-hour mobile repairman or travelling salesman this is classed as working. Routine travel between home and work is not working time.

Working at home

Where a worker takes work home, time worked would only count as working time if it was done on a basis agreed with the employer. If an employer knows that a worker is doing a lot of work at home, and as a result the 48-hour working week is exceeded, it is likely that this would count as working time, as the employer is likely to have implicitly agreed to the work being done in this way.

Working while travelling abroad

Time spent abroad is working time if a worker works for an employer who carries on business in Great Britain.

5.6.2 'Reference period' for the working week

Average working hours per week should not exceed 48 (including overtime) in any period of 17 weeks and employers should take all reasonable steps to ensure the limit is not exceeded.

The number of hours worked each week should be averaged out over 17 weeks or however long a worker has been working for their employer if this is less than 17 weeks. This period of time is called the '**reference period**'.

A collective or workforce agreement cannot modify or exclude the 48-hour ceiling, but in certain circumstances it can extend the period over which hours are averaged.

Workers and employers can agree to calculate the average weekly working time over a period of up to 52 weeks under a workforce or collective agreement. The reference period is also extended to 26 weeks in other circumstances (the 26-week period applies to those workers who are partially excepted from the rest break provisions).

- Doctors in training have a 26-week reference period
- The offshore sector has a 52-week reference period

The actual working week is not specified in the Regulations, but for most it will commence at midnight on Sunday and be for seven days.

The average weekly working time is calculated by dividing the number of hours worked by the number of weeks over which the average working week is being calculated, for example 17. When calculating the average weekly working time, if the worker is away during the reference period because he or she is taking paid annual leave, maternity, paternity, adoption or parental leave, or is off sick.

Work with more than one employer will count towards the individual's maximum working hours in any reference period.

5.6.3 Categories of workers

Workers fall into four categories which are explained below.

(a) **Category 1 workers**

These are workers whose working time is not measured or predetermined, or can be determined by the workers themselves. This is because they are expected to have complete control over the hours they work and because their time is not monitored or determined by their employer. Such a situation is likely to occur if a worker can decide when the work is to be done or may adjust the time worked as they see fit.

Example: A worker who is given the option of working flexitime. However, the Regulations specifically include in this category managing executives (or other persons with autonomous decision-making powers) and family workers. Notwithstanding health and safety obligations, these workers are not subject to any maximum working hours.

(b) **Category 2 workers**

(i) Those whose place of work is distant from their home or whose places of work are distant from one another, eg construction workers on site.

(ii) Those involved in security and surveillance activities where a permanent presence is required to protect property and persons, eg security guards, caretakers.

(iii) Those involved in activities which involve the need for continuity of service or production, and particularly:

- Care workers in hospitals, residential homes and prisons
- Dock or airport workers
- Press, radio, media, post and telecoms workers
- Gas, water, electricity and refuse workers
- Workers in continuous process production
- Research and development workers, and

- Farmers and agricultural workers

(iv) Those who work in activities where there is a *'foreseeable surge of activity'*, ie seasonal peak industries, such as farming, tourism or postal services.

(v) Those whose activities are affected by an unusual or unforeseeable occurrence beyond the control of the employer, or exceptional events, the consequences of which could not have been averted by the exercise of all due care by the employer, or an accident or the imminent risk of an accident.

(c) **Category 3 workers**

(i) Shift workers, when they change shifts and cannot take daily and/or weekly rest periods between the end of one shift and the start of the next.

(ii) Workers carrying out work involving periods which are split up over the day, eg cleaning staff.

These workers are only exempt from the provisions in the Regulations relating to daily and weekly rest periods.

(d) **Category 4 workers**

This is the widest category. Any worker will be exempt from all the principal Regulations' provisions except the maximum working week, but only if there is a relevant collective agreement or a workforce agreement in place.

5.6.4 Night work

Reg.2 defines 'night workers' as anyone who:

- 'As a normal course' works at least three hours of the daily working time during night time

- Who is likely, during night time, to work a certain proportion of the annual working time as defined by a collective or workforce agreement, or

- If the daily working time includes at least three hours of night time often enough for it to be said that they work such hours '**as normal course**'

The words '**as a normal course**', means on a regular basis. There has been a court ruling that a worker who worked at night for one third of his working time was a night worker.

Occasional, or ad hoc, work at night does not make you a night worker.

'Night time' will be a period of **seven hours** or more in duration which must include the period midnight to 5am. Where there is no 'relevant agreement' to determine 'night time', the Regulations have a default period to include 11pm – 6am.

Special health and safety rules apply to night workers.

5.6.5 Length of night work

The 'normal working hours' of a 'night worker' must not exceed an average of eight hours in each 24-hour period. There are special rules for those engaged in working with special hazards and heavy strain. Nightly working time should be averaged out over a reference period, which is usually 17 weeks. This period could be longer if agreed in a workforce or collective agreement.

The **average** hours worked can be calculated over the 17-week reference period. The night worker's average working hours can be determined by the following calculation:

The average hours worked at night are calculated by dividing the number of normal hours worked in the reference period – eg 17 weeks – by the number of days in the period, after the number of rest days which the worker has taken in relation to their entitlement under the regulations has been subtracted.

A |(B – C)

A = the **normal** working hours during the reference period, but not the **actual** hours worked for that period.

B = the number of 24-hour periods included in the reference period.

C = the number of hours during that period which comprise or are included in the weekly rest periods. This figure should be divided by 24 (hours). If workers work less than 48 hours a week on average, they will not exceed the night work limits.

Normal hours of night work include overtime where it is part of a night worker's normal hours of work.

5.6.6 Rest and break periods

The entitlements to rest and break periods are as follows

- A minimum daily rest period of 11 consecutive hours in every 24 hours. The rest period cannot be averaged, but does not apply to shift workers and split-duty workers, eg cleaners.

- An uninterrupted rest break of at least 20 minutes, away from the workstation if possible in every 6 hours of work. Can be added to the above if appropriate.

- Weekly rest: 24 hours per 7 days or 48 hours per 14 days for workers engaged in particular jobs. This is in addition to any daily rest periods. The rest day can be any day of the week: 'Sunday working'.

There are special rules for young workers.

An individual worker cannot opt out of the entitlement to rest periods and breaks. However, a collective or workforce agreement can modify or exclude these entitlements provided an equivalent period of compensatory rest is given.

5.7 Enforcement and remedies

5.7.1 Enforcement

Enforcement is split between different authorities. The limits and health assessment requirements (for night workers), are enforced by the Health and Safety Executive (HSE), local authority environmental health departments, the Civil Aviation Authority (CAA), the Vehicle and Operator Services Agency (VOSA) and the Office of Rail Regulation (ORR).

Sanctions are criminal offences punishable with a fine not exceeding £5,000 per individual offence and, in extreme cases, imprisonment. Various enforcement and prohibition notices may be issued. A failure to keep proper records going back for two years will be an offence.

The entitlements to rest and leave are enforced through Employment Tribunals. Any complaint to a tribunal needs to be made within three months.

5.7.2 Remedies

The Regulations protect workers from being subjected to a detriment if they insist on their rights under the Regulations. A worker is protected against such a detriment on account of:

(a) The refusal to exceed any limit on working time applicable under the Regulations

(b) The refusal to work when entitled to a rest period or break or to forego annual leave

(c) The refusal to sign a workforce agreement or to make, vary or continue any other agreement provided for in the Regulations

(d) Any activities carried out as a workforce representative or a candidate for election as a workforce representative, or

(e) Any allegation made by a worker in good faith that the employer had infringed his or her rights under the Regulations or bringing proceedings to enforce such rights.

There is *no* free-standing right to bring a tribunal claim for a breach of the 48-hour working week, but where the employee is forced to work longer hours and resigns as a result, the excessive working hours may be the basis of a constructive dismissal claim under.

Failure to pay for holidays entitles the worker to bring a claim for unlawful deduction of holiday pay (wages). Failure to pay accrued holiday pay on termination can also give rise to a claim. The worker has three months from the date on which the right should have been exercised to bring a claim. Remedies will normally be an order for compensation and/or payment of the amount owed.

6 Sunday working

6.1 Sunday Trading Act 1994

The Sunday Trading Act 1994 inserted a number of provisions into the Employment Rights Act 1996 relating to shop workers and betting workers. Shop workers are those employed in any retail trade or business, including hairdressers. Both types of worker are entitled not to be dismissed or suffer any other type of detriment for deciding not to work on a Sunday. These workers are entitled to opt out of the employer's requirement to work on Sundays. A three-month notice period is applicable. Where the worker decides to opt out, the employer is not obliged to increase working hours on any other day to compensate for the loss of working time and related remuneration.

Where the employer requires Sunday working within two months of their employment they must provide the worker a written statement explaining their opt-out right. Only one month's opt-out notice need be given.

Any breach will entitle the worker to bring a complaint to the Employment Tribunal within three months of that breach.

7 Discrimination legislation

As described in Chapter 1 – Advertising and recruitment – while the Equality Act has replaced previous discrimination legislation certain parts of the Act have substituted little of the original definition of the protected characteristic. This applies to:

- Age
- Marriage and civil partnerships
- Pregnancy and maternity
- Race
- Religion or belief
- Sex
- Sexual orientation

Given that the Equality Act introduces uniform definitions of:

- Direct discrimination
- Indirect discrimination

- Harassment
- Victimisation

There is little to be gained from studying the previous legislation in minutiae. Therefore this section will provide a synopsis of those statutes that the Equality Act did not alter, or where a new concept was introduced for the first time. Included within this is general advice as to compliance.

7.1 Age

7.1.1 Scope of the Regulations

The Employment Equality (Age) Regulations 2006, came into force on 1 October 2006. The Regulations made it unlawful for employers and a number of other bodies to discriminate on the ground of age. They implemented the age aspect of EC Framework Directive.

The Age Regulations prohibit, in the employment area:

- Direct and indirect age discrimination
- Victimisation and
- Age harassment

They apply to:

- All employers
- Vocational training providers
- Trade unions
- Professional organisations
- Employer organisations, and
- Trustees and managers of occupational pension schemes.

They protect employees (and, to an extent, other workers) of all ages (young and old) and apply throughout the employment process, to recruitment and selection, promotion, training, pay and benefits, dismissal and post-termination relationships.

The legislation makes clear that decisions on selection, recruitment, promotion, training needs, etc, are to be made on the basis of merit and competence, not because the person has reached an arbitrary chronological age. This applies to:

- Employment and vocational training (although schools are exempt)
- Coverage: all workers, job applicants, crown-appointed office holders and some other paid office-holders, eg, company directors, trades union members and members of professional bodies. Unpaid voluntary workers are not covered.
- Post-employment discrimination is covered where the complainant can show a close connection between his/her *former work* and less favourable treatment.

7.1.2 Direct age discrimination

The Regulations provide that direct age discrimination occurs where 'on grounds of B's age, A treats B less favourably than he treats or would treat other persons... and A cannot show the treatment... to be a proportionate means of achieving a legitimate aim'.

The measure taken in respect of a particular person must fall within a set of 'legitimate aims':

- Health, safety and welfare
- Facilitation of employment planning (HR planning/succession planning)
- Particular training requirements for the particular post
- Encouraging or rewarding loyalty
- Requirement for a reasonable period of employment before retirement

In addition, the employer will have to provide further evidence by reference to it being by 'proportionate means'.

7.1.3 Indirect age discrimination

The same definition of **indirect discrimination** as that used for sexual orientation, applies. Indirect discrimination occurs where:

- A applies to B a provision, criterion or practice which A applies, or would apply, equally to persons not of the same age group as B

- That provision, criterion or practice puts persons of B's age group at a particular disadvantage when compared with other persons, and

- B suffers that disadvantage.

The statutory definition of indirect discrimination makes clear that establishing such discrimination will involve a **comparison between the claimant's 'age group'** (a concept introduced by the Regulations with little explanation) and other persons.

The Regulations use the same **proportionality** test of justification for both direct and indirect discrimination. An indirectly discriminatory practice will not be objectively justified if there is a less discriminatory way of achieving the aim in question that would be equally practicable for the employer to implement. For example, a requirement that all job applicants be recent graduates would probably have a disparate impact on older candidates, and the employer's aim might equally be achieved with a test that assessed candidates on their individual merits, focusing on the relevant required skills.

7.2 How Regulations apply to employers

7.2.1 Mandatory retirement ages

The dismissal of employees on their attaining a certain age is the most obvious example of direct age discrimination. These Regulations introduce a **default retirement age** of 65.

The default age means that provided the employer follows a prescribed procedure, they will be able to fairly dismiss an employee for retirement at this age or above. Employers who have a retirement age below 65 will need to objectively justify it. This procedure is dealt with in Chapter 8 – Termination of employment, however it is planned to end the default retirement age from 2011.

7.2.2 Unfair dismissal

Until October 2006, the right to claim unfair dismissal did not apply to employees at or over the 'normal retiring age' for their position or, where there was no such NRA, to employees at or over the age of 65. This limit was removed by the Age Regulations as part of the UK government's implementation of the Framework Directive.

The Regulations insert certain provisions into the Employment Rights Act 1996 to make special provision for retirement dismissals and adds retirement to the existing **potentially fair reasons for dismissal.**

Therefore a procedurally correct dismissal for retirement is automatically fair under the rules. However, if an employer fails to follow the correct procedure and the Tribunal considers that the dismissal is not by reason of retirement, it can rule the dismissal to be unfair and the dismissal will be considered under the normal unfair dismissal provisions. Given that the dismissal will have been effected purportedly by reason of retirement, the employer will run into the difficulty of not having a potentially fair reason for dismissal to put forward as well as not having followed the statutory dispute resolution procedures in relation to the dismissal, in which case, the dismissal will be automatically unfair.

7.2.3 Age-related discrimination – tribunal claims

Any complaint must be submitted within three months of the act of discrimination complained of. There is no cap on the compensation.

7.2.4 Post-employment discrimination

The Regulations provide that certain post termination actions by a respondent are caught by the prohibition on age discrimination in employment.

However, it should be noted that the Regulations providing for post employment discrimination cannot apply retrospectively if they were not in force at the time of the Act.

7.2.5 Pay and non-pay benefits

The government states that employers may continue to grant pay increases and other benefits in accordance with age or experience-based incremental schemes, provided employers can *justify* such schemes. Similarly, this will apply to schemes based on qualifications, professional status, loyalty and seniority. However, this does not close off the right of individuals to bring an age-related indirect discrimination complaint.

Indeed, this is a reminder to employers that they must justify any age-related reward or incentive scheme, whether financial or non-financial. For example, many large organisations retain incremental-based length of service schemes.

7.3 Marriage and civil partnerships

7.3.1 Introduction

The **Sex Discrimination Act 1975** made it unlawful to treat a person who is married or has a civil partner less favourably than a person who is not married or does not have a civil partner on the grounds that they are married or have a civil partnership. The complainant has to show that the employer has treated someone who was not married or in a civil partnership more favourably and, therefore marriage/civil partnership was the reason for the discriminatory treatment. The marriage provisions were introduced because at the time it was common to find employers who would not hire a young married woman because they believed she would leave after a short period of time to have children. The civil partnership provisions were introduced by the **Civil Partnership Act 2004**.

7.3.2 Indirect marriage/civil partnership discrimination

It is unlawful for a person to apply a provision, criterion or practice equally to both married and unmarried people of either sex where it has the effect of having a detrimental effect on a considerably larger proportion of one sex and is to the detriment of the complainant, unless it can be shown to be justified. For example, if an employer tries to deter applicants by imposing unjustifiable requirements such as the length of time the job holder will have to be away from home, this may well be indirect marriage/civil partnership discrimination. However, it may also amount to indirect sex discrimination, because fewer women may be able to satisfy such a requirement.

7.4 Race – Race Relations Act 1976 (Amendment) Regulations 2003

7.4.1 Direct discrimination

A new definition was inserted into the Race Relations Act 1976 (RRAct 1976); covering *'race, ethnic or national origin'*. Because the Regulations were introduced under European Communities Act 1972 they had to transpose the Directive and risked going further than its provisions. This meant that the previous definition of discrimination under the un-amended RRAct 1976 was broader as it also covered *colour of skin and nationality* (which includes citizenship).

The practical effect was that there were two parts to the RRAct 1976 – one applying to race, national and ethnic origins, and the other applying to colour of skin and nationality.

7.4.2 New definition

'A person (A) discriminates against another person (B) if (a) on the grounds of race, (A) treats (B) less favourably than he treats or would treat other persons.'

Race, or ethnic or national origin.

7.4.3 Un-amended definition

'A person discriminates directly if, on racial grounds, he treats one person less favourably than he treats or would treat other persons' Colour (of skin) or nationality. Citizenship can also apply to nationality, but not to race.

7.4.4 Reversal of burden of proof

Under the Race Directive if an applicant has established facts from which it may be presumed that there has been direct or indirect race discrimination, the burden of proof shall be on the respondent to prove that no such discrimination has, in fact, occurred.

The Regulations incorporate the **burden of proof** principle, but this applies to race, ethnic or national origin, but not to colour of skin or nationality.

7.4.5 Harassment: new law

A new section was inserted into the RRAct 1976:

'On grounds of race or ethnic or national origins, (a person) engages in unwanted conduct which has the purpose or effect of (a) violating (another) person's dignity, or (b) creating an intimidating, hostile, degrading, humiliating or offensive environment for him.'

The amended Act also makes it unlawful for an employer to subject an employee or a job applicant to harassment, as newly defined. The Regulations also outlaw harassment meted out in various circumstances by persons including principals in respect of contract workers; partnerships; various trade organisations; qualifying and public bodies; training organisations; persons concerned with the provision of goods and services; and barristers in respect of pupils or tenants.

These provisions apply to employees, workers and contract workers. Liability can rest with 'principals' in respect of contract workers, service contract relationships, partnerships, various trade organisations, providers of goods and services, public bodies, barristers in respect of pupils or tenants and professions.

The provisions create a new self-standing right not to be harassed. The new definition of harassment in the RRA closely follows the definition given in the Race Directive. However, there is one important difference. Under the Directive, the conjunctive wording in the definition of 'harassment' requires an applicant to show that the purpose or effect of the unwanted conduct is (i) to violate dignity and (ii) to damage the workplace environment in one of the ways described. In contrast, the wording of the Regulations requires only that the complainant show that the purpose or effect of the harassment is to violate dignity or damage the workplace environment. The wording chosen by the government is consistent with the protection that the direct discrimination provisions of the RRA, as interpreted by courts and tribunals, has traditionally provided.

7.5 Religion or belief

7.5.1 Introduction

In December 2003 the **Employment Equality (Religion or Belief) Regulations 2003** came into effect.

The Regulations apply only to employment, but employment in the broadest sense. **Political belief** is expressly omitted, but '**profound philosophical convictions similar to religious beliefs**' are included. In other words, non-believers of any religion or religious ethos would be equally protected, however their non-belief will have to be a clear philosophical belief (eg, that there is no God).

7.5.2 Regulations – coverage

The Regulations cover fringe religions and cult groups such as:

- **Church of Scientology** – Not considered as religion in the UK charity law, but accepted as one under the European Convention of Human Rights (ECHR)
- **Druidism** – Not covered under the ECHR
- **Krishna Consciousness** movement

- Moonies

In the final draft Regulations the key terms (eg, 'profound philosophical belief') were *not* defined, leaving them to be determined by case law. But, the draft Regulations did state that '**religion or belief**' means '**any religion, religious belief or similar philosophical belief**'.

Some of the main religions are:

Baha'i	Judaism (Jews)
Buddhism	Paganism
Christianity	Rastafarianism
Druidry	Church of Scientology
Hinduism	Sikhism
Islam (Muslims)	Zoroastrianism (Parsi)
Jainism	Wicca

Certain factors are provided as indicating the characteristics of a protected group, *examples:*

- Existence of collective worship
- Clear belief system
- Profound belief affecting the person's way of life or view of the world

Under the Regulations atheists and agnostics are equally protected as those who hold strong religious beliefs, *but only* where they have a clear set of beliefs related to their non-acceptance of an organised religion or a theology. The express inclusion of the words 'similar philosophical belief' may bring forth claims from vegetarians, vegans, pacifists, fascists and Jedis.

7.5.3 Regulations – Genuine Occupational Requirements (GOR)

The Regulations contain a unique two-tier provision:

- Genuine and determining occupational requirement to be a member of a particular religion, eg, religious orders or teaching in a denominational school.

- Genuine, but not determining occupational requirement: this has a broader range of application, eg, where the organisation has a religious ethos, but the work is not overtly religious, eg, Muslim lawyers. Religion is a requirement, but it will be difficult to argue that all staff must subscribe to the religion.

The Regulations permit an employer to apply the GOR with a measure of discretion. As well as being proportionate in the particular case, it must also be that:

'either the person to whom that requirement is applied does not meet it, or the employer is not satisfied, and in all the circumstances it is reasonable for him not to be satisfied, that the person meets it'.

This assists employers who wish to recruit or promote a person who is genuinely committed to the faith in question, instead of someone who pays 'lip service' to it, eg, a baptised member of the Anglican Church but who is actually a non-believer.

Special rules apply to religious organisations and those with a religious or particular ethos where limited exceptions to appointments apply.

7.5.4 Leave for religious observance

There is no automatic duty on employers to grant all requests for annual leave, special leave or for time off during work for religious observance. Objective justification based on the principle of *proportionality* are permissible, however employers should not define 'religious belief' too narrowly.

Religious observance in the workplace

The Regulations do *not* say employers *must* provide time and facilities for religious observance in the workplace, but employers must guard against indirect religious discrimination. Employees may request time off to celebrate religious and other related observance days and festivals. Of crucial interest for the employer is the requirement to: (a) apply rules objectively, fairly and consistently (keeping careful records will help); *and* (b) to take decisions which avoid indirect discrimination. Employers should be careful not to indirectly discriminate against women who may be less assertive than men in requesting leave, etc. Also, the granting of leave requests by employers based on seniority of service may lead to indirect discrimination because those from minority groups may have less seniority than others.

Standard closures of business

By having such closures (eg, Christmas) it may disadvantage others who will have insufficient leave to enjoy their own religious festivals. Therefore, including public holidays as part of the employee's annual leave entitlement, could lead to a claim of direct discrimination. In addition, employers should reconsider insisting that all staff take public and Bank holidays as leave. Where it is practical for the employer to have employees working on such days, like Easter Monday, this should be considered. For some religions, dates vary from year to year, and, in some cases may not be known to individuals until quite close to the day itself (eg, they are allied to the lunar phases).

Time-off during working day for religious observance eg praying

Where possible, a prayer room should be allocated for this purpose, but there is no legal obligation on the employer to do so. An alternative may be a quiet room or quiet place, but this should not be confused with a general rest room. If an employer were to convert the only rest room into a prayer room this could generate claims of discrimination from those not using the prayer room. Storage facilities for religious ceremonial objects would be good practice. Employers should be aware that in some cases, employees may undertake periods of fasting.

7.5.5 Diet

Social gatherings at work (including formal events) must be organised so as not to disadvantage those for whom alcohol is banned by religion, and so on. Similarly, this rule applies to food supplied at particular venues.

Food at work. Where possible, employers should facilitate staff bringing into work their own foodstuffs that are a necessary part of their diet in accordance with religious requirements.

7.5.6 Dress

The Directive does not provide duties or guidance for employers regarding dress.

Where the employer adopts a specific dress code this should not conflict with the employees' needs wherever possible. Similarly, the employer may have a policy on the wearing of jewellery, tattoos etc. The main justifications for forbidding staff to dress as they wish will be *health and safety* and *corporate image* where the dress/appearance is extreme in nature. In law there are a few regulatory exceptions for employees, eg, Sikhs have a statutory right to wear their turban, when working on building sites and when riding a motorcycle, etc. But, crucially, these rules provide immunity from criminal prosecution rather than being expressed as a universal civil right.

7.5.7 Offensive remarks

An offensive remark may be made by a religious person to a gay or lesbian person, if their lifestyle contravenes their religious beliefs. The employer must take steps to curb such remarks and prevent them from being repeated.

7.5.8 Special working days

The Sunday working rules found in the Employment Rights Act 1996 only applied to those working in retail and betting trades and not to those who work only on Sundays. The Religion, etc, Regulations do not specify any particular rules regarding working days. An employer, may indirectly discriminate unless s/he can show the '**provision, criterion or practice**' can be justified by showing a **business need** which is **proportionate and legitimate** in its application to the individual.

7.6 Sex

7.6.1 The Sex Discrimination Act 1975 – amended by The Sex Discrimination Act 1975 (Amendment) Regulations 2008

Introduction

Discrimination takes three basic forms:

- Direct sex discrimination, including sexual harassment
- Indirect sex discrimination
- Victimisation

In sex discrimination cases the burden of proof is on the employer to rebut the allegation of unlawful discrimination.

Reversal of Burden of Proof

In 2001 the **Burden of Proof in Discrimination Cases Directive** was implemented in the UK by the Sex Discrimination (Indirect Discrimination & Burden of Proof) Regulations. The effect being that once a complainant has *prima facie* established on the primary facts that there is a case to answer, the burden of proof shifts to the respondent employer to positively rebut the allegation. The complainant will have to show evidence of probable or presumable discrimination.

A clear process can be established when a tribunal is hearing a discrimination complaint:

(a) The complainant must show that on the *balance of probabilities* a *prima facie* case of unlawful discrimination has taken place. In other words, on the basis of *primary facts* (above) the complainant must show s/he has suffered treatment on the ground of, eg, his/her sex. Insufficient evidence of treatment based on sex, etc, will mean the case fails. One or more actual or hypothetical comparator(s) must normally be identified to show that the differences are based on sex, etc. The tribunal must ask the question: 'What would have been the treatment of one (or more) comparator(s) if their circumstances had been the same or similar to that of the complainant?' (that is, what if they had also been women or a member of an ethnic group?).

(b) The employer is then given an opportunity to rebut that allegation. The employer must 'positively' show that discrimination did not take place. They may refer to the differences in treatment between one or more comparator(s) to show this. There must be more than just 'unreasonableness' on the part of the employer's actions. There must be clear *inference* of treatment based on sex, etc, for it to be unlawful. Tribunals are empowered to look beyond mere excuses put forward by employers, eg, 'we made a mistake!' For example, they will look beyond claims of incompetence to matters such as:

(i) A record or pattern of discrimination

(ii) The existence of an equal opportunities or diversity policy that is properly framed, communicated and enforced with training

(iii) The culture of an organisation. Critical evidence can be obtained from examining answers to a *questionnaire* which the employer can be asked to complete before tribunal proceedings commence. The employer can only *justify* an unlawful act of race or sex discrimination (or discrimination based on sexual orientation or religion/belief) where it is **indirect**, not direct discrimination. Where the explanation given by the employer is inadequate the tribunal can draw appropriate inferences of discrimination.

(c) Only if the employer's defence is inadequate should the tribunal then address the question: 'Was the treatment less favourable?'. This enables the seriousness of the discrimination to be assessed, which will impact on damages awarded if, indeed the treatment is found to be less favourable.

This approach was further clarified in a later case:

(1) The first stage requires the claimant to prove the existence of facts from which the tribunal could, in the absence of an adequate explanation, conclude that the respondent has committed, or is to be treated as having committed, an unlawful act of discrimination. The words 'could, in the absence of an adequate explanation' indicate that the tribunal is required to make an assumption at the first stage which may be contrary to reality, the plain purpose being to shift the burden of proof at the second stage so that unless the respondent provides an adequate explanation, the claimant will succeed. It would be inconsistent with that assumption to take account of an adequate explanation by the respondent at the first stage.

(2) The second stage, which only comes into effect if the claimant has proved those facts, requires the respondent to prove that it did not commit, or is not to be treated as having committed, the unlawful act. If the second stage is reached, and the respondent's explanation is inadequate, it will be not merely legitimate but also necessary for the Employment Tribunal to conclude that the complaint should be upheld.

Meaning of direct discrimination

An employer directly discriminates against an employee on the ground of sex where s/he treats a woman less favourably than s/he treats (or would treat) a man (or *vice versa*).

Key points

The complainant must show that s/he has been treated less favourably than someone of the opposite sex, and therefore must nominate one or more real or hypothetical comparators of the opposite sex. Where none are provided the tribunal will carry out a comparative exercise, if necessary with a hypothetical comparator.

Although direct discrimination cannot be justified, the respondent can show that the alleged act was not discriminatory, eg, in a selection decision, by showing that the woman was passed over in favour of the male candidate because the latter was demonstrably the better candidate. Because the burden of proof is on the respondent s/he must show proof, eg, candidate application forms, results of tests, etc, or interview notes, all of which contain no sex bias.

Pregnancy and childbirth

This is a special case in sex discrimination law because a comparator is not necessary in order to bring a successful complaint. Regulation 2 of the Sex Discrimination Act 1975 (Amendments) Regulations 2008 has amended the definition of discrimination on grounds of pregnancy or maternity leave to **eliminate** the requirement of a comparator who is not pregnant or not on maternity leave, as the case may be.

Sexual harassment – definition amended by The Sex Discrimination Act 1975 (Amendments) Regulations 2008

The **amended definition of sex harassment** contained in the SDA 1975 provides, as follows:

For the purposes of this Act, a person subjects a woman to harassment if:

he engages in unwanted conduct that is related to her sex or that of another person and has the purpose or effect –

(a) Of violating her dignity, or

(b) Of creating an intimidating, hostile, degrading, humiliating or offensive environment for her.

The Amendment Regulations replaces the previous phrase 'on the grounds of her sex' with the phrase 'related to her sex or that of another person'. As a result, a person complaining of harassment under the Act is no longer required to show that the alleged treatment took place because the complainant was a woman (or a man). A connection or association with sex will, in future, be sufficient to mount a successful harassment claim (provided that the rest of the definition of harassment is satisfied).

The Explanatory Notes which accompany the Regulations gives an example of how this amended definition works.

> Where male colleagues dislike a female colleague and decide to put office equipment on a high shelf to make it hard for her to reach, the old definition may not apply because the men are acting out of dislike and not because she is a woman, ie not 'on the ground of her sex'. Under the new definition, such conduct might be actionable on the basis that it is 'related to sex' because women are, on average, shorter than men.

Further, under the amended regulations, the unwanted conduct need not be directed at the complainant. It will suffice if the complainant witnesses another person being harassed, provided the other elements of the definition are satisfied. Importantly, the witness does not have to be of the same sex as the recipient of the conduct because of the phrasing – unwanted conduct 'related to her sex or that of another person' – encompasses abuse directed towards either sex.

Sexual harassment is dealt with separately from harassment under other heads, eg, race.

It is important to note that harassment of a sexual nature amounts to less favourable treatment on the grounds of sex without the need to establish that the same treatment would not have been meted out to a person of the opposite sex or of a different race. In other words, the treatment is '**gender specific**' and there is no need to look at the treatment of a comparator.

7.6.2 Sexual orientation – The Employment Equality (Sexual Orientation) Regulations

Introduction

The **Employment Equality (Sexual Orientation) Regulations 2003** were introduced on 1 December 2003.

The Regulations do not extend to provide protection in respect of other sexual preferences or specific sexual practices.

The scope of the law

The Regulations are restricted to employment, but in the broadest sense. The Regulations use the definition in the Race Relations Act 1976: discrimination 'on grounds of' sexual orientation, thereby any 'less favourable treatment' on such a ground would be unlawful. This would cover situations where a person whose sexual orientation is not at issue. They may claim protection under the law.

The Regulations provide cover for employees, other types of workers, contract workers, office holders, police, barristers and partnerships. The legislation states protection will extend to 'perceived' sexual orientation, not just actual sexual orientation; this means that unlawful discrimination would take place where a person is discriminated against because the perpetrator believes the 'victim' has a particular sexual orientation, although they may be mistaken in that belief. Sexual orientation means being heterosexual, homosexual, lesbian, bisexual or hermaphroditic. Protection extends to employment, working conditions and pay (including benefits and health insurance, occupational pensions). Two types of restriction in occupational pension scheme benefits will operate:

- Restriction of benefits to opposite sex partners – likely to amount to direct discrimination.

- Restriction of benefits to surviving spouses – unlikely to amount to direct discrimination.

Employer's defence

The Regulations do not expressly use the word 'justification', but instead: 'proportionate means of achieving a legitimate aim'. The government says the words are interchangeable with those used in the Directive: 'appropriate and necessary'.

Exceptions

There are exceptions as with other Regulations: grounds of national security, benefits depending on marital status (eg, private health care) and positive action. In addition, a **Genuine Occupational Requirement (GOR)** can be applied where:

(a) There is a genuine and a determining requirement for a post holder to be of a particular sexual orientation

(b) It is proportionate to apply the requirement in the particular case, and

(c) Either the person to whom that requirement is applied does not meet it, or

(d) The employer is not satisfied, in all the circumstances it is reasonable for him/her to be satisfied, that the person meets it.

There is no list which specifies certain exempt occupations.

Positive action

Positive action is permissible in order to 'prevent or compensate for disadvantages linked to sexual orientation'.

Same-sex partners should be treated in the same way as married or unmarried heterosexual partners, unless the specified restrictions apply. Parental leave applies to time off to care for a child even though the employee has a same-sex partner.

Organised religion

The Regulations permit an organised religion to discriminate against those with a particular sexual orientation in order to comply with the doctrines of that religion, or to avoid conflicting with 'strongly held religious beliefs of a significant number of the religion's followers', and either the person to whom that requirement is applied does not meet it, or the employer is 'not satisfied, and in all the circumstances it is reasonable for him not to be satisfied', that that person meets it.

7.6.3 Sexual Orientation – some practical issues

Dress or appearance

It must be emphasised that protection of manifestations of sexual orientation was not part of the government's aims in introducing the legislation. Only if someone else of a different sexual orientation was treated more favourably because of the manifestations of their sexuality should a successful complaint arise.

A culture of homophobia

A general culture of homophobia is sufficient to succeed in bringing cases of harassment against an employer where there is no specific evidence of an individual being targeted. The use of jokes, catch-phrases, jargon or language and behaviour will require monitoring and, if necessary, changing.

Transfer of undertakings 7

1 Transfer of Undertakings (Protection of Employment) (TUPE) Regulations 2006

1.1 Introduction

The Transfer of Undertakings (Protection of Employment) (TUPE) Regulations 2006 replaced the earlier 1981 Regulations, with effect from 6th April 2006. The 1981 Regulations were brought in to implement the 1977 EC Acquired Rights Directive (as amended by Directive 98/150 EC and consolidated in 2001/23/EC). This means that the rights should be interpreted, as far as possible, in line with decisions of the European Court of Justice (ECJ) under the Directive. The law is difficult and constantly developing through decisions of the ECJ and UK courts.

Developments, therefore, need to be monitored. The Regulations protect employees' rights on the transfer of the business in which they are employed. The transfer could be the result of a legal transfer or merger. The mechanism of the transfer does not matter, provided there is a change of legal person responsible for running the undertaking, who acts as employer. The contracting-out of a part of a business or public sector organisation will be covered by TUPE. A transfer of the majority of shares from one owner to another is *not* covered by the Regulations. Nor do they apply where there is only the transfer of assets, not employees ie the sale of equipment. It is, arguably, one of the more complex areas of employment law.

Broadly speaking, the effects of the Regulations are as follows:

(1) To preserve the continuity of employment and terms and conditions of those employees who are transferred to a new employer when a relevant transfer takes place. This means that employees employed by the previous employer ('the transferor') when the transfer takes effect automatically become employees of the new employer (the 'transferee') on the same terms and conditions (except for certain occupational pension rights). It is as if their contracts of employment had originally been made with the transferee

employer. However, the Regulations provide some limited opportunity for the transferee or transferor to vary, with the agreement of the employees concerned.

(2) The Regulations contain specific provisions to protect employees from dismissal before or after the relevant transfer.

(3) Representatives of affected employees have a right to be informed about a prospective transfer. They must also be consulted about any measures which the transferor or transferee employer envisages taking, concerning the affected employees.

(4) The Regulations also place a duty on the transferor employer to provide information about the transferring workforce to the new employer before the transfer occurs.

(5) The Regulations make specific provision for cases where the transferor employer is insolvent by increasing, for example, the ability of the parties in such difficult situations to vary contracts of employment, thereby ensuring that jobs can be preserved because a relevant transfer can go ahead.

(6) The Regulations can apply regardless of the size of the transferred business: so the Regulations equally apply to the transfer of a large business with thousands of employees or a very small one (shop, pub or garage). The Regulations also apply equally to public or private sector undertakings – and whether or not the business operated for gain or for charity.

Do the Regulations apply to your situation?

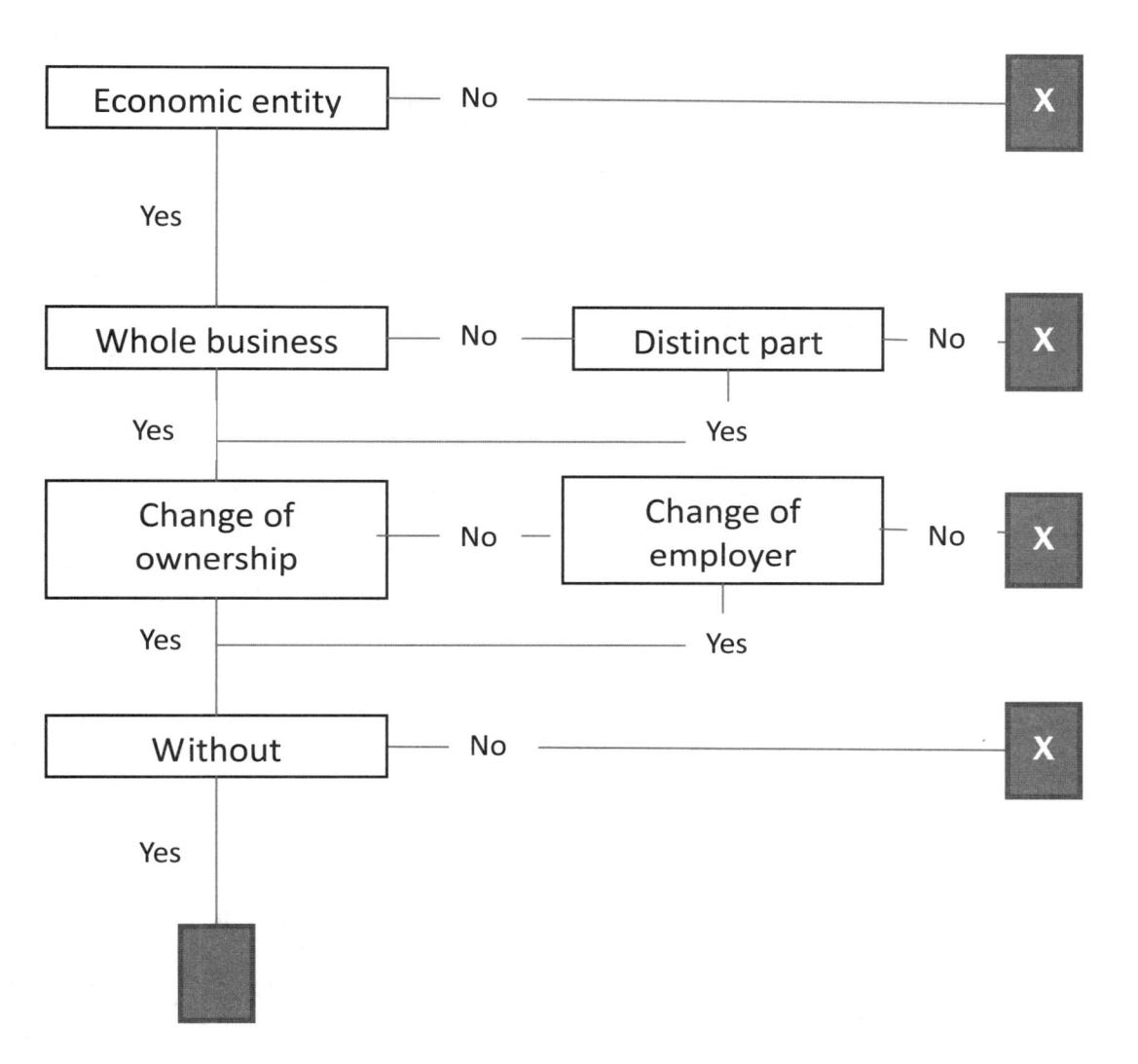

```
Economic entity ── No ─────────────────────── X
      │
     Yes
      │
Whole business ── No ── Distinct part ── No ── X
      │                      │
     Yes ──────────────────── Yes
      │
Change of ownership ── No ── Change of employer ── No ── X
      │                             │
     Yes ─────────────────────────── Yes
      │
Without ── No ──────────────────────── X
      │
     Yes
      │
     [■]
```

7: Transfer of undertakings

2 Regulations explained

2.1 Introduction

The whole aim of the Regulations is to protect **employees** caught up in a transfer. The effect of the Regulations is to transfer intact the contracts of employment of employees working for the transferor to the transferee at the point of transfer. The Regulations do provide for limited opportunity for the transferee or transferor to vary, with the agreement of the employees concerned, the terms and conditions of the employment contracts for a range of stipulated reasons connected with the transfer.

In order for the TUPE Regulations to apply, the service, business or part of the business must be deemed an 'economic entity' in its own right and retain its identity after the transfer.

There are two forms of transfer under the TUPE Regulations.

1. The first type follows the old definition and case law under the 1981 TUPE Regulations – a 'business transfer' and applies when a business, undertaking or part of one is transferred from one employer to another as a going concern. This includes cases where two companies cease to exist and combine to form a third.

2. The second type, introduced in the 2006 TUPE Regulations, and referred to as a 'service provision change', covers when a client engages a contractor to do work on its behalf, or re assigns such a contract – including bringing the work in-house.

2.2 Examples of a transfer of undertakings

To illustrate the concept, consider Transferor (A) is a public sector organisation contracting-out a service (eg, cleaning) to a private sector organisation (Transferee (A)). However, Transferee (A) loses the contract, which is passed to Contractor/Transferee (B). In this transaction (known as a 'second generation transfer') the Transferee (A) becomes the second transferor (B). However, suppose that after some years this contractor also loses the contract and the public sector organisation decides to take the service back in-house. This is known as a 'reverse transfer', whereupon Transferee (B) becomes Transferor (C).

2.3 When the new employer takes over

When the regulations apply and the new employer takes over

- Collective agreements affecting the employees and in force immediately before transfer – insofar as individual contracts of employment are concerned
- Liability in respect of contracts of employment for all transferred employees

This includes:

- Terms and conditions of employment
- Claims regarding pay arrears
- Outstanding legal claims, eg unfair dismissal, discrimination claims
- Personal injury claims
- Disciplinary records
- Contractual requirements covering confidentiality, patents, etc.

3 Dismissals connected with a transfer

Such dismissals or changes will be held to be automatically unfair and unlawful **unless** they are necessary for an economic, technical or organisational (ETO) reason entailing changes in the workforce. The courts to date have tended towards a very narrow interpretation of such reasons.

An example might include redundancies necessitated by the business losing profits after the transfer and facing liquidation. This would be an 'economic' reason.

The case of *Hynd v Armstrong [2007] IRLR 338* involved the redundancy of an employee, immediately before a transfer by the transferor because the transferee required one less employee. The question which this raised was 'can the transferor dismiss for redundancy when the redundancy will be in the transferee's business?' It was held by the court in session that it couldn't. It ruled that the transferor had no ETO reason to dismiss, because the redundancy situation was the transferee's. In practical terms, if liability for automatic unfair dismissal is to be avoided, any redundancies as a result of the transfer should be implemented by the transferee.

The House of Lords has ruled that any dismissal 'connected' with a transfer is automatically unfair. This means that a dismissal several weeks before a transfer or several months (or even years) after the transfer could fall under the ambit of the TUPE Regulations.

4 Consultation on transfers

There is a duty on both the transferor and transferee to inform and consult representatives of their employees who may be affected by the transfer or measures taken in connection with the transfer.

The Regulations state that trade union representatives or elected representatives of the affected employees must be consulted. If there are no representatives in place it is expected that representatives will be elected for this purpose. Where the number of employees is small it is possible, with their agreement, to consult directly with them.

The information must be provided sufficiently in advance of the transfer to give adequate time for consultation and must include:

(a) Notification that the transfer will take place, approximate timing and the reasons

(b) The legal, economic and social implications of the transfer for the affected employees

(c) Whether the employer intends to take any action which will affect the employees and, if so what action will be taken

(d) Where the previous employer is required to give the information, he or she must disclose whether the prospective new employer envisages carrying out any action which will affect the employees, and if so, what.

The term 'measures' is used in the legislation. These can mean actions or changes for example a relocation of the employees to the new employer's office, or a change in the way that work is processed or a new organisation structure.

Where the previous employer is required to give the information, he or she must disclose whether the prospective new employer envisages carrying out any action which will affect the employees, and if so, what. The new employer must give the previous employer the necessary information to meet the requirement.

The consultation with the representatives of employees must be **in good time** with **a view to reaching agreement**. It is important to understand that there is no stipulated time requirement, and that the consultation periods for redundancy are not to be treated as a guidance. The length of time will be determined by the complexity of the transfer, whether any measures are required, the frequency with which the representatives can be consulted and how well the consultations progress. (Note: the parties do not have to reach agreement.)

If there are special circumstances which make it not reasonably practicable for an employer to fulfil any of the information and consultation requirements, s/he must take such steps to meet the requirements as are reasonably practicable.

The transferor and transferee are jointly and severally liable for the transferor's failure to inform and consult. So it is incumbent upon the transferee to ensure a robust process and one in which they participate as necessary.

If there is failure to consult, employees can apply to the tribunal and if successful can be awarded a sum of up to 13 weeks' wages.

A factor that is frequently overlooked is that the transferor is also expected to consult with its own employees regarding any measures that it envisages taking in connection with the transfer – prior to the transfer. For example once the new employees transfer in it may reorganise a department which may result in potential job losses.

5 When do regulations apply?

5.1 Relevant transfers: TUPE definition

TUPE applies if there is a relevant transfer. Due to the requirements of TUPE many employers are tempted to see if they can circumvent the Regulations, however the most prudent approach is to assume they do apply and then consider whether they don't. The definition of relevant transfer has 2 limbs.

The first limb, Regulation 3(1)(a) is substantially the same as the definition under the 1981 Regulations and applies on a Business Transfer ie:

> 'the transfer of an undertaking, business or part of an undertaking or business situated immediately before the transfer in the United Kingdom to another employer where there is a transfer of an economic entity **which retains its identity**'.

Economic entity means: 'an organised grouping of resources which has the objective of pursuing an economic activity, whether or not that activity is central or ancillary'.

The second limb, Regulation 3(1)(b) applies on a Service Provision Change, see sections 5.3 and 5.4 below.

The main points arising from the application of both limbs of the definition in Regulation 3 are as follows:

(a) The undertaking does not have to be in the nature of a commercial venture

(b) A sale or other disposition may transfer the undertaking eg the contracting out of cases referred to below, and

(c) Share transfers are excluded – that is the sale of the business by a sale of their shares.

5.2 Business Transfer test: has the undertaking retained its identity?

The definition of a relevant transfer in Regulation 3(1)(a) (a Business Transfer) is substantially the same as the definition of a relevant transfer under the 1981 Regulations. The best approach is to first ascertain if there is 'an economic entity that retains its identity'.

An economic entity means an organised grouping of resources which has the objective of pursuing an economic activity, whether that activity is central or ancillary. There are two stages which must be proved:

(1) That the undertaking was a stable economic entity prior to the transfer
(2) That the entity was transferred in a recognised form.

The above are broad guidelines taken from case law as to when TUPE will apply, but the particular facts of every case will be important.

One of the most helpful cases to date is *Spijkers v Gebroeders Benedick Abattoir CV*. This provides a shopping list of criteria to decide if there is an economic entity which retains its identity:

'Does the undertaking in question retain its identity after the transfer so that is has the same or similar activities as before?'

In order to establish this the following should be considered as an overview of the type of undertaking in question:

- Whether tangible or intangible assets are transferred (eg, buildings, stock and intellectual property respectively)
- Whether 'goodwill' is transferred
- Whether customers or clients are transferred
- Whether contracts are transferable and actually transfer
- The **intention** to transfer employees (and whether those employees **do transfer**)
- The degree of similarity of the activities before and after the transfer (it does not have to be identical), and
- The duration of any interruption in activities of the undertaking.

It is important to note that not all or even most of these factors need to be present for a transfer to arise. In some circumstances, there need not be a discrete and identifiable stable economic entity before the transfer. It is sufficient if a part of a larger stable economic entity becomes identified for the first time as a separate economic entity on the occasion of the transfer.

5.3 Service Provision Change: is there a transfer?

Whether there is a transfer of an undertaking historically caused most difficulties where there was a change of contractor. In many contracting out cases it was difficult to assess whether the economic entity retained its identity. For example, in labour intensive undertakings (such as contract cleaning) employees were the only real asset so if staff did not transfer it was difficult to determine whether a relevant transfer had occurred.

To resolve this difficulty the definition of a relevant transfer in the TUPE Regulations is wider than the definition of a relevant transfer under EC law and previous 1981 Regulations. The second limb of the definition of a relevant transfer in Regulation 3(1)(b) provides that the TUPE Regulations will automatically apply to a Service Provision Change ie:

(1) Where a client ceases to carry out activities on its own behalf and delegates the carrying out of the activities to a contractor ('contracting out or outsourcing')

(2) Where a contractor ceases to carry out the activities for the client which are then carried out instead by a subsequent contractor ('second-generation contracting out or 'outsourcing' or 're-tendering'), or

(3) Where a contractor or a subsequent contractor ceases to carry out activities for a client which then carries out the activities itself ('contracting in or insourcing')

It must be the case that immediately before the Service Provision Change there is an organised grouping of employees situated in Great Britain which has its principal purpose of carrying out of the activities concerned on behalf of the client (that is, the person from whom services were originally outsourced).

5.4 Service Provision Change: exceptions

There will not be a relevant transfer under the Service Provision Change definition if:

(a) The client intends to use the contractor for a single specific event or task of short term duration; or

(b) The activities concerned consist wholly or mainly of the supply of goods for the client's use.

If one of the exceptions applies there may still be a relevant transfer as a result of the Business Transfer definition.

6 Legal considerations of a transfer

(a) Which employees are affected?

(b) How is the transferee affected?

(c) Automatically unfair dismissals upon a transfer

(d) The defence of an 'economic, technical or organisational reason entailing a change in the workforce' ('ETO Reasons')

(e) Attempts to vary terms and conditions

(f) Duty to inform and consult

(g) Remedies

6.1 Which employees are affected?

(a) Only workers who are employees are affected. This does not include independent contractors.

(b) Employees employed immediately before the transfer or those who would have been employed if they had not been unfairly dismissed for a reason related to a transfer. This does mean that an employee who is reassigned to another part of the business before the transfer can be excluded from the transfer.

(c) Employees assigned to the business or part of the business transferred (other than on a temporary basis). This is often a source of contention during a transfer, as the number of employees and subsequent employment costs can be significant. The crux of the test is where the employee is predominately employed. This will often be determined by identifying where the majority of their time is spent. Ultimately, if agreement cannot be reached or an employee objects, the fact of the matter is for the tribunal to decide.

(d) Employees who object to being employed by the transferee will not transfer. If they do so their employment ends automatically on the date of the transfer. It is not legally considered to be a dismissal and the employee will have no right to a redundancy payment. The transfer will then operate to terminate their employment, for practical purposes this is treated as a 'resignation'.

6.2 How is the transferee affected?

The Regulation states:

On the completion of a relevant transfer:

(a) All the transferor's rights, powers, duties and liabilities under or in connection with any such contract, shall be transferred by virtue of this regulation to the transferee; and

(b) Any act or omission before the transfer is completed, of or in relation to the transferor in respect of that contract or a person assigned to that organised grouping of resources or employees, shall be deemed to have been an act or omission of or in relation to the transferee.

There is no transfer of criminal liability.

The transferor and transferee are jointly and severally liable for the transferor's failure to inform and consult.

In practice most businesses want to know how to dispose of, or take over a business with the minimum of extra financial exposure as a result of the TUPE Regulations. It is therefore customary for transferees to seek indemnities from transferors in respect of any sums which may become payable as a result of the TUPE Regulations.

Regulation 4(11)

Regulation 4(11) applies to an employee who resigns with immediate effect before the transfer in response to a repudiatory breach of contract. It codifies the case of Oxford principle and provides that an employee can resign if substantial changes to his/her working conditions to his/her detriment are proposed on the basis of the transfer. This will be deemed to be a dismissal with notice.

Pensions

Occupational pension schemes are excluded from the TUPE Regulations in so far as they cover old age, invalidity or survivor's benefits (early retirement benefits transfer). Accrued pension rights should be preserved but there is probably no entitlement to continued membership or contributions.

The Pensions Act 2004 and the Transfer of Employment (Pension Protection) Regulations 2005 have introduced a minimum occupational pension entitlement to transferred employees who had such entitlement with their employers before the transfer. The minimum 'safety net' requires the new employer to match employee contributions up to 6% of salary into a stakeholder pension, or offer an equivalent alternative. There is no requirement that the post-transfer pension is equivalent to the original scheme. In the public sector, the government has said it will continue to follow the more generous policy, set out in Annex A to the Cabinet Office Statement of Practice.

Such a change in the pension scheme from final salary to stakeholder should be covered as one of the proposed changes (or measures) included in the consultation process.

6.3 Automatically unfair dismissals upon a transfer

Any dismissal because of a transfer is automatically unfair unless it is for an ETO reason.

Regulation 7 states:

Where either before or after the relevant transfer, any employee of the transferor or transferee is dismissed, that employee shall be treated for the purposes of Part X of the 1996 Act as **unfairly dismissed** if the sole or principal reason for his dismissal is:

(a)   Transfer itself; or

(b)   **A reason connected** with the transfer that is not an economic, technical or organisational reason entailing changes in the workforce (an "ETO Reason").

This paragraph applies where the sole or principal reason for the dismissal is a reason connected with the transfer that is an economic, technical or organisational reason entailing changes in the workforce of either the transferor or the transferee before or after a relevant transfer.

6.4 The ETO reason defence

To qualify as an ETO defence, an ETO reason must be one entailing changes in the workforce. The courts have held that this means a change in the numbers of people employed or a change in the employee's particular functions.

The fact that the transferor will achieve a better sale price, or that the transferee will not proceed unless staff are dismissed is not an ETO reason as it does not relate to the **conduct of the business or entail a change in the workforce**.

Any dismissal must still be fair in all the circumstances. Therefore even if an ETO reason is established, a failure to consult or consider other opportunities will render any dismissal unfair.

6.5 Attempts to vary terms and conditions of the employees' contracts

Article 3 of the Acquired Rights Directive states that employees are entitled to insist on all of the rights under their old contract.

However, is an agreed variation between an employee and the transferee effective? The House of Lords has held that even a consensual and advantageous change will not bind employees, if the transfer is the reason for the alteration.

On addressing the issue of when changes can be made, the House of Lords indicated as follows:

'There must, at least may, come a time when the link between the transfer and the variation is broken.'

However, there is no 'rule of thumb' governing the length of time. Often a 12-month moratorium is referred to, but this is not true, this must be assessed on a case by case basis.

The new TUPE Regulations provide some help for employers and contain a limited exception to the bar on changing terms and conditions. Changes will be void if the sole or principal reason is:

(a)   The transfer itself; or
(b)   A reason connected with the transfer that is not an ETO reason.

Where an ETO reason is the sole or principle reason for changes to terms and conditions of employment, or the changes are unconnected with the transfer, they will be valid.

This means that if the transferee subsequently makes changes that affect all employees within the workforce (ie those who worked in the business before the transfer and those who have subsequently transferred into it) for example a reduction in working hours, this could be applied to the transferred employees as the decision was made to the whole business as part of ongoing business activity and not connected to their transfer.

6.6 Duty to inform and consult

6.6.1 Employee Liability Information

In addition, under the TUPE Regulations the transferor must provide to the transferee Employee Liability Information ie:

(a) The identity of the employees who will transfer

(b) The age of those employees

(c) Information relating to any collective agreements which apply to those employees

(d) Information contained in the statements of employment particulars for those employees

(e) Instances of any disciplinary action within the preceding two years taken by the transferor in respect of those employees in circumstances where the statutory dispute resolution procedures apply

(f) Instances of any grievances raised by those employees within the preceding two years in circumstances where the statutory dispute resolution procedures apply, and

(g) Instances of any legal actions taken by those employees against the transferor in the previous two years, and instances of potential legal actions which may be brought by those employees where the transferor has reasonable grounds to believe such actions might occur.

The information must be given in writing or in other forms accessible to the transferee at least two weeks before the transfer unless special circumstances exist (in which case it should be given no later than the date of the relevant transfer). It must be updated if changes occur before the transfer.

This is likely to be particularly useful where there is no legal relationship between the transferor and transferee.

6.6.2 Information and Consultation of Employees Regulations 2004 ('ICE Regulations')

The ICE Regulations currently apply to businesses with at least 50 employees. Where applicable, they require employers to recognise a Domestic Works Council ('DWC') and consult with the DWC on a variety of topics including 'decisions likely to lead to substantial changes in work organisation or in contractual relations'. This includes TUPE transfers.

Provided that the employer notifies the DWC in writing **before** it is obliged to inform and consult under TUPE, that it intends to do so, the ICE Regulation obligations will cease to apply in relation to the transfer.

6.7 Remedies

(a) A claim for damages for unfair dismissal is the main remedy for employees dismissed or who have had their contract unlawfully varied as a result of the transfer. Claims must be made within three months of the effective date of termination (EDT) and are dependant on the employee having sufficient continuity of employment.

(b) Employees can also ask for the tribunal to make a declaration that the variation was void. Therefore, their employment continues under their old terms and conditions.

(c) Re-engagement/re-instatement can also be requested in a claim for unfair dismissal in the usual way.

(d) If there is failure to consult, employees can apply to the tribunal and if successful can be awarded a sum of up to 13 weeks' wages.

(e) If the transferor fails to provide Employee Liability Information or if the information provided is inaccurate, the Transferee can apply to the Employment Tribunal. The tribunal can make a declaration and award compensation for any loss which the transferee has incurred because the Employee Liability Information was not provided. Compensation must be at least £500 for each employee in respect of whom information was not provided, unless the tribunal considers that it would be unjust or inequitable to award this sum.

Termination of employment 8

1 Introduction

In this chapter we look at the various ways that someone's employment ends. This ranges from dismissal to retirement. Naturally this is usually one of the most contentious matters that any employer has to manage. As well as reviewing the relevant legislation the chapter also include Employment Tribunals, the ACAS Code of Practice and compromise agreements.

2 Outline of the provisions

The right of an employee not to be unfairly dismissed created by statute bears little relation to a common law breach of contract (see section 8); a dismissal may well be lawful under the common law but still be unfair under the statutory provisions now contained in the Employment Rights Act 1996 (ERA 1996). In a claim for **unfair dismissal** it is breach of the statute which is the important factor and the remedies available to the claimant are **reinstatement, re-engagement** and **compensation.**

An employee who has been dismissed by the employer may be entitled to:

- Bring a case before an Employment Tribunal for unfair dismissal; and/or
- Claim a redundancy payment.

Not all **workers**, however, are entitled to the protection provided by the statute. In order to be eligible to bring a claim for either unfair dismissal or a redundancy payment a person must:

(a) Be an **employee**
(b) Have been **continuously employed** for the requisite period
(c) Not have validly **contracted-out** of his/her rights
(d) Not be within an **excluded class**
(e) Bring the case within the **time limits**

2.1 Employees only

Employees are defined as individuals who work under a contract of employment, ie a *contract of service* or apprenticeship, whether express, oral or in writing.

2.2 Continuity of employment

In order to present a statutory claim, normally, the employee must have been continuously employed for at least one year prior to the date of the dismissal. There are some exceptions where reduced or no continuity is required, for example, in respect of trade union membership or dismissal related to pregnancy where there is no qualifying period. There are no limitations placed on employees because of hours worked.

The period of continuity will normally start from the day on which the employee starts work (normally the date specified in the contract) – the **date of commencement, and ends** at the **effective date of termination** (ie, EDT, but called the **relevant date (RD)** in redundancy cases). In calculating periods of continuous employment a month means a **calendar month** and a year means **twelve calendar months** so that, for example, an employee commences employment on 30 January 2007 and works continuously for the employer from that date, the period of one year's service will be complete on 29 January 2008.

The effective/relevant date of termination: The EDT/RD is the date on which the notice expires *or* if the employee gives counter notice which is shorter than the employer's notice, the date on which the counter notice expires. If the dismissal is lawfully without notice, (that is **summary dismissal)**, the EDT/RD is the date on which the notice takes effect.

Where the dismissal was unjustifiably without notice *or* where shorter notice than was required was given, the proper statutory notice is added to the actual date of dismissal to find the EDT/RD. This will be the case even if the employee was entitled to a longer period of notice under their contract. For example, in the case of employee X who commenced employment on 1 March 2010 and who had no breaks in continuity of employment:

If X is dismissed wrongfully without notice on 25 February 2011 s/he will be entitled to add one week's statutory minimum notice to the actual date of termination (X has been employed longer than four weeks, but less than one year) which will give an effective date of termination as 4 March 2011. X will, therefore, be eligible to present a claim. In respect of fixed-term contracts which expire without being renewed the effective/relevant date is the date on which the contract expires.

The period of employment must be continuous in order to give the employee a right to claim; if it is **broken** the employee will commence a new period of service after that break, and will not be entitled to add the old period of service to the new employment. Continuity will be **preserved** when the employee is absent from work owing to the following reasons.

(a) A **temporary cessation of work** where the employer lays-off the employee or places the employee on short-time working because of lack of work.

(b) The incapability of the employee to attend work in consequence of illness or injury, where no contract of employment exists subject to the rule that not more than 26 weeks count between any periods of employment, which themselves count for continuity purposes.

(c) **An arrangement** between the employer and the employee such as granting **extended leave**, for example where secondment is granted. Retrospective arrangements cannot preserve continuity.

(d) Periods of statutory maternity, adoption, paternity or parental leave.

(e) Where the employee successfully claims unfair dismissal and is **reinstated or re-engaged**.

(f) Where an employee is **re-engaged** after receiving a redundancy payment and it is a term of the re-engagement that s/he repays the redundancy payment to the employer: in these circumstances the period of continuous employment will be unbroken. Specifically, receipt of a *statutory* redundancy payment breaks continuity for the purposes of qualification for a further statutory redundancy payment or claiming unfair dismissal. The exception is where having received the payment the employee is re-instated or re-engaged by the employer on terms which require him/her to repay the redundancy statutory payment in full.

(g) Continuity may be preserved by reason of **custom and practice** where it was established prior to the beginning of the absence.

(h) Where an employee has engaged in **industrial action** and returns to work, the continuity of employment will not be broken, but the period during which the employee was taking the action cannot count towards the total continuity period.

(i) Where there is a change of employer, continuous employment will be preserved where:

    (i) A business or undertaking is transferred from one person to another

    (ii) An employee of an employer is taken into the employment of an associated employer

    (iii) One body corporate is substituted for another body corporate by Act of Parliament

    (iv) The employer dies and their personal representative(s) continues to employ the employee, and

    (v) There is a change in the partners who employ the employer.

2.3 Automatically unfair dismissal

For all the dismissals listed below, the employee can bring an unfair dismissal claim from the start of their employment, ie they do not need at least one year's continuous employment.

A dismissal will be unfair where the reason or the principal reason for the dismissal or redundancy is:

- Because of their trade union membership, trade union non-membership, trade union activities or proposed activities, or use or proposed use of trade union services

- Because they failed to accept an unlawful inducement from an employer to give up their trade union rights or to disapply a collective agreement

- Because they failed to accept an offer made by an employer to induce them to become a trade union member

- Because they refused to make a payment in lieu of union membership, or objected to their employer deducting a sum from their wages or salary to make such a payment

- For exercising or seeking to exercise rights relating to trade union recognition procedures

- For exercising or seeking to exercise their right to be accompanied at a disciplinary or grievance hearing, or to accompany a fellow worker at such a meeting

- For reasons relating to jury service

- On grounds relating to pregnancy, childbirth or maternity

- For taking, or seeking to take, maternity leave

- For taking, or seeking to take, paternity leave

- For taking, or seeking to take, adoption leave

- For taking, or seeking to take, parental leave

- For taking, or seeking to take, time off for dependants

- For taking, or proposing to take, certain specified types of action on health and safety grounds

- Because, subject to certain conditions, the employee was a shop worker or a betting worker and refused to work on Sundays or gave, or proposed to give, an 'opting-out' notice to their employer

- For reasons relating to the Working Time Regulations 1998

- For performing, or proposing to perform, any duties relevant to their role as an occupational pension scheme trustee
- For performing, or proposing to perform, any duties relevant to their role as an employee representative or as a candidate to be such representative or as a participant in the election of such a representative
- For making a protected disclosure
- For having sought, in good faith, to assert a statutory employment protection right
- For reasons relating to the national minimum wage
- For requesting flexible working arrangements
- For taking lawfully organised official industrial action lasting 12 weeks or less (or more than 12 weeks in certain circumstances)
- For reasons relating to the Transnational Information and Consultation of Employees Regulations 1999
- On grounds related to the Part-time Workers (Prevention of Less Favourable Treatment) Regulations 2000
- On grounds relating to the Fixed-term Employees (Prevention of Less Favourable Treatment) Regulations 2002
- For reasons relating to the European Public Limited-Liability Company Regulations 2004
- For reasons relating to the Information and Consultation of Employees Regulations 2004
- For reasons relating to the Occupational and Personal Pension Schemes (Consultation by Employers and Miscellaneous Amendment) Regulations 2006
- For exercising or seeking to exercise the right to be accompanied at a meeting to consider a request not to retire, or for exercising or seeking to exercise the right to accompany a fellow employee at such a meeting
- For reasons relating to the European Cooperative Society (Involvement of Employees) Regulations 2006
- For reasons relating to the Companies (Cross-Border Mergers) Regulations 2007
- For reasons relating to them making a request for time to study or train
- For reasons relating to the European Public Limited-Liability Company (Employee Involvement) (Great Britain) Regulations 2009

- In relation to them being on a 'prohibited list', ie a blacklist of individuals who are currently or used to be trade union members or who currently or used to take part in trade union activities

A dismissal will also be unfair where the employee was dismissed:

- On grounds of retirement without the employer having first complied with their duty to consider a request by the employee not to retire.
- On the transfer of an undertaking or part of an undertaking, and the transfer itself, or a reason connected with it, is the main reason for the dismissal. This is unless it can be established that the dismissal was for an economic, technical or organisational reason entailing changes in the workforce.

2.4 Automatically fair dismissals

Automatically fair dismissals

There are two categories of automatically fair dismissals:

(a) Dismissed on grounds of national security
(b) Dismissal for taking part in unofficial industrial action

An employer can dismiss employees during a strike, lockout or other forms of industrial action unless the individual action is 'protected' (maximum 12 weeks). However (except in health and safety cases or a case where the dismissal was on maternity-related grounds) an Employment Tribunal has no jurisdiction to determine a complaint of unfair dismissal from an employee dismissed while participating in unofficial industrial action.

2.5 Employee validly contracting-out of his statutory rights

Normally, an employee cannot sign away their right to bring an action before an Employment Tribunal (to claim, for example, unfair dismissal or redundancy pay). There are a number of exceptions, however, to this section. A **conciliation officer** of ACAS may **promote an agreement** between the parties in a dispute under which the employee accepts the agreement in full settlement of their claim.

An ACAS arbitration offer may reach a decision as to the fairness or otherwise of a decision. Both parties must voluntarily enter into the individual arbitration process. The right of access to the tribunal is thereby nullified.

Compromise agreement between the parties, which include undertakings not to take proceedings before an Employment Tribunal are binding provided that:

- It is in writing
- It relates to a particular complaint (ie, proceedings) which is being compromised

- The claimant has received **independent advice** from a *named* qualified lawyer (that is a barrister or an advocate or a solicitor or a fellow of ILEX) as to the terms and effect of the proposed agreement, particularly its effect on the complainant's ability to pursue his or her rights before an Employment Tribunal. Legal advice will be independent if it is given by a lawyer who is not acting for the employer, or where applicable, the other party to the dispute or a person connected with that other party

- The agreement must identify the adviser

- There must be in force, when the adviser gives the advice, a contract of insurance or an indemnity covering the risk of a claim by the employee/adviser

- The agreement must expressly state that the conditions regulating compromise agreements have been satisfied.

There are no practical difficulties associated with compromise agreements. Nevertheless, there are a number of common difficulties which do occur.

A failure to comply with any of the above statutory requirements will render the agreement void, leaving the claimant at liberty to pursue the claim that the agreement purported to settle. The claimant receiving independent advice is particularly important. To prevent agreements failing for this reason, the employer will often contribute to the legal costs of the employee in obtaining such advice. It should be noted that there is no requirement for the agreement to contain a certification or signature from the independent adviser.

Practical difficulties with compromise agreements

The rules governing compromise agreements are aimed at safeguarding the interests of the employees entering into them. But employers will need to be on their guard that some technicality does not invalidate the agreement, leaving the employee free to take a tribunal complaint regardless of the agreement.

A compromise agreement must relate to the 'particular complaint'. It means that the particular proceedings must be clearly identified, either by a generic description such as 'unfair dismissal' or by reference to the section of the statute giving rise to the claim. It is not sufficient for a **compromise agreement** to use 'a rolled-up expression such as "all statutory rights"', nor even to identify the proceedings only by reference to the statute under which they arise.

- If actual proceedings are compromised, the particulars of the proceedings and of the allegations made in them should be spelled out by means of a brief factual and legal description

- If an anticipated claim is compromised, the particulars of the nature of the allegations and of the statute under which they are made or the common law basis of the alleged claim should be spelled out by means of a brief factual and legal description

- **Compromise agreements** should be tailored to the individual circumstances of the case. It is not good practice to draft a standard form of **compromise agreement** that lists every form of employment right known to the law.

Therefore it appears that an agreement cannot include a catch-all phrase covering any or all statutory complaints that might be open to the individual concerned. Where an agreement relates to complaints covered by different statutes, it will be necessary to make reference to each relevant statute and provide a brief factual and legal description. This is because the compromise agreement provisions, which are inserted separately into each relevant Act, require that the agreement states that it satisfies the conditions 'under this Act'.

Please note that a compromise agreement will have the effect of preventing an individual from taking a claim under statutory sources to the tribunal or court, but not prevent them from bringing a claim for breach of contract. However, a tribunal can hear a claimant's claim for breach of contract only in so far as the claim 'arises or is outstanding on the termination of the employee's employment'.

2.6 Excluded employees

Four examples of excluded employees are listed below.

(a) **Employees who are above 'normal' retirement age**

An employee is prohibited from claiming if on or before the EDT s/he has attained the age, which in his/her employer's undertaking, is the 'normal' retirement age for employees holding the same position. The retirement age must be the same for men and women. This means that an employer may have a normal retirement age of, say, 67 years, entitling employees to claim unfair dismissal. 'Normal' retirement age is determined by assessing the expectations of the employment group generally having regard to the employer's policy and previous practices.

In most circumstances the contractual retirement age will be the normal retiring age. This age can be 65 or above. An employer is unable to set a lower age than 65 unless this is objectively justifiable. The retirement procedures introduced on 1 October 2006 mean that employers have to: give employees advance notice of retirement; and tell employees that they can ask to work for longer. Employers who want to terminate the employee's employment before the default or normal age must have another fair reason for dismissal and follow the normal dismissal procedures. Where there is no contractual or normal retirement age in an enterprise, employees aged 65 or over may not normally bring a claim for unfair dismissal, provided the employer has followed the correct procedures.

(b) **Employees who fall into other certain excluded classes**

These include crews of fishing vessels where the employee is not remunerated otherwise than by a share in the profits or gross earnings, where the employee has validly contracted out, and police officers. Also, where the employment contract is illegal.

(c) **Employees who participate in unprotected industrial action**

With the introduction of twelve-week **protected industrial action** any dismissal will be automatically unfair. However, there remain circumstances in which an employee may be fairly dismissed when taking industrial action. The basic reasons are that the industrial action itself is unlawful (eg, unofficial or secondary action), or the dispute has lasted more than twelve weeks and the employer has taken 'reasonable procedural steps' to try to bring the dispute to an end. In practice, it is very unlikely that such dismissals would take place other than in exceptional cases in the current climate.

(d) **Claims excluded if 'out of time'**

A claim for unfair dismissal must be made within three months of the EDT, inclusive of the first day, whereas a claim for redundancy pay and for unfair dismissal arising out of selective dismissal during industrial action must be brought within six months.

3 Unfair dismissal

3.1 Types of dismissal

In order to be entitled to a statutory redundancy payment *or* to claim unfair dismissal an employee must have been dismissed within the definition of the Act. The employee has the burden of proving that a **dismissal** has taken place. If the employee has resigned without coercion or the contract has come to an end by mutual agreement or frustration then there has been no dismissal and, therefore no claim can be made.

If dismissal is proved the employer **must show** that the reason or the principal reason for the dismissal was fair as defined by the Act. The Employment Tribunal must then decide if it was **fair or unfair** to dismiss the employee for that reason. This will depend upon whether in the circumstances the employer acted **reasonably** in treating it as a sufficient reason for dismissing the employee. If the employer is unable to show that the reason for dismissal was fair the employee will be entitled to one of the remedies laid down by the Act.

It may be unfair because it was not reasonable to dismiss for the particular reason or it may be unfair because the employer failed to follow a fair procedure. However failure to follow additional fair procedures will not in itself make the dismissal unfair if the employer shows they would have decided to dismiss the employee even if they had followed the procedures.

Where are unfair dismissal claims heard?

(a) **Employment Tribunal**

Their jurisdiction to hear complaints on a variety of matters is now very wide. Each tribunal comprises a legally qualified Chairman and two lay members. When submitting a complaint to the tribunal the complainant will have to complete a form ET1 and send it to the Regional Office of Tribunals. On receiving the claim, the tribunal decides whether to accept it. If everything is in order, the claimant will be sent a standard acknowledgement form (ET5). The form states when the ACAS conciliation period will end. A copy of the claim will be sent to the employer (known as the respondent) who will have 28 days to respond. The respondent will be asked to complete the form ET3. In many cases a Conciliation Officer from ACAS will contact both parties to seek conciliation, and if successful they will sign the legally-binding form COT3.

Most claims to tribunals will have to be submitted within three months of the act complained of, eg act of discrimination, or date dismissal took effect. The tribunals have wide powers to determine their own procedures. The three month period can be extended by the Employment Tribunal where this requirement has not been met.

(b) **EAT – Employment Appeal Tribunal**

Appeals on a point of law are made from the Employment Tribunal to the EAT. It is for the Employment Tribunal to decide who is telling the truth (ie to base its decision on the facts of the case, and then apply the law to those facts). However, only on points of law can an appeal be made to the EAT and the higher courts. A point of law may be that the Employment Tribunal allegedly misinterpreted the law or ignored a part of the law in reaching its decision.

Remedies for unfair dismissal

Unfair dismissal complaints are determined by an Employment Tribunal. If the tribunal finds that the dismissal was fair, it will dismiss the application.

If, however, the tribunal finds the dismissal unfair, remedies are

- Re-instatement (to original post), or
- Re-engagement (same employer, different job) and/or
- Compensation (this is most commonly provided, in 99% of successful claims).

> There are four headings of compensation
> - Basic award (calculated on age and service) up to the equivalent of 20 years' service based on a formula, but capped
> - Compensatory award for loss of earnings, fringe benefits, loss of pension, expenses for job hunting – setting up new employment and loss of statutory rights
> - Additional award (if employer fails to comply with re-instatement/re-engagement order)
> - Special award (in trade union and health and safety cases where re-instatement/re-engagement is not practicable or complied with).

3.2 The dismissal

A dismissal takes place in any one of the following situations:

- Termination by the **employer** with or without notice – (termination by employer)
- Lapse of a **limited-term contract** without renewal, or
- Where the employee terminates the contract with or without notice in circumstances such that s/he is entitled to do so without notice by reason of the employer's conduct (**constructive dismissal**).

(a) **Employer termination**

Normally, there is no problem in determining whether or not there is a dismissal. There can be no doubt that an employer who tells the employee that s/he is 'sacked' is dismissing the employee, but there may be instances in which it is *not* so obvious whether the employer by their words or conduct is dismissing the employee. Is there, for example, a dismissal where an employee is told 'to get out' or to 'remove himself/herself from sight?' Where the words spoken are ambiguous, the effect of the statement has to be considered in the light of the surrounding circumstances and, in particular, the conduct of the parties and what happened before and after the disputed dismissal. Questions to ask are:

(i) What was the situation in which the words were spoken?

(ii) Were they spoken 'in the heat of the moment'?

(iii) Would any reasonable employer or employee have understood the words to amount to a dismissal?

Similarly, a resignation under **threat of dismissal** may, in fact amount to a dismissal. An employee who is told to resign or be 'sacked' may feel that they have no choice but to resign. The resignation will, nevertheless be treated as a dismissal provided s/he can show that there was a certain and immediate threat.

(b) **Expiry of fixed - (limited-) term contract**

A fixed-limited-term refers to a contract which has a defined beginning and end. An employee who is employed under a limited-term contract is treated as dismissed if the term expires and is not renewed. You will note that any waiver to claim unfair dismissal or for a redundancy payment is invalid.

(c) **Constructive dismissal**

Essentially, constructive dismissal takes place when the employer's behaviour constitutes a **repudiation** of the contract and the employee accepts the repudiation by resigning.

The **test** for establishing whether the employer's conduct was such as to entitle the employee to leave and claim constructive dismissal is a **contractual** one. Therefore, before resigning an employee needs to consider which contract term the employer has broken.

Written reasons for dismissal

An employee (with one year's service) whose employment is terminated, or whose fixed-term contract expires without being renewed, is entitled to receive, on request, a written statement of the reasons for dismissal or non-renewal of their fixed-term contract. The request can be oral or in writing.

Employers are required to comply with the request within 14 days.

An employee dismissed at any time during pregnancy or statutory maternity leave is entitled to receive from her employer a written statement of the reasons for her dismissal, regardless of:

- Whether or not she has requested one, and
- Her length of service

The written statement can be used as evidence in any subsequent proceedings, eg unfair dismissal complaint.

3.3 The importance of the contract test

The test for constructive dismissal requires three criteria to be present. An employee will only be able to claim constructive dismissal where:

(a) The employer's conduct constitutes a **significant breach** going to the **root of the contract** or shows that the employer no longer intends to be bound by the essential terms of the contract. The breach must therefore be **repudiatory**, that is fundamental, such as instigating a major change in the terms and conditions of the employment contract without the employee's consent. A minor change in terms will not be sufficient for a constructive dismissal claim to be made. There does not have to be one major breach. There maybe a series of breaches, where each breach in isolation might not constitute a significant and fundamental breach, but taken together they do – the 'last straw' doctrine. Conduct of a line manager or supervisor may amount to a repudiatory breach by the employer provided the act was done **in the course of employment**. In recent years claims of constructive dismissal have been based on bullying and harassment at work.

(b) The employee **left** because of the breach.

(c) The employee did **not** waive the breach by **affirming** the contract. An employee who continues in their job for a significant period of time after the employer has breached the contract may be regarded as having affirmed the contract and will lose their right to claim unfair dismissal. Although a formal assertion by the employee that they have not accepted the breach or waived it is not necessary, the employee must leave because of the breach. Generally, there should be no delay between the repudiatory breach by the employer and the employee leaving. However, if the employee makes their objection to the breach clear and continues in their job for **a limited period** thereafter, for example while seeking alternative employment, they will not be regarded as having affirmed the contract and will be able to rely on the breach as grounds for a claim of constructive dismissal. This is known as *'working under protest'*.

3.4 Reason for the dismissal

Once the employee has proved to the Employment Tribunal that they have been dismissed the **burden shifts** to the employer to show the reason, or if there was more than one, the principal reason for the dismissal. In order to establish that the dismissal is **fair** the employer must firstly prove that the reason for the dismissal falls within one of **six categories**. The tribunal must then satisfy itself that the employer acted **reasonably** in dismissing the employee for the reasons given. Whether the employer acted reasonably will depend upon the circumstances and the steps taken by the employer before dismissal. These facts will normally be apparent from all the evidence presented to the tribunal.

3.5 Establishing a fair reason

Where an employee claims unfair dismissal, it is for the employer to show, on a balance of probabilities, that the dismissal was for one of the six potentially fair reasons. (This is not to show the dismissal itself was fair – that is for the tribunal to decide on the balance of probabilities.) (However, it is also open to a claimant to show that a dismissal was for a prescribed reason, rendering it automatically unfair). The six reasons which may lead to a fair dismissal by the employer:

1. Capability or qualification (ie, incapability)
2. Conduct (ie, misconduct)
3. Redundancy
4. Retirement
5. Prohibition under a statutory provision (sometimes known as 'statutory bar')
6. Some other substantial reason (often abbreviated to 'SOSR').

The reason for the dismissal must **exist** and be **known** to the employer at the time of the dismissal so that it is not generally possible to rely on any subsequently discovered misconduct.

3.6 Matters to be considered

The elements are:

- Capability plus qualifications
- Lack of competence
- Ill health
- Qualification
- Conduct

(a) **Capability and qualifications**

Capability is defined under the Act as 'capability assessed by reference to skill, aptitude, health, or any other physical or mental quality'. Qualification means 'any degree, diploma or other academic, technical or professional qualification relevant to the position which the employee held.' Thus, dismissal under the capability reason can be based on the **ability** to do the job; that is failing to reach the employer's expected level of performance through incompetence or through **illness** or **sickness**. An employer will be expected to treat incompetence and illness very differently, eg an employee who is incompetent may be given a warning and told to improve; however, it would not be appropriate to treat a sick employee in that way. This element of **procedural fairness** is discussed further on in this chapter.

(b) **Lack of competence**

There are a number of reasons why an employee may be incompetent; it may stem from inherent incapability to do the job or from **laziness, negligence** or **attitude**. Under the heading of conduct it is relevant to consider incompetence stemming from inherent incapability, since negligence, laziness and so on, are more appropriately dealt with under **conduct**.

It is important to note that the employer need not prove in the Employment Tribunal that the employee actually was incompetent. The employer need show only that s/he genuinely and reasonably believed that the employee was incompetent. The test is as follows.

(i) Did the employer honestly believe that the employee was incompetent or unsuitable for the job?

(ii) If so, was such belief held on reasonable grounds?

(iii) In forming such a belief, did the employer carry out a proper and adequate investigation?

Skill is referred to in the definition of capability as covering both managerial and manual skills. **Aptitude** may include such factors as facets of the employee's character, such as lack of interpersonal skills required. The incapacity must relate to the job the employee is employed to do and the duties which are laid down in the contract. The employer must prove that the employee was actually incapable of doing that job. Clearly, the employee must be aware of the standards which s/he should be reaching and if s/he is found to be performing poorly the employer will be expected to inform the employee of that fact. If the employee is left in ignorance of the relevant standards or the failure to meet those standards, a dismissal based on poor performance may well be found to be unfair.

In this respect it is very important for an employer to follow the ACAS **Code of Practice on Disciplinary and Grievance**. The Code recommends that steps be taken to ensure that all employees are aware of the standards of work performance and conduct which are satisfactory, *and* those which are not and will probably give rise to disciplinary action. Breaches of conduct and satisfactory levels of performance should be identified with specific disciplinary penalties. Moreover, this provision is considered an essential part of the 'Rules of Natural Justice'.

[The Code can be downloaded at *www.acas.org.uk*]

Many employers will distinguish in their disciplinary procedures between:

(i) Poor performance
(ii) Incapability due to ill health
(iii) Incapability due to ability or qualifications.

(c) **Ill health**

Where the dismissal is based on incapability because of ill health the considerations are different. The law draws a distinction between cases of **long-term** and **short-term** sickness. In the case of consistent periods of **short-term sickness** the procedure which should be followed is similar to that adopted in misconduct cases but the dismissal will be for some other substantial reason (SOSR), whereas long-term absence may be for reasons of capability.

In cases of short-term absence there is no obligation for the employer to obtain medical evidence, but if investigation reveals an underlying cause for the absences, such as clinical depression for example, the tribunal will expect the employer to obtain relevant medical evidence. In dealing with persistent short-term illness the employer should have regard to the nature of the illness, the relative length of the illness, the role which the employee plays within the business and the impact of the illness on the rest of the workforce. The employer must act **sympathetically** and demonstrate a measure of **understanding** which may involve **issuing cautions and warnings** as to the consequences of persistent absence. ACAS recommends counselling, advice and discussion, followed by a period for **improvement**.

In cases of **long-term sickness** the decision whether or not to dismiss is a matter for the employer to decide on the medical evidence available. First, the nature and length of the illness may frustrate the contract, in which case dismissal is irrelevant.

If the contract is not frustrated the issue of whether the dismissal was fair will depend upon the **procedure** adopted by the employer. The tribunal will look to see if the employer acted sympathetically and whether the employee was consulted at all stages.

The employer should always act from an informed view on the basis of proper medical information. The **Access to Medical Reports Act 1988** provides that the employer is entitled to make enquires of the employee's doctor only where the employee consents. Furthermore, the employer cannot insist that the employee undergo a medical examination unless it is expressly provided for in the contract; however, if an employee refuses, a subsequent unfair dismissal claim may easily fail. The worker may also have rights under the Data Protection Act 1998 or the Access to Health Records Act 1990 to health records held on him/her by the employer or any external doctor working for the employer.

Once medical evidence has been obtained the employer must consult with the employee. In the light of the medical evidence obtained, and after consultation, the employer should make the decision on whether to dismiss, taking into account the nature of the employee's situation and the needs of the business. A final, but *critical* consideration is whether the employee should be treated as a person with a 'protected characteristic' – disability, under The Equality Act 2010.

(d) **Qualification**

This means any **academic** or **technical** qualifications relevant to the position that the employee holds. Dismissals on the grounds of qualification will be those where the employee loses a qualification or fails to obtain a qualification or has a bogus qualification which is a condition of employment. The qualification must be one which is necessary for the performance of the employee's duties.

(e) **Conduct**

Misconduct is one of the most common reasons for dismissal but establishing whether a dismissal is fair will depend on the circumstances of each case. Conduct which may be acceptable on the shop floor may not, for example, be acceptable in a professional office. The procedure used by the employer in each case will be closely examined by the tribunal. In particular, the tribunal will look to see how far the employer's procedure complies with the principles of the **ACAS Code of Practice on Disciplinary and Grievance**. The tribunal will also explore whether the employer holds a genuine belief in the guilt of the employee.

A distinction is drawn between **gross misconduct** which may justify **summary dismissal** (that is instant dismissal) and **less serious misconduct** which is not usually sufficient grounds for dismissal unless it is repeated and continues despite warnings or is aggravated by other circumstances. The ACAS Code of Practice suggests that employers '…should give examples of acts which the employer regards as acts of gross misconduct. These may vary according to the nature of the organisation and what it does, but might include things such as theft or fraud, physical violence, gross negligence or serious insubordination'; this will normally be covered in the contract of employment and/or the disciplinary procedures or rules.

It does not follow, however that *only* gross misconduct indicated in the contract will warrant summary dismissal; if circumstances of the case show that the misconduct complained of was of a very serious nature the summary dismissal might be fair, even though specifically not stated in the contract. Nor does the conduct have to be blameworthy in the sense that the employee need not necessarily be to blame for his or her conduct. There is no exhaustive list of misconduct which justifies dismissal or gross misconduct to justify summary dismissal.

This section contains further information on conduct.

(a) **Conduct inside employment**

    (i) **Absenteeism/lateness**

        Conduct of this kind will usually not amount to gross misconduct; thus, dismissal for a first offence will not be fair except in special circumstances. Where the lateness or absenteeism is persistent provided that the employer has acted reasonably and followed appropriate procedures the employer may be justified in dismissing. A distinction should be made between a series of short-term absences and a period of absenteeism due to serious ill-health, but both should be properly investigated before any disciplinary action is taken.

    (ii) **Disobedience of reasonable orders**

        Clearly, an employee may be dismissed for refusing to obey a **reasonable** order made in accordance with the terms of the contract of employment. The duty of the employee is to obey reasonable lawful orders only. A dismissal for disobedience of an unreasonable or unlawful order will be unfair. What is a reasonable order is a **question of fact** to be decided in all the circumstances of the case, including whether the employee had a valid reason for refusing. Generally, if a reasonable order made in accordance with the contract of employment is refused, the employer would be justified in dismissing unless the employee had a good reason for the refusal. An employee who does not comply with the employer's rules may also be guilty of disobedience entitling the employer to dismiss, even though the rules are not strictly contractual terms but collateral to the contract such as management instructions, eg, in Works Rules. In addition, refusal to do something which is outside the contract of employment *may* constitute disobedience providing a fair reason for dismissal, for example where the employee refuses to undertake non-contractual overtime without valid reason.

    (iii) **Dishonesty**

        Acts of dishonesty such as fraud and theft of the employer's property will amount to a fair reason for dismissal. The employer does not have to act as a court or apply similar rules, but provided that they properly **investigate** the matter and establish a **genuine belief** in the employee's guilt, they will be justified in dismissing even if the employee is later found to be not guilty of the offence alleged. It would appear that where misconduct has occurred, for example, a theft has taken place and the employer has several suspects but cannot discover the actual employee responsible, provided they have reasonable grounds for believing one of the employees is guilty they may dismiss all.

(iv) **Violence or fighting**

Violence or fighting with colleagues at the workplace is likely to constitute gross misconduct. But the employer must have sufficient evidence on which to dismiss. If the dismissal is to be fair, the employer must consider all the relevant circumstances based on a thorough investigation including the status of the employee and any provocation, and mitigation. Also, the employer should generally act consistently.

(b) **Conduct outside employment**

Misconduct outside employment will in some cases amount to a fair reason for dismissal. The conduct in question must generally be such that it has an **adverse** effect on the employer's business, for example because it makes the employee unsuitable for the job or unacceptable to other employees, or brings the employer's business into contempt. The abuse of drugs or alcohol may also give rise to disciplinary action. However, employers should note that even where they have a reasonable belief that an employee has committed a serious criminal offence outside work which could damage their reputation, they should conduct a reasonable investigation and follow a proper procedure to avoid a claim of unfair dismissal.

4 Redundancy

4.1 Introduction

An employer may fairly dismiss an employee by reason of redundancy. A redundancy situation exists where the employee is dismissed for a reason wholly or mainly due to:

(a) The fact that the employer has ceased or intends to cease carrying on the **business** for the purposes of which the employee was employed by them; or

(b) The fact that the requirements of that business for employees to carry out work of a particular kind in the **place** where the employee was so employed by the employer have ceased or diminished; or

(c) The fact that the requirements of that business for employees to carry out **work of a particular kind** have ceased or diminished.

4.2 Cessation of business at the place of employment

Where there is a total closure of business, (not a transfer of the undertaking), few legal problems arise and there is no **requirement** to look behind the closure of the business. Most problems occur where there is a change in location or where the business closes down in one particular place but continues elsewhere. The employer may offer a position to the employee at the new location, in which case, first it will be necessary to look to see how substantial the move is; for example, an employee who refuses to move to an adjacent premises close-by and claims a redundancy payment is unlikely to be viewed sympathetically by a tribunal.

Second it is necessary to consider the employment contract to see whether it contains a mobility clause. If **no mobility clause** is included and the employer ceases business at the place where the employee works, the dismissal *will* be by reason of redundancy. Even where there is a mobility clause it may still not mean that the employer can rely on it in a case of redundancy. Where the business is changing location and the employer attempts to move an employee to a place of work which is outside a location which is described with sufficient clarity in his or her terms of employment, that employee may refuse to transfer and make a claim for a redundancy payment.

An employee who refuses an offer of suitable alternative employment in a redundancy situation will not be able to claim a redundancy payment. This could include the situation where the job offered is at a different location to the place in which the employee was employed. Reasonable alternative work is discussed below.

4.3 Cessation or diminution in requirement for employees of a particular kind

The House of Lords said that the meaning of the words 'diminution in the need for employees to carry out work of a particular kind' meant that two questions should be asked:

(a)   Had the employer's business requirements caused work of a particular kind to have diminished?

(b)   Was the dismissal of employees wholly or mainly attributable to that state of affairs?

The key word here is 'attributable' and means that any employee 'affected' by a downturn in business could be placed in the redundancy selection pool. Obviously a situation could arise in an organisation where the work of one or more employees might not be affected by any cessation or diminution in the employer's business requirements for employing other staff and, therefore they should *not* be placed in the pool, but there would have to be a clear separation, eg different locations.

4.4 Variation of duties giving rise to redundancy – work of a particular kind ceases or diminishes

Where there is a fundamental change in the nature of the job, so that work of a particular kind has diminished or ceased and an employee is dismissed as a result, this will amount to a redundancy. However, a mere reallocation of duties, or introduction of new working methods or **different working hours** which the employee refuses to agree to and which leads to a dismissal will not amount to a redundancy, but may be due to '**some other substantial reason**', provided the employer can show a sound business need for the change. However, a **reduction** in working hours may give rise to redundancy.

4.5 Fair redundancy

Where an employee is made redundant the dismissal must be **fair** and must relate to the **workplace** situation. Thus, where an employee is selected for redundancy and no real redundancy situation exists, the employee will have been unfairly dismissed. The essence of a fair redundancy is **fair selection**, providing reasonable **warning** and **consultation** with the employees or their representatives and a **fair procedure** for handling the redundancy. The criteria for good industrial practice are set out below and should only be departed from where some good reason is shown (although it has been accepted that not all of the criteria are relevant to small businesses). The criteria are:

(a) The employer should give as much **warning** as possible of impending redundancies to enable the trade union (employee representatives) and employees to take appropriate steps.

(b) The employer will **consult** the trade union as to the best means by which the desired management result can be achieved fairly and with as little hardship to the employees as possible, and will seek an agreement on the criteria for selection. (There are statutory obligations shown below.)

(c) Whether or not an agreement as to criteria has been reached, the employer will seek to establish **fair objective** and selection criteria.

(d) The employer will seek to ensure that the selection is made **fairly** in accordance with the criteria and will consider any trade union (employee) representations made.

(e) The employer will ascertain whether **other employment** could be offered as an alternative to dismissing employees.

An employer who fails to follow the required procedure may find that the redundancy dismissal is held to be unfair for lack of procedure. In addition, even though the reason exists there may be an unfair dismissal if the employee can show that they fall within the provisions relating to automatically unfair redundancy dismissal. It is important to note however that these guidelines are not binding principles of law.

An employer can normally be expected to provide evidence as to the steps which were taken to select the employee, to consult and to seek alternative employment. Thus evidence of redundancy criteria, attempts to find alternative employment will need to be produced.

Further points relating to a fair redundancy dismissal are:

(i) **Notice periods** operate in the same way as those for any other termination with notice.

(ii) **Warning of redundancy** does not constitute a repudiation of the contract, and is therefore, not a dismissal.

(iii) **Once a redundancy payment has been offered** and a *subsequent* arrangement is made for the employee to retire early instead, care must be taken to withdraw the offer of redundancy pay.

4.6 Unfair selection for redundancy

There is no one fair method of selection, but the employer should seek to agree the criteria for selection with the representatives of the employees concerned. The main criteria may include

- Experience
    - Skill
    - Health

- Attendance

- Efficiency of the employee-performance and productivity

- Length of service, if it is established that it demonstrates business knowledge, otherwise there is a risk that the criteria constitutes discrimination

- Whatever the criteria chosen it must be fair and not constitute discrimination, such as requiring part-timers to be dismissed instead of full-time employees. The decision must be objectively based.

A matrix of the above criteria may be the best approach.

The process for selecting employees for redundancy must be clear and based on criteria which are consistent (ie, not variable or capricious), fair, reasonable and objectively based (eg, not based on one manager's opinion). The criteria applied must be applied in a reasonable, fair and objective manner.

Last In First Out may give rise to indirect sex or racial or disability discrimination. Performance, discipline, absenteeism and sickness are acceptable as criteria, but assessment must be unbiased, objective, fair and accurate. Any connection with **pregnancy** would be unlawful, and previous absence due to maternity leave or disability should not be included. Important periods of employment should not be omitted from any formula including those while an employee was absent on maternity leave.

Employers should be wary of using the following criteria.

- **Employee attitudes or personality**, other than where a **psychometric test** is used as part of a range of criteria. This technique could be valid if the organisation was facing massive cultural change, otherwise there are strong ethical reasons for not using such a method. **Personal data** must always be fairly and objectively used.

- Although the **criteria used must be divulged** to employees they are not entitled to know the ratings or assessment levels of all employees subject to selection for possible redundancy or those not eventually selected. An over detailed analysis of the way in which the criteria is applied is not necessary.

- Employers have acted unfairly when they withheld from the individual employees their assessment ratings for a redundancy selection exercise.

4.7 Warning and consultation

A fundamental requirement for the employer who is likely to make redundancies is to properly consult with individual employees and/or employee representatives. The legal provisions can be best addressed by asking and answering a series of questions.

(a) **What should be the overall objective of consultation?**

It should include ways of '…avoiding the dismissals…reducing the numbers of employees to be dismissed….of mitigating the consequences of the dismissals….*and with a view to reaching agreement…*'

The consultation must focus on the '*consequences*' of the employer's proposals before actual individuals had been identified.

(b) **Who must be consulted?**

Collective consultation

'…appropriate employee representatives are either of a recognised trade union……or in default of this situation, the employer may choose employee representatives who were not elected or appointed by the affected employees…….but who have authority from those employees to receive information and be consulted about the proposed dismissals on their behalf…..or the employer may choose to consult employee representatives specifically chosen for the purposes of redundancy consultation…..providing they are elected in accordance with s 188(A)(1)'.

- 'Affected employees' will include not only those who will be at risk of redundancy, but those who might be affected in some other way by the redundancies, eg, additional work spread across fewer staff.

- 'Appropriate representatives' will include representatives of recognised independent trade unions and elected or appointed employee representatives. Where there is one or more recognised trade unions their representatives must be consulted. Where no union exists the employer may choose to consult with existing employee representatives (eg, those elected under the Information and Consultation Regulations 2004) *or* to elect a special forum of representatives.

- Where there is no trade union, no existing employee representatives *and* no employee puts themself forward for election the employer cannot consult collectively, but they *must* then consult individually each affected employee.

Election rules in cases where employee representatives are to be specially elected

(a) The employer shall make such arrangements as are reasonably practical to ensure that the election is fair.

(b) The employer shall determine the number of representatives to be elected so that there are sufficient representatives to represent the interests of all the affected employees, having regard to the number and classes of those employees.

(c) The employer shall determine whether the affected employees should be represented either by representatives of all the affected employees or by representatives of particular classes of those employees.

(d) Before the election the employer shall determine the term of office as employee representatives so that it is of sufficient length to enable relevant information to be given and consultations to be completed.

(e) The candidates for election as employee representatives are affected employees on the date of the election.

(f) No affected employee is unreasonably excluded from standing for election.

(g) All affected employees on the date of the election are entitled to vote for employee representatives.

(h) The employees entitled to vote may vote for as many candidates as there are representatives to be elected to represent them; or, if there are to be representatives for particular classes of employees, for as many candidates as there are representatives to be elected to represent their particular class of employee.

(i) The election is conducted so as to secure that:

- So far as is reasonably practicable, those voting do so in secret, and
- The votes given at the election are accurately counted.

Individual consultation

This operates at two levels:

(i) 'If, after the employer has invited affected employees to elect representatives, the affected employees fail to do so within a reasonable time, he shall give to each affected employee the information ....'.

(ii) It is important to note that even if individual consultation takes place, once the decision to dismiss particular individuals has taken place, the employer should communicate with each individual about the arrangements for him or her to be dismissed. However, there is no general rule that if collective consultation is 'adequate' then individual consultation should also follow.

(c) **When should consultation take place?**

(i) Notify the Department for Business, Innovation and Skills (BIS) by letter or using form HR1. The form can be downloaded from the website. BIS must receive the notification on form HR1 at least:

- 30 days before the first redundancy where there are 20 to 99 proposed redundancies and before the individuals have received personal notice of termination

- 90 days before the first redundancy where there are 100 or more proposed redundancies and before the individuals have received personal notice of termination

A copy of the notification form must also be given to the employees' representatives. Late notification, or failure to notify is liable to a fine up to £5,000.

(ii) 'In good time', when redundancies are 'proposed'. (**Note** the EC **Collective Redundancies Directive** states that it should commence when redundancies are first 'contemplated', which is arguably at an earlier stage).

(a) Consultation to begin 30 days before the first dismissal takes place where 20 – 99 employees in one establishment are to be dismissed within 30 days; or

(b) 90 days before the first dismissal takes place where 100+ employees in one establishment are to be dismissed within a period of 90 days or less.

A strict interpretation of these rules means that the employer should identify the date of the first dismissal and count back to the start of the consultation period. It is not absolutely necessary that the consultation commences when redundancies are first 'proposed'.

Where an employer who has already begun consultations about one group of proposed redundancy dismissals and later finds it necessary to make a further group redundant the employer does not have to add the numbers of employees together to calculate the minimum period for either group.

(c) Consultation should take place when a fixed-term contract expires.

8: Termination of employment

(*) Employers should not issue redundancy notices of dismissal to individuals until the consultation process has closed.

(d) **How should consultation take place?**

The consultation process involves disclosing **information**, which should include:

(i) Reason for redundancies

(ii) Numbers and description of employees affected (including the total numbers of employees employed at the relative establishments)

(iii) The number of proposed dismissals, including a description of the individuals

(iv) Proposed redundancy selection criteria

(v) Proposed method of dismissals

(vi) Time-scales proposed

(vii) Proposed method of calculating redundancy pay and any other parts of the severance package.

Once consultation is underway, the information should be disclosed as soon as is practical.

(i) Consultation should take place with appropriate employee representatives.

(ii) Redundancy selection criteria: these are important because they may render the dismissals as unfair.

The Information and Consultation of Employees ('I & C') Regulations 2004 give employees in larger firms rights to be informed and consulted on an on-going basis about issues in the business they work. This includes decisions on collective redundancies.

The rights given by the I & C Regulations are in addition to the consultation rights. An employer proposing to make collective redundancies must comply with the requirements detailed above, even if they have established separate consultation arrangements as a result of the I & C Regulations. For example, if a trade union is recognised in respect of employees affected by proposed collective redundancies, the employer must consult representatives of that union, even if there is a separate group of employees' representatives set up as a result of the I & C Regulations. Where there is a separate group of employees' representatives set up as a result of the I & C Regulations, the employer would only have to consult that group if s/he had agreed to do so as part of a 'negotiated agreement' made under the I & C Regulations. An employer who is subject to the standard information and consultation provisions in the I & C Regulations need not consult employees' representatives under those provisions if s/he notifies those representatives in writing on each occasion that the TULR(C)A 1992 consultation duties are triggered that s/he will be consulting under TULR(C)A 1992.

(e) **Are there any defences the employer can use for not properly consulting?**

Yes, but they are very limited, primarily the '**Special circumstances**' defence, that the employer took all reasonable steps in the circumstances to fulfil the statutory obligations.

(f) **Must the employer follow a redundancy consultation/dismissal procedure?**

Common law

There is no general rule on this, but the procedure must be a fair one, otherwise this might render any dismissal unfair. This could include retraining, redeployment, avoiding compulsory redundancies through natural wastage, voluntary severance, short-time working and reductions in overtime. Possibly counselling and an outplacement service could be provided, but this reflects best practice, not law.

Contract of employment

(i) Any procedure expressly enshrined in the contract or incorporated through a collective agreement must be followed. In addition, cases have shown that through custom and practice a redundancy procedure might be binding on the employer.

(ii) The **statutory rules** are discussed in the sections above.

(g) **What penalties are available against the employer for a failure to consult properly, other than individual claims of unfair dismissal?**

If the employer fails to consult, the remedy is to complain to an Employment Tribunal. Compensation may then be awarded to the employee.

Where there is a failure to consult, an Employment Tribunal can order the employer to pay appropriate compensation to individual employees, up to a maximum of 90 days pay for each employee. The Employment Tribunal must take into account the seriousness of the employer's failure.

(h) **Through consultation with affected employees can an employee who will not be made redundant, put him/herself forward for voluntary redundancy instead?**

Yes. This could involve '*bumping*' which is a process of transferring the employee who is to be made compulsorily redundant to a post vacated by an employee who would like to be made redundant. The process is no more than a paper exercise and both employees need not actually transfer jobs before the dismissal takes effect.

NB: A voluntary redundancy is still a redundancy and there is no loss of rights or entitlements.

4.8 What is the employee entitled to if selected for redundancy?

(a) To be given proper **notice**, based on the contract of employment *or* the minimum statutory requirement, if greater.

The **minimum** statutory notice period to be given by an **employer** is:

(i) One week's notice to an employee who has been continually employed for one month but less than two years

(ii) One week's notice for each whole year of continuous employment for an employee with two years or more, but less than 12 years continuous employment

(iii) At least 12 weeks notice for continuous service of 12 years or more.

Note: A contract of employment can specify rights to longer notice than the statutory minimum.

(b) To be offered **reasonable alternative employment** by the employer where this is practical. If the alternative employment commences within **four weeks** of the ending of the original employment s/he may lose their entitlement to statutory redundancy pay if a reasonable offer of work is refused without good reason.

Where an offer of alternative work is made **after notice of dismissal** the alternative work can begin any time within four weeks of the original contract coming to an end. The employee then has a further four weeks in order to carry out the work. **If s/he continues** in work after that period, continuity of employment will be guaranteed for the whole period. **If s/he leaves** before the end of the four-week period s/he will be treated as having been dismissed when the original contract terminated, and lose the redundancy payment. The consideration of **alternative** employment for the employees selected for redundancy will often be an important part of a fair and reasonable redundancy procedure.

However, as a general rule, tribunals will expect an employer with sufficient resources to take reasonable steps to ameliorate the effects of redundancy, including giving detailed consideration to whether suitable **alternative** employment is available.

Suitability of alternative employment

Inevitably, the question of **suitability** must be determined on a case-by-case basis and will entail a detailed consideration of the employee's circumstances. This can be compared to the proper approach towards the question of whether an employee has unreasonably refused a suitable **offer** of **alternative** employment. The personal circumstances of the employee are crucial to that question: the employee's decision to refuse the employer's **offer** has to be judged, looking at it from his or her point of view, on the basis of the facts as they appear (or ought reasonably to have appeared) at the time the decision was made.

Factors which will be taken into account are: the approximation of pay, nature of duties and status as well as domestic circumstances, the perceived capabilities of the employee and extra travelling required.

Where the employee under notice secures **alternative employment with another employer** and is subsequently offered reasonable alternative work instead of redundancy this will not automatically make the refusal of such work reasonable, but it will greatly influence the tribunal's decision.

Trial periods can be extended by mutual agreement (eg, to conduct training), and further job offers can be made. In all these situations the employee retains the right to a redundancy payment, providing that the extension of a trial period was contractually provided before notice expired, and in the case of the latter before the first alternative job period expired.

(c) **Time-off to look for work**. An employee who is under a notice of dismissal by reason of redundancy and who has been continuously employed for two years or more is entitled to paid reasonable time-off to look for work. If the employer unreasonably refuses to give time-off the employee may present a complaint to an Employment Tribunal within three months of the alleged refusal.

(d) **Redundancy pay**. An employee who has been dismissed by reason of redundancy and who is eligible (within the rules discussed above) is entitled to a **statutory redundancy payment**. The employee's entitlement to redundancy pay will be calculated by applying a **formula** based on **age, length of service and a week's pay**, but *not* on loss actually suffered. Working back from the date of termination of employment, the employee is entitled to: Statutory redundancy pay, in addition to any contractual monies owing.

Age of employee	Number of weeks' pay
Under 21	Half a week's pay for each year of employment/service
22 – 40	One week's pay for each year of employment/service
41+	One and a half week's pay for each year of employment/service

Service before the age of 18 does not count.

There is a maximum statutory limit on the amount of weeks' pay that may be reckoned and this figure is reviewed annually. Employers can pay in excess of the statutory minimum.

4.9 Factors to be taken into account when managing redundancy

Factors to be taken into account are as follows.

(a) **Resignation and early retirement**

An employee who resigns voluntarily is not entitled to a redundancy payment. The employee may, however retain the entitlement to pay if, after receiving notice of redundancy, the employee gives notice of termination which would expire earlier than the employer's notice. If the employer objects to the employee leaving early they may request that the employee withdraws the notice and give warning that they will contest an application for redundancy pay in the tribunal.

(b) **Misconduct**

An employee who is dismissed for misconduct will *not* be entitled to a redundancy payment even if they later become redundant.

(c) **Industrial action**

An employee will *not* be entitled to a redundancy payment if they engage in non-protected strike action during the period of redundancy notice or after the employee has given notice claiming redundancy pay on account of short time working or lay-off.

Individual rights (including a redundancy payment) will be lost if the employee is dismissed during a trial period for a reason not connected with suitability for the new work, for example, misconduct.

The definition of a fair dismissal relating to redundancy is defined as 'any dismissal not related to the individual'. This can extend to the definition of a dismissal for 'some other substantial reason'.

5 Retirement

5.1 Mandatory retirement ages

The dismissal of employees on their attaining a certain age is the most obvious example of direct age discrimination. Indeed a mandatory retirement age is a frequent issue discussed by government and employers. In the most recent legislation, the Equality Act 2010 confirmed a number of issues. It:

- Removed upper age limits on unfair dismissal and redundancy

- Introduced a national default retirement age of 65, making compulsory retirement below 65 unlawful unless objectively justified. The default age was then phased out and abolished in October 2011.

- Gave all employees the right to request to work beyond 65 or any other retirement age set by the company

Employers who still want to enforce retirement will need to objectively justify it.

5.2 Retirement

The Regulations make special provision for retirement in terms of both the non-discrimination rule and the law on unfair dismissal. For a dismissal automatically to be deemed retirement, the employer must, between six and 12 months before the date of dismissal, notify the employee of his or her right to request not to retire on the intended date of retirement. If that requirement is observed, and the dismissal then takes place on the intended date of retirement, the dismissal will not be unlawful age discrimination.

If that requirement is not observed, whether or not the dismissal is deemed to be retirement will be determined by the tribunal according to the extent to which the employer has complied with the rest of the procedural duties and the statutory procedure.

The statutory retirement procedure is as follows:

- Between six and 12 months before the employee's intended retirement date the employer must notify them in writing of the intended retirement date and their right to request to work beyond their intended retirement date if they want

- If the employee makes a request to work beyond their intended retirement date, the employer will have to meet with them to discuss it

- If the employer wholly or partly refuses the request, the employee has the right to appeal against the decision

- The employee has the right to be accompanied at any meeting to discuss their retirement and any subsequent appeal meeting

6 Some Other Substantial Reason (SOSR)

6.1 Introduction

This ground for dismissal provides the employer with a potentially very broad reason for a fair dismissal. It permits the employer to rely on some factor which does not fall within the other fair reasons for dismissal. The employer can rely on *any* reason provided that they can show that the reason justifies dismissal which does not run contrary to law. The Court of Appeal has stated that in deciding whether the reason for dismissal falls within the scope of 'SOSR' the tribunals have to consider if the reason *could* justify the dismissal of an employee holding the position that the dismissed employee held. In other words, different types of reasons could justify dismissal of employees holding different positions. A substantial reason is one which is not trivial or unworthy but one which would justify the dismissal. It is not possible to provide a comprehensive list of fair/SOSR dismissals but examples are given below.

- Necessary reorganisation of the business

- Necessary economies in the running of the organisation, eg, pay reduction

- Protection of the interests of the company, eg, failure of employee to sign a reasonable and necessary restrictive covenant or there is a genuine risk arising from an employee's relationship with a competitor

- Expiry of fixed-term contract

- Imprisonment of employee (although may also be frustration of contract)

- Dismissal of employee who was engaged to cover the work of an employee on maternity leave.

- Dismissal of an employee (not redundancy) before or after a transfer of undertakings for an Economic, Technological or Organisational reason.

- When trust and confidence breaks down because of the employee's actions in a situation that might otherwise give rise to a misconduct dismissal, in which the employee's behaviour disrupted the work environment, constituted a breach of the express and implied terms of the contract and caused a breakdown in the relationship with the employer.

In **rare** cases pressure on the employer to dismiss an employee comes from some **third party** such as customers or fellow employees, for example to dismiss an employee because of fear of personal violence. In this type of case the employer might rely on SOSR to justify a dismissal, providing it does not amount to 'third party harassment' as described in the Equality Act where employers may be liable for harassment of their employees by third parties, such as customers and clients.

However, the most common reason justifying dismissal under this provision is **business needs**. Provided the employer can show that there is a **genuine business reason** for the change in working patterns or reorganisation which has triggered a dismissal it will fall within a potentially fair dismissal for SOSR. Thus, an employee who is dismissed for refusing to agree to changes to his/her employment contract or to working rules (which the employer proposes to make for business reasons), such as a change in shift patterns or an increase in working hours, or a reduction in pay, for example, may be found to have been fairly dismissed.

7 Fairness of the dismissal

Although the employer may be able to show that the reason for the dismissal falls within one of the six permitted grounds that does not necessarily mean there has been a fair dismissal. The tribunal must, in addition, be satisfied that the employer acted **reasonably** when dismissing.

Strictly speaking, the employer does not have **to prove** that they acted reasonably, because the burden of proof is neutral. In practice, however, they will be required to present considerable evidence to the tribunal or court as to how they dealt with the employee and, possibly how they dealt with similar cases in the past.

Whether the employer acted reasonably in treating the reason as sufficient cause to justify dismissal is determined in accordance with **equity** and the **substantial merits** of the case.

The tribunal or court will consider two main aspects when determining the reasonableness of the employer's dismissal: **actual fairness** and **procedural fairness**.

7.1 Fairness and criminal convictions

In situations where criminal charges are laid against an employee or the employee is arrested, an employer should not conclude that the employee is automatically guilty. The prudent employer will wait until the outcome of the criminal trial is known.

Where the employer *does* dismiss they must show a reasonable belief in the employee's guilt at the time of dismissal and act reasonably in treating the guilt as a reason for dismissal.

Where the employee's guilt is connected to an offence committed **outside work** a hearing should be held to determine the effect on the individual's employment.

7.2 Actual fairness of the decision

First, the tribunal or court must satisfy themselves that the employer **acted fairly** in dismissing, having regard to the reasons given by the employer.

- The starting point should always be the *words themselves* used by the employer
- The tribunal must consider the **reasonableness** of the **employer's** conduct *not* whether the tribunal considered the dismissal to be fair
- The tribunal must, therefore *not* substitute its own decision as to what was the right course of action for that employer to adopt
- In many cases there will be a **band of reasonable responses** to the employee's conduct within which different employers will take different views
- It is the function of the tribunal to determine whether, in the particular circumstances, the decision to dismiss fell within the **band of reasonable responses which a reasonable employer might have adopted**. If the dismissal falls within the band it is fair, if it falls outside the band it is unfair (but note the second and third points above).

The **range of reasonable responses test** is the standard test used to assess the fairness of any dismissal. It is important to remember the question to be addressed is what a **reasonable employer** might have done in the circumstances, *not* what the tribunal or court believe should have specifically been done if they were in the place of the employer. Each case must be considered **on its own merits**, but a number of general principles will be relevant.

(i) Has the evidence shown that the employer has complied with the pre-dismissal procedures which a reasonable employer could and should have applied in the circumstances of the case?

(ii) Where there is a contractual appeal process, has the employer carried it out in its essentials?

(iii) During the disciplinary/appeals hearings has the employer dealt fairly with the employee?

7.3 Other matters to be considered by the tribunal

(a) **Matters known to the employer**

The dismissal must be fair in the light of the information known to the employer at the time the employee was dismissed. However, where there has been an internal appeal, the employer should take into account factors which come to light during the appeal.

(b) **Size of the undertaking**

The size and resources of the undertaking should be considered when addressing the question of reasonableness. An employer with a small workforce may, for example be acting reasonably in dismissing an employee who is absent through sickness for a long period because the employer is not able to find other employees to cover the work of that employee. On the other hand, an employer who has a large workforce and who dismisses in similar circumstances may be acting unreasonably.

(c) **Consistency**

The employer must act consistently in applying the rules and the tribunal or court will look to see how the employer treated other employees in similar circumstances. If it is found that the employer acted inconsistently in dismissing then such a dismissal may be unfair. To summarise, employers should try to deal with matters in a consistent way, but not slavishly reach identical decisions.

(d) **Work record and length of service**

This factor is particularly important in cases of misconduct. A work record may, for example show that the employee has had a good employment record over a considerable time with the employer, in which case it would be reasonable to take this into consideration when dealing with the alleged misconduct.

(e) **Alternative employment**

An employer will not generally have acted reasonably if they have not considered the possibility of alternative work. This is particularly so in cases of illness, capability or redundancy, but may apply to other situations, except in cases of gross misconduct where the trust and confidence in the employee is irreparably broken.

(f) **Reasonable belief of the employer**

In relation to the reason for dismissal, the employer must be able to show that they held a **genuine belief** that they had a justified reason for dismissing, for example that they genuinely believed that the employee was guilty of theft.

A case involving misconduct dismissal, would be expected to consider a **three-stage** test to determine whether the employer entertained a reasonable suspicion amounting to a belief in the guilt of the employee.

(i) The employer must establish the **fact(s)** of the genuine belief that the employee was guilty of misconduct

(ii) It must be shown that the employer had in his/her mind reasonable grounds upon which to sustain that belief at the material time (ie, at the time the decision to dismiss was taken), and

(iii) At the stage which the employer formed that belief, and on those grounds, the employer must have carried out as much **investigation** into the matter as was **reasonable** in all the circumstances of the case.

8 Procedural fairness

Procedural defects in relation to the dismissal may render the dismissal **unfair**. **The ACAS Code of Practice No. 1, Disciplinary and Grievance Procedures (which was revised with effect from April 2009)** and 'Discipline and grievances at work: the ACAS guide' that complements the Code set out the principles which employers should follow when drawing up a disciplinary procedure and when handling a disciplinary matter. According to the Code:

- Employers and employees should raise and deal with issues promptly and should not unreasonably delay meetings, decisions or confirmation of those decisions.

- Employers and employees should act consistently.

- Employers should carry out any necessary investigations, to establish the facts of the case.

- Employers should inform employees of the basis of the problem and give them an opportunity to put their case in response before any decisions are made.

- Employers should allow employees to be accompanied at any formal disciplinary or grievance meeting.

- Employers should allow an employee to appeal against any formal decision made.

A good disciplinary procedure will help employees maintain standards of performance and conduct maintenance and help the employer to deal with those who do not. Larger employers will be expected to have written disciplinary procedures which are based on the principles of the Code, while smaller employers may have less formal procedures.

The procedures themselves will depend on the nature of the employment but should stipulate fair treatment, be **non-discriminatory**, be applied **consistently** and **reviewed** regularly.

The fact that the disciplinary procedures are simply in place is not sufficient. All employees must know and understand the procedures and the likely consequences of breaking the rules for the procedures to be effective. Where discipline regarding performance is concerned the tribunal will look to see whether the employer had an operable appraisal scheme and provided training and employee support.

8.1 Disciplinary hearing and appeals procedure

The ACAS Code incorporates the **Rules of Natural Justice**. These are principles which should be applied and can been identified from an analysis of the case law; they include the following.

(a) The employee should know the nature of the accusation against them in **sufficient detail**, and be given adequate time to allow them to prepare their case.

(b) The employee should be given the **opportunity** to state his case. Although it is *not* necessary that the accused employee should be present throughout the hearing, providing his interests are safeguarded by his representative, he must be given the chance to plead his side of the case and present a defence or argue mitigating factors. A sensible employer would, however take all reasonable steps to ensure the employee is present throughout the proceedings.

(c) The person holding the inquiry must be **impartial**. Thus, a person who is a witness to, or a principal character in the events should not also act 'as judge' in the proceedings. To avoid bias the person who undertakes the investigation should not be the person who takes the final decision to dismiss, otherwise the dismissal may be found to be unfair because it is contrary to rules of fairness and natural justice.

(d) The employee should be allowed the right to have another person speak on their behalf or at least to accompany them, otherwise a subsequent dismissal may be unfair (**right of accompaniment**).

(e) The employee should be informed of their **right of appeal**. Absence of an appeal or review procedure is one factor to be considered in determining fairness but will not itself make a dismissal unfair. On the other hand, an employer who fails to allow the employee to exercise their right of appeal to which they are contractually entitled, will not have acted fairly. In relation to the appeal procedure itself, a number of issues should be considered.

(i) The ACAS Code of Practice contains guidelines for an appeals procedure.

(ii) In order to avoid bias the person who carried out the disciplinary hearing should *not* carry out the appeal. A person who investigates the original disciplinary offence may well become so involved with the matter that they take it up as their own cause. Ideally the person who is responsible for the original dismissal should not be involved in the appeal.

(iii) The appeal panel may only make its decision based upon the same ground as the original dismissal. In other words, it cannot turn a dismissal for misconduct into a dismissal for incapability. It can, however, accept fresh evidence to either confirm the original decision to dismiss or to uphold the employee's appeal.

(iv) Where there was a breach of procedure in the original hearing an appeal which is a total rehearing of the case may rectify that defect.

8.2 Disciplinary sanctions

The employer may apply one of a number of sanctions, the ultimate penalty being dismissal. If the employer does dismiss, the sanction of dismissal must be within the *reasonable band of responses*. As noted above, the ACAS Code of Practice suggests the practice that should be followed:

(a) Where misconduct is confirmed or the employee is found to be performing unsatisfactorily it is usual to give the employee a written warning. A further act of misconduct or failure to improve performance within a set period would normally result in a final written warning.

(b) If an employee's first misconduct or unsatisfactory performance is sufficiently serious, it may be appropriate to move directly to a final written warning. This might occur where the employee's actions have had, or are liable to have, a serious or harmful impact on the organisation.

(c) A first or final written warning should set out the nature of the misconduct or poor performance and the change in behaviour or improvement in performance required (with timescale). The employee should be told how long the warning will remain current. The employee should be informed of the consequences of further misconduct, or failure to improve performance, within the set period following a final warning. For instance that it may result in dismissal or some other contractual penalty such as demotion or loss of seniority.

However, these are *only* guidelines and the appropriate action clearly depends upon the type and seriousness of offence. Where the employee has committed a number of different offences the employer can probably add together such warnings to gain a true picture of the employee upon which to make the decision.

As a matter of good practice, warnings should, however be wiped-off the record after a reasonable time, normally after one or two years. Warnings which are kept, must be kept in accordance with the Data Protection Act 1998. Finally, in order to have the appropriate effect the warning must be sufficiently specific; in particular the final warning should be a definite warning that a further offence will lead to dismissal.

An employer who does not dismiss may have a number of alternative sanctions against the employee including the following:

Fines, deductions or suspension without pay

The employer must have contractual consent or obtain written permission to apply such a penalty, otherwise it may amount to an unfair constructive dismissal or entitle the employee to claim unlawful deduction of wages against the employer.

Demotion or disciplinary transfer

Any change by the employer of the terms of the contract, without the consent of the employee, including a change in duties, constitutes a breach of contract and may give rise to a claim for constructive dismissal. Even where there has been a constructive dismissal, however, it does not follow that the tribunal will find the dismissal unfair. Any sanction should take account of:

- Any provocation
- Any mitigating factors
- The employee's length of service, good record or outstanding disciplinary warnings/sanctions on file.

8.3 Right of accompaniment

Workers attending a disciplinary or grievance hearing have a right to be accompanied by a work colleague or union official. The statutory rights are that the companion:

(a)   Will have the right to address the hearing (if the employee desires it)

(b)   May confer with the employee

(c)   May put the employee's case to the hearing on behalf of the employee

(d)   May respond on behalf of the employee to any points put forward at the hearing, and

(e)   May sum up the case for the employee.

The companion has no legal right to:

(a) Answer questions on behalf of the employee

(b) Address the hearing in any way against the wishes of the employee, and

(c) Use his/her powers to prevent or deter any other party to the hearing to fully explain their evidence/case to the hearing.

If the employee's companion is not available for a hearing the employee may propose a reasonable alternative time. The right to be accompanied is limited in law to where a disciplinary hearing could result in the following:

(a) Administration of a formal warning to the employee
(b) The taking of some other action in respect of the employee
(c) The confirmation of a warning issued or some other action taken.

In other words, the right to be accompanied only arises where **formal** action is taken against the employee by the employer.

9 Termination involving dismissal at common law

Summary of termination of contract:

Not involving dismissal:	Involving dismissal:	Unfair dismissal:
1. Frustration 2. Resignation 3. Mutual agreement (eg retirement) 4. Expiry of fixed-term contract (although a dismissal under statutory provisions) 5. Dissolution of partnership or winding-up of a company	Dismissal instigated by employer: 1. With notice 2. Without notice	Fair reasons for dismissal: 1. Capability or qualification 2. Conduct (ie, misconduct) 3. Redundancy 4. Retirement 5. Prohibition under a statutory provision (sometimes known as 'statutory bar') 6. Some other substantial reason

At common law a contract of employment may be terminated in several ways. The parties to the contract may agree various terms and must adhere to those terms. Only if either the employer or the employee terminates the contract in breach of those terms will the other party be able to claim damages for breach of contract. The employer or employee may, for example, terminate the contract without notice or justification in which case the common law will enable the injured party to claim damages to the extent of the **loss**, ie, wages for the notice period to which s/he was entitled. The employee will not, however, be entitled to claim damages for the

manner of the dismissal and is thereafter required to mitigate the loss, eg, find another job quickly. This point will be discussed below.

The main ways in which a contract comes to an end at common law may be divided into those which involve a **dismissal at common law** *and* those which require **no dismissal**.

Termination which may not involve dismissal at common law

Examples of this are:

(a) Frustration – contract comes to an end through no fault of either party
(b) Resignation by the employee
(c) Mutual agreement between the parties
(d) Expiry of a fixed-term contract
(e) Dissolution of a partnership or winding-up of a company

Termination involving dismissal at common law

Examples of this are:

(a) Employer dismisses with notice

(b) Employer dismisses without notice which may be:

 (i) Summary, ie, justified by way of breach by the employee (eg, gross misconduct) or

 (ii) Wrongful, ie, not justified under the terms of the contract; the best example being a failure to give contractual notice

10 Termination without dismissal

10.1 Frustration of the contract

Frustration occurs when, without fault of either party, the contract becomes impossible or unlawful to perform, or where there has been such a change in the significance of the contractual obligation that the performance of it would be fundamentally different from what the parties originally intended.

If a contract is frustrated, it comes to an end automatically by operation of law and neither party will be in breach or be able to claim against the other, other than for wages due up to the date of frustration. The two major events which have been held to be capable of frustrating a contract are long-term illness and imprisonment of the employee.

10.2 Frustration through illness

Long-term or permanent illness or injury which prevents the employee from performing duties may frustrate a contact. The courts have, however been reluctant to find contracts of employment frustrated because of sickness since it leaves the employee without any remedy. Moreover, it can undermine the statutory rights of the employee to claim unfair dismissal.

(a) The court must guard against too easy an application of the doctrine of frustration, especially when redundancy occurs and when the true reason may be a dismissal by reason of disability or other form of discrimination.

(b) An attempt to decide the relevant date may help to determine *in the mind of the court* whether it really is a true frustration situation.

(c) There are a number of factors which may help to decide the issue as they may each point in one or other direction. The factors which must be considered are:

   (i) The provisions of the contract, especially sickness absence and sick pay, (eg, do they point to acceptance by the employer of long-term absence?)

   (ii) The length of employment

   (iii) How long the employment could have been expected to last except for the absence

   (iv) Whether or not the employee held a key post

   (v) The nature of the illness, the prospects for recovery, and expected length of absence

   (vi) The need for the employer's work to be done (ie, whether the employer can afford for the work not to be carried out)

   (vii) Whether wages have continued to be paid

   (viii) The acts and statements of the parties, and

   (ix) Whether a reasonable employer be expected to wait longer.

The courts are reluctant to apply the doctrine of frustration because it undermines statutory rights which have been made clearer since the introduction of the Disability Discrimination Act 1995 (DDA) and subsequently the Equality Act 2010.

10.3 Imprisonment of the employee

If a prison sentence is imposed on an employee and the employer refuses to keep the job open for the employee's return, does the prison sentence amount to frustration of the contract? The employer may allege that it has come to an end by frustration because the employee can no longer perform the contract and that there is no further liability on the contract. The employee may argue that there has been no frustration of the contract since the imprisonment was his/her own fault and has nothing to do with the employer, so the contract has come to an end by dismissal. If the court accepts the employee's argument the employee may then be entitled to bring an action for unfair dismissal, even though in the majority of cases the dismissal would be justified and fair.

10.4 Resignation of the employee

An employee who resigns will generally have no rights under common law. It is the employee and not the employer who has terminated the contract. The employee must give **proper notice** in accordance with the contract otherwise they will be in breach unless the resignation is in response to a fundamental breach by the employer when this may give rise to a constructive dismissal.

> **Notice to be given by an employee**
>
> Unless otherwise stated in their contract an employee is required to give at least one week's notice if employed for one month or more. This minimum is unaffected by longer service.

The resignation must be purely voluntary; if pressure is placed on the employee to resign or s/he is dismissed, this could operate as a dismissal by the employer and enable the employee to make a claim for unfair dismissal. In such circumstances the employee may claim that the employer's behaviour was such that s/he was entitled to resign, alleging constructive dismissal.

10.5 Mutual agreement

An employment contract may be terminated by the mutual agreement of the parties. You should note that an automatic termination contract term, that is a term which states that the contact will come to an end automatically on the occurrence of an event is unlikely to be upheld. Mutual agreements not contingent on the **happening of an event** will, however be enforceable, eg, employer and employee expressly agree that the latter will resign and the contract end on a specific date.

10.6 Expiry of a fixed-term contract

At common law a fixed-term contract will expire at the end of the fixed-term and there is no dismissal in law. But, under The Fixed-term Employees (Prevention of Less Favourable Treatment) Regulations 2002 expiry of such a contract is a dismissal even though the parties have agreed an end-date. A fair dismissal will be for 'some other substantial reason'. Fixed-term contracts may contain notice periods known as a 'break clause'. This entitles the parties to bring the contract to an end earlier than the end-period. Some break clauses are inserted with reference to certain reasons, eg, illness or criminal conviction. Unless there is a break clause early termination will be a breach of contract unless:

(a) The other party has breached a fundamental term of the contract (eg, gross misconduct); or

(b) The termination is by mutual agreement.

The **Fixed-term Employees (Prevention of Less Favourable Treatment) Regulations 2002** provide that a fixed-term contract will terminate:

(a) On the expiry of its specific term

(b) On the completion of a particular task, or

(c) On the occurrence or non-occurrence of any other specific event other than the attainment of the employee of any normal and *bona fide* retirement age.

To have a policy of terminating fixed-term contracts once they had reached 51 weeks in duration, in order to avoid employees having sufficient service to claim unfair dismissal and other rights is likely to be viewed as a '**detrimental**' practice.

Receipt of a **statutory** redundancy payment breaks continuity for the purposes of qualification for a further statutory redundancy payment or claiming unfair dismissal. The exception is where having received the payment the employee is re-instated or re-engaged by the employer on terms which require the employee to repay the redundancy statutory payment in full. Where the employee receives a redundancy payment from the transferor in a transfer of undertakings situation, but is transferred to the service of the transferee employer without dismissal, the redundancy payment will not be counted as a statutory redundancy payment and, therefore continuity is preserved.

10.7 Dissolution of a partnership or winding-up of a company

Where a partnership is the employer, a change of partners will not usually affect the employees' contracts of employment. However, where the contract is of a personal nature, ie, the identities of the parties are of fundamental importance, and the relevant partner leaves, the employment contract is automatically terminated.

Where there is a compulsory winding-up of a company the employees' contracts will be automatically terminated.

These common law rules are superseded by statute which provides that the liquidation (insolvency) of a company or the dissolution of a partnership shall be treated as dismissal for the purposes of **redundancy**.

11 Dismissal with notice

A contract of employment for an indefinite term (a 'permanent' contract) can be terminated at any time by either party by giving proper notice. Provided the notice given accords with the terms of the contract there will be no further liability of either party under the common law.

In the unlikely event of there being no notice period stated in the contract a term is implied by law that the contract can be terminated by **reasonable notice**. What is 'reasonable' will depend upon the circumstances of each case; for example, the more senior the employee the longer the notice period required. The common law rules are complemented by statutory provisions which lay down statutory minimum periods of notice which must be given. The statutory minimum notice periods are set out and these prevail over any shorter contractual period and **cannot** be over-ridden.

The minimum legal notice period to be given by an employer is:

(a) One week's notice to an employee who has been continually employed for one month but less than two years

(b) One week's notice for each whole year of continuous employment for an employee with two years or more, but less than 12 years continuous employment

(c) At least 12 weeks notice for continuous service of 12 years or more.

Assuming that the employee does not have a **contractual obligation** to accept pay in lieu of notice, the employer may choose to give the employee payment in lieu of notice. Strictly speaking, the employee could refuse to accept the payment in lieu and bring an action for breach, but in practice, providing the payment is at least equivalent to the amount which the employee would have received in damages (assessed under the normal rules of contract), there would be no point in the employee refusing the payment in lieu.

12 Dismissal without notice

12.1 Wrongful dismissal

There may be circumstances in which the employee acts in such a way as to enable an employer to dismiss them without giving notice, for instance, if the employee commits a repudiatory breach of the contract. A justified dismissal without notice is called a **summary dismissal**. On the other hand, if the employer dismisses the employee without notice, or with short notice without justification this may be a **wrongful dismissal** and may entitle the employee to sue for damages for breach of the contract regardless of the length of time employed by that employer.

Wrongful dismissal can be defined as dismissal by the employer where there is a common law breach. The most common examples of wrongful dismissal are failure to give proper notice or where the employer has failed to follow their own disciplinary procedure correctly.

Remedies are limited to compensation for loss of earnings only. This type of action has normally been taken in the civil courts, but a breach on termination can now be pursued in the Employment Tribunal. Damages are the principle remedy and will encompass the amount due under due contract (had it been correctly performed).

13 Summary dismissal

In order to justify summary dismissal the employee must have breached an important (fundamental) express or implied term of the contract, ie, committed a **gross misconduct**. This breach will go to the '**root of the contract**'. There are a number of well recognised grounds on which the employer may dismiss an employee summarily, including:

- Refusal to obey reasonable orders
- Dishonesty
- Gross neglect
- Gross misconduct
- Any offences stipulated in the contract as being '*very serious*'.

The critical factor in deciding whether summary dismissal is justified in all these cases is the seriousness of the breach. One single act may be insufficient to justify summary dismissal unless it is very serious in its nature, whereas a persistent pattern of misconduct is more likely to provide grounds for such dismissal. Furthermore, misconduct outside the workplace is less likely to entitle the employer to dismiss summarily.

Whilst in such a cases, no previous warnings are necessary, the correct disciplinary procedure must be followed. This means that in most cases of gross misconduct a reasonable investigation of the facts should be undertaken.

Also when writing to the employee inviting them to the disciplinary hearing, it should be made clear that due to the severity of the allegation the outcome of the hearing could be dismissal.

In addition to summarily dismissing an employee who is in breach of contract, the employer may also be entitled to an **indemnity** from the employee for any loss suffered because of the breach. The employee may, for example, have breached the **duty of good faith** by revealing trade secrets causing loss to the employer, in which case the employer would have a claim for the loss incurred. In practice, however, this remedy is not often pursued by the employer since the employee will often not be in a financial position to meet an award of damages.

If an employer summarily dismisses an employee without good reason the contract will not come to an end until the employee accepts the breach, and until that time certain contractual rights and obligations survive (in particular rights and duties in respect of disciplinary procedure). It should be noted, however, that the courts will often **infer** that the breach has been accepted. In practice, this places the onus on the employer to show that the breach has not been accepted. In constructive dismissal cases this can be equated to the employee waiving the employer's conduct, and continuing to work.

14 Unjustified dismissal without notice

If the employer dismisses the employee without notice in circumstances where they are not entitled to do so this will amount to a wrongful dismissal.

If the employee is wrongfully dismissed they will be able to claim damages. The amount of damages which they will be able to claim is limited to the equivalent of net wages during the notice period plus damages for loss of other benefits to which they were entitled under the contract.

This may cover lost commission and fringe benefits such as a company car and pension rights, but no account is taken of the manner of the dismissal, for example for injury to feelings or false allegations. The employee, is however under a duty to **mitigate the loss** and must take steps to find alternative employment as soon as possible, but will only be expected to look for work of a similar kind at a similar level. Because of the limited damages which most employees could claim, the common law is considered in most cases to give an inadequate remedy for this reason and any employee who has been dismissed wrongfully and who qualifies for protection under the legislation will usually take an action for unfair dismissal.

15 Damages for breach of contract

Damages for breach of contract are assessed as follows.

Loss of wages. The starting point for the calculation in the case of a contract for an *indefinite period* is the wages which the employee would have earned during the proper contractual notice period.

Additional loss. In addition to the loss of wages, an employee may claim for loss of other benefits to which s/he was entitled under the contract such as commission. Generally, only pecuniary loss can be claimed and not loss for injured feelings for example, but, in exceptional cases, actors and apprentices have been able to claim for loss of future prospects.

Duty to mitigate. The employee is under a duty to mitigate the loss and when the contract has been terminated s/he must try to find other employment. If s/he refuses suitable alternative employment or does not seek employment s/he will not be entitled to damages in respect of the loss which would have been mitigated.

Benefits reducing the loss. Where the employer has paid money in lieu of notice to the employee this will be taken into account in assessing the damages awarded. Additionally, certain other benefits such as unemployment benefit will be set-off against the damages awarded.

Tax and National Insurance. The general rule is that any income tax and National Insurance contributions which would have been paid on the wages, if earned, will be deducted in assessing damages payable.

Trade unions, employee communications and participation

1 Introduction

In this chapter the legislation associated with the scope of trade unions and their rights are reviewed along with the issues of recognition and industrial action.

The chapter also looks at the legislation associated with formal employee communication and the National Works Councils Directive.

1.1 What is a trade union

A trade union is: '......*an organisation (temporary or permanent)*

(a) Which consists wholly or mainly of workers of one or more descriptions and whose principal purposes include the regulation of relations between workers of that description or those descriptions and employers or employers' associations; or

(b) Which consists wholly or mainly of.....constituent or affiliated organisations [and their representatives whose principal purpose is the regulation of relations as in (a) above or between its constituent or affiliated organisations].' *(**Definition of a Trade Union (Trade Union and Labour Relations (Consolidation) Act – TULR(C)A 1992, s.1 (1))**

The definition can also include a body which is 'concerned with the professional interests of its members'.

The union must have some form and structure, although a formal constitution is not required.

1.2 Legal status

Trade unions are unincorporated associations (and, therefore, do not have any legal identity at common law); this means a union is the sum total of its members. Statute, however has provided them with certain limited legal personality and attributes to enable them to operate effectively within the law. They are to:

(a) Make contracts

(b) Sue or be sued in its own name (the latter being subject to the immunities for civil action)

(c) Be a defendant in criminal proceedings

(d) Own property, which *must* be vested in trustees, and

(e) Be subject to judgements, orders and awards and any other court orders.

Because a trade union does not have general *legal personality* it cannot sue others for libel, slander and so on. The above legal status depends on a union being deemed '**independent**' of the employer by the Certification Officer. Non-independence would, for instance exist where the employer established an in-house staff association which could not collectively bargain with the employer and call for strike action by the employees. In other words, an independent union is one which is not under the domination of the employer and is free from interference from any other body.

In order to establish 'independence' the union does *not* have to be 'listed' by the Certification Officer (as was the case during the period of the Industrial Relations Act 1971 –1974). For a union which does, however, register with the Certification Officer there are certain tax exemptions and *prima facie* evidence of it being a trade union in any legal proceedings. The Certification Officer may withdraw independent status from a union at any time. The union may subsequently appeal against this decision before the EAT, on a question of fact *or* law. Where an unlisted union is involved in a legal dispute and claims 'independence', those legal proceedings will be stayed pending a finding by the Certification Officer.

2 Recognition

2.1 Recognition for the purposes of collective bargaining

An independent union which can gain recognition from an employer for the purposes of collective bargaining enjoys certain legal rights which were first established in the 1970s:

(a) The right to be **provided with information** for the purposes of collective bargaining (eg, annual profits)

(b) The right to be **consulted on health & safety matters**

(c) The right to be **consulted about proposed redundancies** from amongst the respective workforce

(d) The right to be **consulted about a proposed transfer of undertaking** in which the respective union has members

(e) The right for its officials to be given **reasonable paid time-off** to carry out trade union duties, and for its members to be given reasonable unpaid time-off to carry out union activities

(f) The **right to information** on **occupational pensions**, and

(g) The **right to be consulted and informed about training** for the employer's workers.

2.2 The meaning of union recognition and collective bargaining

Recognition means that a trade union is recognised by one employer, or two or more associated employers, to any extent, for the purposes of collective bargaining.

Collective bargaining is defined as 'negotiations relating to or connected with' one or more of the following matters:

(a) Terms and conditions of employment or physical working conditions

(b) Engagement, non-engagement, termination or suspension of employment, or the duties of employment, of one or more workers

(c) Allocation of work or the duties of employment as between workers or groups of workers

(d) Matters of discipline

(e) Facilities for union officials

(f) A worker's membership or non-membership of a trade union; and

(g) Machinery for negotiation or consultation or any other procedures relating to (a) – (f) above, including recognition, and the right of a union to represent workers.

Collective agreements are *only* enforceable between union(s) and employer(s) in common law if the parties expressly or implicitly intend to be bound. Otherwise, they will be binding in honour only.

The TULR(C)A 1992 takes this further by stating that there is a presumption in law that a collective agreement will *not* be legally binding except where a contrary intention is expressed in *writing*.

Incorporation: Although not legally enforceable between the parties the terms of collective agreements are commonly *incorporated* into individual employee's contracts of employment and these terms subsequently have the same legal force as any other contractual term. Typically, **express** reference will be made in the employee's Statement of Principal Terms and Conditions along the lines:

'.......your terms and conditions may be changed from time to time as a result of agreements made between (the employer) and the Staffs' Side/X trade union .....' Whether any term of a collective agreement has been incorporated into an individual contract of employment is a matter of law.

Sometimes, in the absence of express terms, the courts will be prepared to imply incorporation. However there must be 'recognisable contractual intent' between employee/employer for the incorporation to take effect.

There must be evidence that the employee has accepted incorporation. Incorporation may also be achieved by custom and practice (where the incorporation is certain, notorious and reasonable and is an accepted industry or employer practice). This would be the case where the employer had always acted upon increases agreed in national or regional collective bargaining of which they were, however, not a participant. Subsequent detachment from such an arrangement may give rise to a variation of contract.

3 Rights of independent recognised trade unions

3.1 The right to be provided with information for the purposes of collective bargaining

The information must be provided in accordance with good industrial relations practice so that failure to disclose would materially impede the conduct of collective bargaining. Examples of specific information are contained in the **ACAS Code of Practice No. 2 on Disclosure of Information to Trade Unions for Collective Bargaining Purposes (1998)**.

Where the information provided is genuinely relevant for collective bargaining the union may make other (lawful) use of that information. Certain categories of confidential information are protected from disclosure, eg, trade secrets or where disclosure would cause substantial injury to the employer's undertakings.

A trade union which reasonably believes that an employer has failed to disclose certain information may appeal to the Central Arbitration Committee (CAC) for a declaration to that effect. Failure to abide by the declaration could render the employer liable to an award, and an order amending the terms and conditions of employment of any employee affected.

3.2 The right to consultation on health and safety matters

The **Health and Safety at Work Act 1974** entitles recognised trade unions to appoint safety representatives. The Act obliges every employer with such safety representatives to consult them on promoting and developing effective health and safety measures. Where two or more safety representatives request the establishment of a safety committee the employer must comply with this request.

Arrangements for consultation, appointment of safety representatives and the functioning of safety committees are provided in the HSE guide **'Consulting Employees on Health and Safety'** *(www.hse.gov.uk)*. Where there is no recognised trade union, employers must either consult directly with employees *or* elected representatives.

3.3 The right to be consulted about proposed redundancies from amongst the workforce

This right becomes effective where the employer is proposing to dismiss at least 20 employees within a period of 90 days. The purpose of the consultation must be to reach agreement on how the redundancies will be managed, including mitigating the effects on individual employees.

3.4 The right to be consulted about a proposed transfer of undertakings in which the respective union has members

In situations of proposed employee transfers employers' duty to consult on a transfer is similar to the duty on mass redundancies (above).

The employer must inform and consult either the trade union or, if there is none, with correctly elected employee representatives. If a representative is not elected then the information will be given to the affected employee. The affected employees may be those of the transferor or transferee. Although the duty to consult is that of the employer, they must also pass on any measures which the transferee envisages. The transferee must give the transferor this information. The purpose of the consultation must be to reach an agreement on how the transfer should be conducted.

3.5 Trade union officials – paid time-off

An employer who recognises an independent trade union for the purposes of collective bargaining is obliged to grant reasonable paid time-off to an employee who is an official of that union. The time-off must be for the **purposes of carrying-out official duties** which are connected with any matters that fall within the Act (TULR(C)A 1992).

The law was changed in 1989 so that the type of activity for which a trade union official could claim paid time-off was restricted. A government minister said in the House of Commons during the Parliamentary debate on the changes:

A union official should not '......have a licence to go round stirring-up trouble at their workplace or at other people's workplaces and being paid for doing so by the employer for whom they are supposed to be working'. **[Hansard: January 1989]**

The restricted duties now must concern either negotiations (added in 1989) with the employer (not associated employers) *or* other functions which the employer has agreed that the union official may perform. Any negotiations for which time-off is sought must be on matters in respect of which the union has been recognised by the employer for the purposes of collective bargaining. The negotiations or functions must be 'related to or connected with' matters which fall within s 178 (2). Requests for time-off to *undertake training* must relate to those items listed in s 178 (2). Inter-union discussions are not covered as a permissible reason for time-off. The attendance by the official at a meeting or to undertake training must be required by the respective union, and approved by the union or by the TUC.

The **ACAS Code of Practice No. 3 on Time-off for Trade Union duties and Activities (January 2010)** provides guidelines on the circumstances and duration of granting time-off.

'The subject connected with collective bargaining may include one or more of the following:

(a) Terms and conditions of employment, or the physical conditions in which workers are required to work. Examples could include:

- Pay
- Hours of work
- Holidays and holiday pay
- Sick pay arrangements
- Pensions
- Learning and training
- Equality and diversity
- Notice periods
- The working environment
- Operation of digital equipment and other machinery;

(b) Engagement or non engagement, or termination or suspension of employment or the duties of employment, of one or more workers. Examples could include:

- Recruitment and selection policies
- Human resource planning
- Redundancy and dismissal arrangements;

(c) Allocation of work or the duties of employment as between workers or groups of workers. Examples could include:

- Job grading
- Job evaluation
- Job descriptions
- Flexible working practices
- Work-life balance;

(d) Matters of discipline. Examples could include:

- Disciplinary procedures
- Arrangements for representing or accompanying employees at internal interviews
- Arrangements for appearing on behalf of trade union members, or as witnesses, before agreed outside appeal bodies or employment tribunals;

(e) Trade union membership or non membership. Examples could include:

- representational arrangements
- any union involvement in the induction of new workers;

(f) Facilities for trade union representatives. Examples could include any agreed arrangements for the provision of:

- accommodation
- equipment
- names of new workers to the union;

(g) Machinery for negotiation or consultation and other procedures. Examples could include arrangements for:

- collective bargaining at the employer and/or multi-employer level
- grievance procedures
- joint consultation
- communicating with members
- communicating with other union representatives and union full-time officers concerned with collective bargaining with the employer.'

(See: www.acas.gov.uk).

3.6 Trade union members – unpaid time-off

Employers are obliged to grant reasonable **unpaid** time-off to an employee who is a member of an independent recognised union to carry out specified trade union activities. The time-off may, therefore be taken during working hours. Any form of activity **'in furtherance or contemplation of a trade dispute'**, eg, planning a strike is excluded.

Activities covered would include hearing trade union officials explain an offer of a pay rise from the employer.

3.7 Remedies

Failure on the part of an employer to agree to time-off gives the trade union official or member concerned the right to present an application for redress to an Employment Tribunal. Where the complaint is justified the tribunal will make a declaration to that effect and may order compensation to be paid the individual concerned. An application may also be made in respect of non-payment by the employer, in which case the tribunal may make an order for the individual to receive the sum due. Any complaint to the Employment Tribunal must be made within three months of the date of the act complained of.

3.8 Disclosure of information on pensions

Trustees of an occupational pension scheme are obliged to disclose certain information to recognised trade unions/members. Particular rules apply to basic scheme information, constitution/rules of scheme, and annual reports. Failure to comply can lead to civil penalties applied by the Occupational Pensions Regulatory Authority.

3.9 Information and consultation on training

The **Employment Relations Act 1999** allowed a recognised union the right to be invited 'from time to time' to send representatives to a meeting to be:

- Consulted about the employer's policy on training for workers within the bargaining unit

- Consulted about the employer's plans for training for those workers during the period of six months starting with the day of the meeting, and

- Informed about training provided for these workers since the previous meeting

- The employer should 'take account of' any written observations during any four-week period following a meeting, so the power to influence training policy is very limited.

The relevant information should be provided for the union representatives no later than two weeks before each meeting to enable them to 'participate meaningfully'. Complaints by a union should be to the Employment Tribunal.

4 Trade union membership and refusal of employment

It is unlawful to refuse an individual employment on the grounds of being or not being a member of a trade union. In addition, their unwillingness to accept a requirement to become a member of a union or to cease being a member, or their suffering financial penalty for the same reasons (eg, deductions in wages) is unlawful.

4.1 Remedies

An individual who believes they have a complaint under the above must submit an application to the Employment Tribunal within three months of the conduct complained of. The employer and the relevant trade union may be joined in the action where it is alleged the latter exercised pressure on the former. The tribunal may order compensation. Also, the tribunal may recommend that the respondent takes action to obviate or reduce the effect of their conduct. Where an employee has been dismissed and the tribunal's order for reinstatement or re-engagement has not been complied with, the tribunal may make an order for a special award.

Union membership agreements ('closed shop') whether they be pre-entry or post-entry, are unlawful.

5 Detriment on trade union grounds

5.1 Statutory provisions

All employees, regardless of length of service, are protected against being subjected to any *detriment* as an individual by *any act or any deliberate failure to act*, by the employer if the act or failure takes place for the sole or main purpose of:

(a)   Preventing or deterring the employee from being or seeking to become a member of an independent trade union, or penalising the employee for doing so

(b)   Preventing or deterring the employee from taking part in the activities of an independent trade union at an appropriate time (eg, outside working hours or at customarily agreed times during working hours), or penalising the employee for doing so

(c) Preventing or deterring the employee from making use of trade union services at an appropriate time, or penalising the employee for doing so, or

(d) Compelling the employee to be or become a member of any trade union or of a particular trade union or of one of a number of particular trade unions.

5.2 Remedies

On successful complaint to the Employment Tribunal a compensatory payment is payable. If a tribunal finds a complaint to be well-founded, it must make a declaration to that effect and may make an award of compensation to the employee. Compensation should be such an amount that the tribunal considers just and equitable having regard to the infringement of the complainant's right by the employer's action, and any loss which is attributable to the employer's action.

6 Dismissal for trade union reasons

S 152(1) TULR(C)A 1992 (amended by the Employment Relations Act 2004) provides that it is automatically unfair dismissal if the principal reason for the dismissal of the employee is that s/he:

- Was, or proposed to become a member of an independent trade union
- Had taken part, or proposed to take part, in the activities of an independent trade union at an appropriate time
- Had made use, or proposed to make use, of trade union services at an appropriate time
- Had failed to accept an offer made in contravention of section 145A or 145B, or
- Was not a member of any trade union, or of a particular trade union, or one of a number of particular trade unions, or had refused, or proposed to refuse to become or remain a member. (This upholds the unlawfulness of a 'closed shop'.)

6.1 Remedies

A complaint must be lodged with the Employment Tribunal within three months beginning with the effective date of termination. A basic award and a compensatory award may be ordered by the tribunal.

7 'Compulsory' trade union recognition (introduced by the 1999 Employment Relations Act)

7.1 Introduction

In this section we examine rules for unions to seek compulsory recognition and the right to negotiate with employers for the purposes of collective bargaining.

7.2 The sources of statutory trade union recognition

In June 2000 the trade union recognition laws came into effect. They are set-out in Schedule 1 to the **Employment Relations Act 1999** – this was inserted into the TULR(C)Act 1992 Schedule A1 which is where the detailed provisions can be found. This Schedule has been amended by: the tribunals, courts and Enforcement Act 2007 and the Employment Relations Act 2004. It has also been partially repealed by the Employment Relations Act 2004. This Schedule is divided into a number of relevant Parts.

7.3 The rules on seeking compulsory recognition

The following provisions in Part I of the statute summarises the basic procedures for seeking and determining recognition, but halt when the employer accepts the majority of the workforce want a union and recognises one or complies with a Central Arbitration Committee (CAC) declaration. At that point the employer enters into collective bargaining with the trade union, but once the statutory recognition procedure is triggered there are legal constraints on the exact nature of the subsequent collective agreement.

(a) **Application by union to CAC for recognition**

Part I sets out the procedure under which an independent trade union (TU) can apply to the CAC (**Central Arbitration Committee**) for a declaration requiring a specific named employer to recognise the TU as being entitled to conduct 'collective bargaining' on behalf of a group or groups ('bargaining unit') of workers.

The CAC will only issue such a declaration where:

(i) The 10 per cent test is satisfied. This is satisfied if members of the union (or unions) constitute at least 10 per cent of the workers constituting the relevant bargaining unit, and

(ii) A majority of the workers constituting the relevant bargaining unit would be likely to favour recognition or the union (or unions) as entitled to conduct collective bargaining on behalf of the bargaining unit. (Majority = at least 40 per cent of the workers constituting the bargaining unit).

This process is limited to employers who employ 21 or more workers.

There must not already be in force a collective agreement entitling one or more TUs to conduct collective bargaining on behalf of any workers in the bargaining unit, although there are some very specific exceptions. The compulsory recognition procedures are not a means of introducing multi-unionism.

There is no strict burden of proof in satisfying the above provisions. CAC must be 'satisfied' of the relevant matters. However, although it appears unnecessary and surprising in reaching a number of decisions the CAC has referred to its reliance on the 'balance of probabilities' for determining these matters.

The Central Arbitration Committee

The Central Arbitration Committee is a permanent independent body with statutory powers whose main function is to adjudicate on applications relating to the statutory recognition and derecognition of trade unions for collective bargaining purposes, where such recognition or derecognition cannot be agreed voluntarily.

In addition, the CAC has a statutory role in determining disputes between trade unions and employers over the disclosure of information for collective bargaining purposes, and in resolving applications and complaints under the following regulations. The areas of dispute with which the CAC currently deals are:

i. Applications for the statutory recognition and derecognition of trade unions
ii. Applications for the disclosure of information for collective bargaining
iii. Applications and complaints under the Information and Consultation Regulations
iv. Disputes over the establishment and operation of European Works Councils
v. Complaints under the employee involvement provisions of Regulations enacting legislation relating to European companies, cooperative societies and cross-border mergers

The CAC and its predecessors have also provided voluntary arbitration in collective disputes. This role has not been used for some years.

Objectives are:

1. To achieve outcomes which are practicable, lawful, impartial, and where possible voluntary.
2. To give a courteous and helpful service to all who approach us.
3. To provide an efficient service, and to supply assistance and decisions as rapidly as is consistent with good standards of accuracy and thoroughness.
4. To provide good value for money to the taxpayer, through effective corporate governance and internal controls.
5. To develop a CAC secretariat with the skills knowledge and experience to meet operational objectives, valuing diversity and maintaining future capability.

(The CAC website *www.cac.gov.uk*)

(b) **The 'ten per cent' test**

Naturally, some employers are dismissive of the fact that at least ten per cent of workers are already TU members, but the truth is that many employers simply do not know exactly how many are in membership of one or more TUs. To attempt to clarify matters CAC often asks the employer to provide a list of workers in the bargaining unit and requests a list of members from the

TU for the same bargaining unit. Neither list will be disclosed to the other party, and CAC has refused to comply with such a disclosure request from employers. The two lists can then be compared to see if it appears that ten per cent are indeed members of the TU.

(c) **The 'majority likely to support test'**

This is a fairly difficult and contentious area. In practice, unions with less than 50 per cent membership in their proposed bargaining unit will usually seek to introduce evidence of employee support by, for example, petitions that aim to demonstrate that a majority of employees want recognition. The CAC adopts a broad-brush approach stressing that it is not a mathematical test and that each particular CAC panel will rely on its own experience of recognition issues.

(d) **Existing recognition**

The CAC will not admit an application for recognition under the statutory procedure if 'there is already in force a collective under which a union is (or unions are) recognised as entitled to conduct collective bargaining on behalf of any workers falling within the relevant bargaining unit.' If there is an overlap of only one employee between the bargaining unit claimed by the union and that already granted to another union, the application will fail. It is possible for an employer to recognise a trade union other than that which brings the CAC claim, even if the first union has no real strength or membership in the bargaining unit.

(e) **Deciding the bargaining unit**

Where CAC is required to determine the bargaining unit because the parties cannot agree on one themselves it must consider the need for the bargaining unit to be 'compatible with effective management', and moreover to take into account:

(i) The views of the employer and the TU

(ii) Existing bargaining arrangements – national and local

(iii) The desirability of avoiding small fragmented bargaining units within an undertaking

(iv) The characteristics of workers falling within the proposed bargaining unit and any other employees of the employer whom the CAC considers relevant, and

(v) The location of the workers.

(f) **CAC declaration**

Once a declaration has been issued the employer and the TU should agree a 'method of collective bargaining'. Where they cannot agree, one or both parties may apply to CAC to impose a method. The potential difficulty for both parties in pursuing this option is that the method of collective bargaining imposed by CAC cannot be unilaterally ended by either party before the end of a three-year period, except through the de-recognition procedures.

(g) **Ballots**

Of course, CAC may decide to declare a union is recognised without the need for a ballot (where the majority of workers in the bargaining unit are already members of the union).

However, where certain conditions exist, CAC may decide that a ballot of the workers in the identified bargaining unit must take place to clearly determine whether the TU should be recognised even though there is a majority of union members in the bargaining unit.

These conditions are that:

(i) It is 'in the interests of good industrial relations', as determined by the CAC

(ii) A 'significant number' of the TU members inform CAC they do not want the union (or unions) to conduct collective bargaining on their behalf

(iii) There is 'membership evidence' that casts doubt on the members' wishes that the union should conduct collective bargaining on their behalf.

Also, a ballot may be held where CAC concludes that there has been a change in the bargaining unit or where there is a shortfall in membership below 50 per cent.

For recognition to take place the CAC must issue a declaration of recognition, but only where a majority of voters in the ballot and more than 40 per cent of all workers in the bargaining unit have voted for recognition.

The ballot may be at the workplace, be postal or a combination of both, at the decision of CAC. A Code of Practice on the balloting arrangements has been issued that contains guidance on the detailed workings of the ballot (Department for Business Innovation and Skills – *Access and unfair practices during recognition and de-recognition ballots* and *Industrial action, ballots and notice to employers*). The union and the employer are under a duty to co-operate generally to ensure the ballot is properly carried out and to co-operate with the person appointed to conduct the ballot.

A TU that fails to gain recognition is prohibited from re-applying for statutory recognition for three years.

Ballots may also be necessary for de-recognition of the union.

(h) **Access to workers**

Where a ballot is held in connection with the recognition or de-recognition procedures the TU must be allowed access to workers in the period leading up to the ballot.

8 The rules on seeking compulsory collective bargaining rights

8.1 Introduction

The rules found in Part II of the statute deal with the situation where, having been recognised by an employer, the TU abandons the compulsory route prematurely because the employer has decided to recognise the TU. But, once the statutory procedures are triggered the parties are now constrained by the type of collective agreement they may draw up.

Part II contains a specification for the satisfying conditions of '**an agreement for recognition**'. The parties' agreement must now satisfy these conditions. Where disagreement arises over the content of the agreement either party can appeal to the CAC for the agreement to be imposed. In other words, either party will ask the CAC to impose a method of collective bargaining in the same way as described above for a Part I recognition. However, there is one difference: although the agreement cannot be terminated for three years the employer does not have to follow any special de-recognition procedure to bring it to an end.

8.2 Part III

The flexibility sought by many TUs and employers is found in Part III of the Act. This permits the parties or CAC to select a new bargaining unit if changes to the employer's business mean that the original bargaining unit is no longer appropriate. A slightly different procedure exists where the original bargaining unit has ceased to exist and, therefore, the original bargaining arrangements should be terminated.

8.3 Imposed collective bargaining

Where recognition has been settled and, even where with the assistance of the CAC, the parties have attempted to agree on collective bargaining arrangements and failed, either party may then apply to CAC for it to specify the formal bargaining arrangements.

The bargaining method to be adopted is known as the '**specified method**' and will be legally enforceable. However, the agreement, including its legal status can be amended by joint agreement.

It is important to differentiate voluntary collective bargaining and 'specified' collective bargaining. The latter only includes bargaining in respect of:

- Pay
- Hours
- Holidays, and
- The two parties are required to establish a Joint Negotiating Body (JNB) to discuss/negotiate these rights.

JNB members must be given paid time-off for JNB meetings plus a two-hour pre-meeting and a day-long preparation meeting prior to the full meeting of the JNB. Reasonable time-off must also be given to consult with members and facilities provided to enable the whole process to be completed. Similarly, the rules on disclosure of information for the purposes of collective bargaining must be followed.

CAC is empowered to depart from the specified method when fixing the bargaining method where it thinks appropriate.

9 De-recognition

9.1 How de-recognition occurs

This occurs where the employer takes the positive step to terminate all agreements with the TU and prevents the TU acting on behalf of and representing the workers in the former bargaining unit insofar as the employer is concerned with respect to collective bargaining.

Either the employer or workers may seek de-recognition. A ballot will be called by CAC where:

(a)   The employer's application to end recognition is accepted by CAC; and/or
(b)   The workers' application is similarly accepted.

This covers voluntary and automatic statutory recognition, and situations where the parties cannot satisfactorily resolve their differences without resorting to a ballot.

10 Summary time-scale of the recognition procedures

10.1 Basic pre-conditions

(a) Employer has 21+ workers
(b) Request must be from independent trade union

↓

Employer must respond in 10 days (these refer to working days).

↓

Recognition or a further 20 days in which employer can negotiate with the TU on the bargaining unit and the terms of recognition [Opportunity for employer to avoid statutory scheme]

↓

| Either party can ask ACAS for help | → | No agreement: CAC asked to examine the case |

↓

Case resolved
CAC can declare an agreement and 'recognition'. CAC will assist in identifying the method of bargaining. [Employer cannot break agreement for 3 years]

↓

Employer rejects request for recognition.

↓

TU applies to CAC. CAC must identify the bargaining unit and determine whether TU has majority support amongst workers therein. If no majority the claim for recognition is dismissed.

↓

But, if the ten per cent rule is satisfied, *and* CAC is satisfied that a majority of the bargaining unit *'would be likely to favour recognition'*, *and* the employer still rejects the application

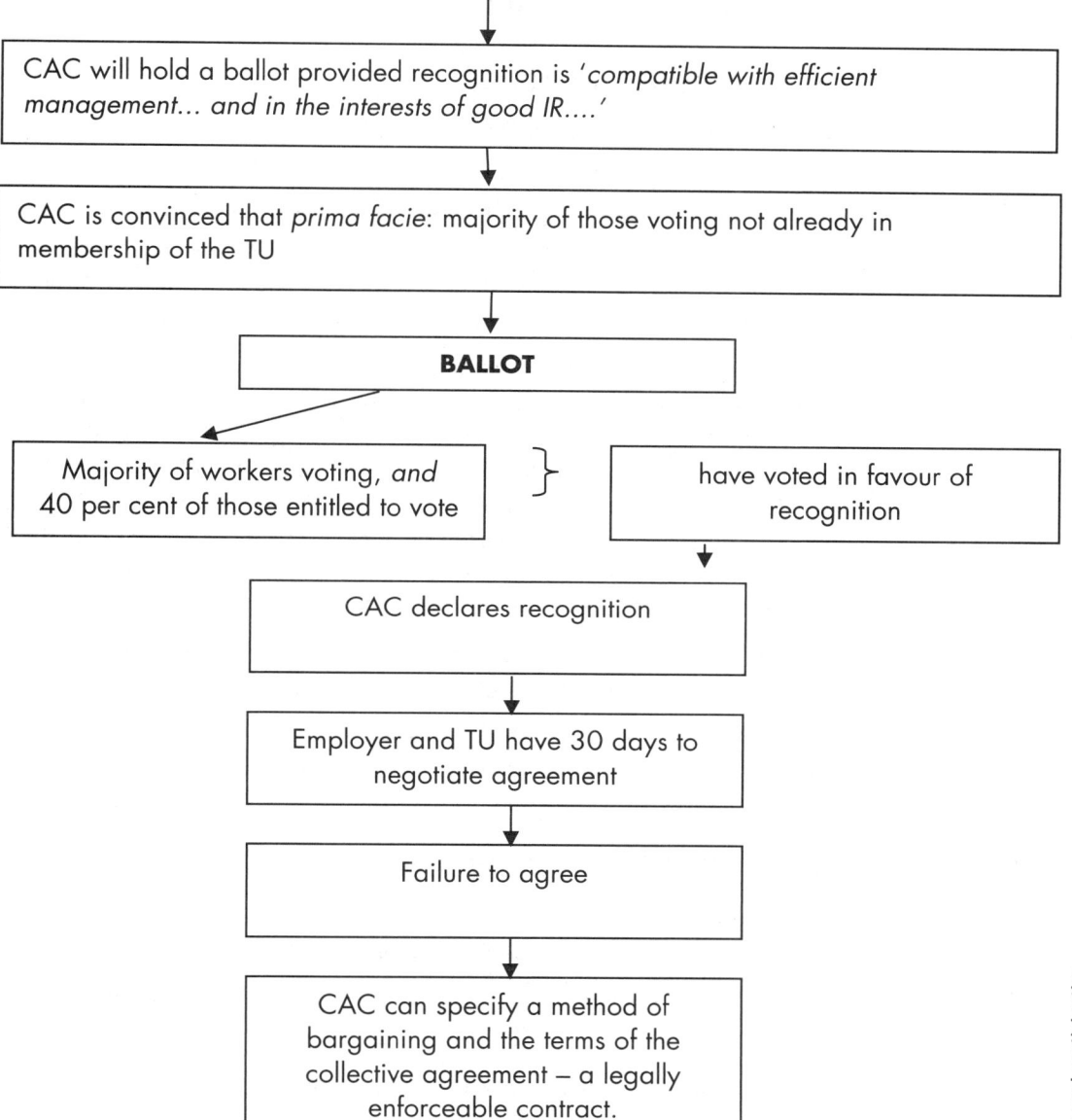

```
                    ↓
┌─────────────────────────────────────────────────────────────┐
│ CAC will hold a ballot provided recognition is 'compatible   │
│ with efficient management... and in the interests of good IR....' │
└─────────────────────────────────────────────────────────────┘
                    ↓
┌─────────────────────────────────────────────────────────────┐
│ CAC is convinced that prima facie: majority of those voting  │
│ not already in membership of the TU                          │
└─────────────────────────────────────────────────────────────┘
                    ↓
              ┌──────────┐
              │ BALLOT   │
              └──────────┘
              ↙          ↘
┌──────────────────────────┐   ┌──────────────────────────┐
│ Majority of workers      │   │ have voted in favour of  │
│ voting, and 40 per cent  │ } │ recognition              │
│ of those entitled to vote│   │                          │
└──────────────────────────┘   └──────────────────────────┘
                    ↓
         ┌──────────────────────┐
         │ CAC declares         │
         │ recognition          │
         └──────────────────────┘
                    ↓
         ┌──────────────────────┐
         │ Employer and TU have │
         │ 30 days to negotiate │
         │ agreement            │
         └──────────────────────┘
                    ↓
         ┌──────────────────────┐
         │ Failure to agree     │
         └──────────────────────┘
                    ↓
         ┌──────────────────────┐
         │ CAC can specify a    │
         │ method of bargaining │
         │ and the terms of the │
         │ collective agreement │
         │ – a legally          │
         │ enforceable contract.│
         └──────────────────────┘
```

[**NB**: It must be appreciated that the above summarises the provisions of the statutory recognition procedure which is highly complex!]

11 Industrial action and picketing

11.1 Definition of industrial action

According to the Employment Rights Act 1996 a 'strike' is:

'.....the cessation of work...or a concerted refusal...to continue to work for an employer...done as a means of compelling their employer or any employed person or body of employed persons, or to aid other employees, in compelling their employer or any employed person or body of employed persons, to accept or not to accept terms or conditions of or affecting employment'.

However, it should be noted that this definition specifically relates to continuity of employment. **Industrial action** relates to steps taken by employees which may not go as far as an outright strike – for instance, a **'work-to-rule'**, **'go-slow'** or refusal to undertake certain duties. Similarly, there is no specific definition of industrial action short of a strike. Any form of 'strike' will generally constitute gross misconduct and a repudiatory breach of contract on the part of the employee concerned, entitling the employer to subsequently summarily dismiss. A threat to go on strike at some future date would not normally constitute a breach of contract.

Industrial action short of a strike will normally constitute a repudiatory breach of contract insofar that the implied terms of:

- Not wilfully obstructing the employer's business, and
- Mutual trust and confidence will have been breached.

11.2 Trade union liability in industrial action

Insofar as industrial action is concerned, the following protection is afforded to a union provided it strictly remains in 'contemplation or furtherance of a trade dispute':

- Immunity from inducing another to break a contract or interfere with its performance
- Immunity from threatening to break a contract or inducing another to threaten to break a contract, and where the
- Dispute is between workers and **their** employer.

Immunity can be **removed** by:

(a) Failure to conduct a proper secret ballot

(b) Undertaking secondary industrial action

(c) Undertaking unlawful picketing (including secondary picketing)

(d) There is a trade dispute but the action has not been called in contemplation or furtherance of that dispute

(e) Failure to provide the required notice of official industrial action to employers likely to be affected, following the ballot

(f) The action is intended to promote union closed shop practices, or to prevent employers using non-union firms as suppliers

(g) The action is in support of any employee dismissed while taking unofficial industrial action

(h) The action involves unlawful picketing.

Should a trade union lose immunity it may be liable for damages as a result of a civil action in tort as follows:

(a) Direct inducement of another to breach a contract, or interfere with the performance of a contract

(b) Indirect inducement to breach a contract by unlawful means

(c) Intimidation – threatening to induce a breach of contract or interfere with the performance of a contract, and/or

(d) Conspiracy to commit one of these torts (unless repudiated by the union).

These are known as the **economic torts**.

12 The economic torts

12.1 Direct inducement of a breach of contract

For a trade union to commit a tort outside the protection of the statutory immunities it must have known that the employee's contract with the employer will have been broken by their inducement of the employee to take industrial action.

Where the TU operates within the statutory framework for calling industrial action the union will be protected by the immunities. However, where a commercial contract is broken the union will no longer be protected from immunity. Several employers used this tort as a cause of action against unions during the 1980s.

12.2 Intimidation

This tort occurs where there is a **threat** of the use of unlawful means, resulting in direct or indirect harm to the plaintiff (employer).

```
        ┌─────────────────────────────┐
        │ Trade union (which must     │
        │ foresee or intend harm to the│
        │ employer)                   │
        └─────────────────────────────┘
                    │         │
                    ▼         ▼
┌──────────────────────────┐     ┌──────────────────────────────┐
│ Direct threat of industrial│   │ Indirect threat of industrial │
│ action                    │    │ action through its members    │
│                          │     │ who are employees of the      │
│                          │     │ employer                      │
└──────────────────────────┘     └──────────────────────────────┘

        ┌─────────────────────────────┐
        │ Employer                    │
        │ Suffers harm eg they decide to│
        │ shut down a premises or cancel│
        │ an order                    │
        └─────────────────────────────┘
```

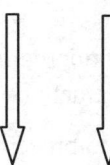

12.3 Conspiracy

Conspiracy occurs when **two or more** persons commit an unlawful act *or* carry-out a lawful act by unlawful means. The conspirators need **not intend** to cause harm, but nonetheless harm is caused to the employer.

12.4 Indirect or direct inducement to break a contract

This can be described diagrammatically.

Direct inducement

Direct intimidation

The diagram below shows how **direct inducement to break a contract** can take place.

This would occur where the union placed direct pressure on the employees.

SHOP STEWARD (representing trade union)	**FULL-TIME UNION OFFICIAL**

```
Plans with one or more
employees who are union         ←——— Direct inducement ———┐
members for them to break their                            │
contract of employment                                     │
                                                           │
CONTRACT OF EMPLOYMENT                                     │
subsequently broken with employer                          │
                                                           │
Their EMPLOYER – suffers        ←——— Direct intimidation ──┘
harm
```

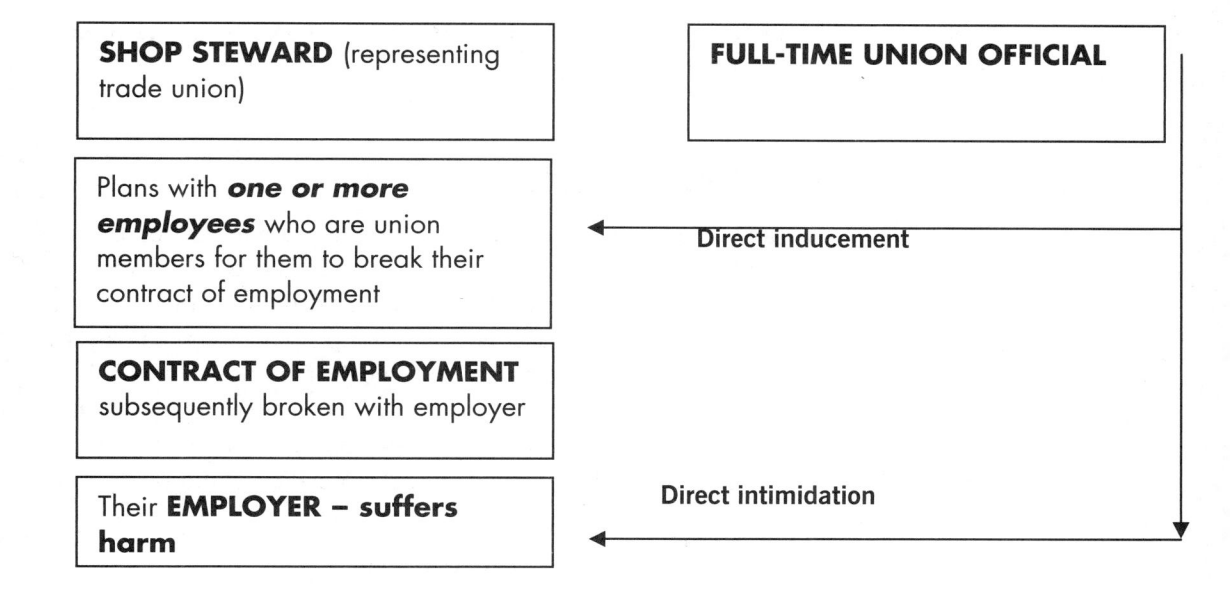

12.5 Intentional interference with a contract, trade or business

The unlawful action may not actually cause a breach. Interference occurs where conduct of the union deliberately prevents or hinders a party from performing a contract. The conduct must be with knowledge of the relevant contract or recklessness as to its existence.

The respective trade union may be liable if the above torts are committed with the endorsement or authorisation of the union. This can be done by anyone empowered to do so by the union's rules, the principal executive committee, president or general secretary of the union, or other union committee, group or person with the role of organising/co-ordinating industrial action. The trade union can avoid liability if it repudiates the action. To do this certain steps must be strictly followed.

(a) The employees (union members) concerned and the local union 'official' **responsible** and the employer concerned must be unequivocally informed of the repudiation as soon as reasonably practicable by a 'responsible person' eg, member of Executive Committee, President or General Secretary

(b) The union or its local officials must not act **inconsistently** with the repudiation

(c) The repudiation must be 'public', and

(d) A statement must be included informing the members that anyone dismissed while taking *unofficial* industrial action will have no right to claim unfair dismissal if the protected period does not apply.

A defence used by a union that it did not have control over its officials, stewards or members will be subject to the utmost scrutiny by the courts.

13 Secondary industrial action

It is unlawful for a trade union to induce an employee to break their contract of employment (or to interfere with the performance of a contract (eg, a commercial contract) or to induce another to do so) where that contract **is not** with the employer party to a particular dispute. In other words, where the employer of those employees who break their contracts (or any other contract) at the behest of the union is **not** a party to the trade dispute in question, the action will fall outside the immunities. It cannot, therefore be argued that within the terms of the narrowed immunities the union is engaged in a dispute with this employer in 'contemplation or furtherance' of a trade dispute.

The following can be considered to be **'secondary'** action:

(a) Where all employer members of an Employers' Association are in dispute with their workers and those of one employer assist other workers of an employer other than their own, **even though both** employers are members of the same association

(b) Inducing a breach of a contract for services issued to self-employed and freelance workers (this is deemed to be a breach of a 'contract of employment')

(c) Pressure to impose trade union membership or recognition – this includes enforcement of a union membership agreement, closed shop, dismissal of a worker for union membership or non-union membership

(d) Pressure to require a commercial contract or other contract be performed by union or non-union members

(e) Pressure to require tenders for work to be submitted or not considered for tender based on union membership or non-union membership.

The restriction of the immunities to exclude *all* secondary action has resulted in a number of cases where the union organising the industrial action has disputed the exact identity of the employer in question. An employer will not normally succeed in denying involvement in a trade dispute because of manipulation of corporate identity. Courts have long been prepared to look behind the 'corporate veil' at the practical identity of the employer. However, where secondary action is carried out an 'employer is not to be treated as party to a dispute between another employer and workers of that employer'; and where more than one employer is in dispute with the workers, the dispute between each employer and the workers is to be treated as a separate dispute.

14 Unofficial industrial action

14.1 Takes place where:

- The action is not authorised or endorsed by the trade union
- The employee taking the action is not a member of a trade union concerned (unless s/he is among those taking part who are members of a union which has authorised or endorsed industrial action), and
- All employees taking industrial action are not members of a trade union.

Immunity is also lost where industrial action is called because an employer has dismissed one or more employees because they were engaged in unofficial industrial action (and therefore have no right to complain of unfair dismissal).

15 Ballots for industrial action

The requirement to lawfully ballot prior to industrial action introduced in full in 1993 represents probably the most significant narrowing of the immunities for unions.

However, there was some lessening of the effect of the law as a result of the **Employment Relations Act 1999**. These changes are indicated below.

15.1 Statutory requirement

Industrial action that is immune from civil action must be preceded by a lawful ballot which conforms to *all* of the following statutory requirements:

(a) **The date of the ballot** is the last day on which votes may be cast. Normally, votes may be cast in the ballot for a period lasting no longer than four weeks.

(b) **Any subsequent industrial** action must be called within four weeks of midnight on the day on which the ballot closed. This period may be extended to *eight* weeks if the union and employer agree (to reduce the risk of misunderstanding, both parties may find it helpful for such agreements to be in writing).

(c) **The ballot must fulfil strict criteria. A Code of Practice** on industrial action balloting *Industrial action ballots and notice to employers* is published by the Department for Business, Skills and Innovation. The Code of Practice came into effect on 1 October 2005. Although compliance is not compulsory a court or tribunal will take into account its use or otherwise as evidence of good practice.

(d) **Ballots must be fully postal** and therefore secret.

(e) **Content of ballot paper**: There are strict rules on the content of the ballot paper, although there is scope for framing the questions as the union wishes. But the following must be asked:

'Are you prepared to take part in (or to continue to take part in) a strike? – YES/NO'.

'Are you prepared to take part in (or to continue to take part in) industrial action short of a strike? – YES/NO'.

The ballot must also contain a statement which reads:

'If you take part in a strike or other industrial action, you may be in breach of your contract of employment'.

(f) **Members' entitlement to be balloted**: All members who will be called upon to take part in the industrial action must be balloted. Specifically:

'Entitlement to vote in the ballot must be accorded equally to all members of the trade union who it is reasonable at the time of the ballot for the union to believe will be induced by the union to take part or, as the case may be, to continue to take part in the industrial action ....'

S 230(2) provides that:

'..... so far is reasonably practicable, every person who is entitled to vote...... has a voting paper sent to him by post at his home address or any other address which he has requested the trade union to treat as his postal address.....be given a convenient opportunity to vote by post'.

Failure to comply can be disregarded if the failure is accidental and on a scale not likely to affect the outcome of the ballot.

(g) **A majority of members entitled to vote** (**NB** not just those voting) must vote in favour in order for the industrial action to be protected by the immunities. A majority vote must be obtained in accordance with the union's rule book if its provisions go further than the statutory provisions.

(h) **New members**. The union concerned may 'induce' non-members and new union members who joined after the ballot to participate in the industrial action, but not take unjustifiable action against the latter if they refuse to participate.

(i) **Meaning of 'workplace'**. A separate ballot must be held for each workplace *unless:*

    (i) At least **one** of its members at each workplace is **affected** by the dispute.

Example

Overtime is worked at workplaces A, B and C where there is a dispute over the rate paid. One aggregate ballot can be held covering all three workplaces. But at workplace D no overtime is worked, so D must have its own ballot.

(ii) The union ballots members in a particular **occupational group** who are employed by a particular employer or group of employers (one aggregate ballot will cover the whole group).

(iii) The union ballots **members** who are employed by a particular employer or group of employers. (See (m) below).

(j) An independent scrutineer must be appointed.

(k) **Notification of industrial action to the employer.** The union must notify the employer of:

- Its intention to hold a ballot calling for industrial action
- The results of the ballot, and
- Its intentions in respect of the industrial action.

(i) **The pre-ballot information must include:**

– Notice of the ballot in writing, not later than the seventh day before the intended opening day of the ballot (with sample ballot paper provided no later than the third day before the opening of the ballot)

– The date of the opening of the ballot

– The total number of employees concerned

– Categories of employees to which the employees concerned belong and the number of the employees concerned in each of these categories

– Details of the workplaces at which the employees concerned work and the number of them who work at each of those workplaces.

There are special information requirements for employees who have payments to the union deducted from their wages.

(ii) **After the ballot:**

As soon as it is '**reasonably practicable**' after the close of the ballot, the trade union must inform the '**relevant employer**' and its members of the results of the ballot. Details must include how many:

– Votes were cast
– Votes were cast in favour of industrial action
– Votes were cast against industrial action, and
– Votes were spoiled.

(iii) **Notice of industrial action:**

Thereafter the union must notify the '**relevant employer**' of the proposed industrial action. (ii) above and (iii) may be combined. This is known as the '**relevant notice**'. It must contain:

- A statement as to whether the industrial action will be continuous or discontinuous (eg, every Monday), and the dates on which the action will take place

- A statement that the notice is for a qualifying purpose

- A statement providing information 'in the union's possession as would help the employer to make plans and bring information to the attention of those of his employees whom the union intends to induce or has induced to take part, or to continue to take part, in industrial action' (the 'affected employees'). Unions will have to provide details of:

    - Categories of workers involved
    - Workplace involved
    - The total number of workers involved
    - Number of workers in each category
    - Number of workers at each workplace but **will not** have to **name the individual employees**.

(l) **Suspension of industrial action:** Should the industrial action be suspended (other than for reason of a Court Order) a fresh period of notice should be given to the employer. In certain cases the employer will seek an injunction from the courts to restrain a union organising fresh industrial action because it will be argued that the action is separate from the previous period of industrial action. If successful, the employer may oblige the union to repeat the process of balloting and notification (as laid-out in (a) – (m)).

Note: the courts cannot enforce a ballot where one has not taken place.

(m) **Note** on meaning of workplace: as the premises at or from which a person works (in the case of a single workplace), or (in any other case) the premises with which the person's employment has the closest connection. The employer does not have to actually 'occupy' the premises.

(n) **Period of effectiveness of a ballot:** The general rule is that a ballot will be effective for four weeks starting with the date of the ballot. This period can be extended by up to eight weeks by agreement between the employer and the union.

Where there are intervening legal proceedings that halt the period of the industrial action it may be extended to a period of 12 weeks subject to certain rules being satisfied. Extension of a period of effectiveness of a ballot is not automatic.

16 The Citizen's Right of Action – s 235A

16.1 Definition

Any individual who claims that a trade union or other person has done, or is likely to do, an unlawful act to induce any person to take part, or to continue to take part, in industrial action and an effect or likely effect is, or will be, to prevent or delay the supply of goods or services or to reduce the quality of those supplied, can apply to the High Court for an order to restrain that action. If the court finds the claim to be 'well founded' it must make an order requiring the person against whom the proceedings are brought – which could be a trade union – to take steps to ensure that:

- There is no, or no further, inducement to take or continue to take part in the industrial action; and
- No person does anything after the order is made as a result of unlawful inducement prior to the making of the order.

Normally, an **interlocutory injunction** may be granted and if there is non-compliance it will constitute a **contempt of court**. The Citizen's Right enables an individual to get an order restraining the unlawful organisation of industrial action. It does not provide any other remedy.

The individual does not have to demonstrate an intent towards himself/herself – only that the likely effect would be to prevent the supply of goods/services. Because there is no tort the statutory provision circumvents the scope of liability constrained in the economic torts, and so the individual applicant does not have to show any loss.

17 Picketing

17.1 Definition

'It is lawful for a person in contemplation or furtherance of a trade dispute to attend...at or near his place of work...for the purpose only of peacefully obtaining or communicating information, or peacefully persuading any person to work or abstain from working'. **[S. 220 TULR(C)A 1992]**.

In other words, although picketing is not a form of industrial action it is normally an extension of it by those employees involved in the strike to persuade other workers not to enter the employer's premises or to deter the delivery of goods or services by other workers.

A Code of Practice on Picketing (re-issued in 1992), although not binding in law, will be taken into account in legal proceedings. One of the most important parts of the Code is paragraph 51 which states that a picket should not exceed **six persons** at any exit or entrance, and that frequently a smaller number will be appropriate.

17.2 Liability of unions in organising and maintaining a picket

Although there is a statutory 'right' to picket insofar that lawful picketing is permitted this does not offer significant protection to pickets or to unions involved from the economic torts. Picketing which constitutes action outside the above definition and the Code of Practice is open to civil and criminal liability. Also, a criminal offence may be committed during the course of picketing which otherwise remains immune from civil liability.

Secondary picketing is now outside the immunities.

The vulnerability of those engaged in picketing can be best understood by assessing each part of the definition:

(a) '...a person in contemplation or furtherance of a trade dispute...'

   The cause of the picket must directly relate to a trade dispute which falls within the scope of the Act. A former employee may picket the premises of his/her former employer but only where the dismissal gave rise to the instant dispute.

(b) '...to attend ...at or near his place of work...for the purpose only of peacefully obtaining or communicating information...'

   This wording follows that inserted into the **Trades Disputes Act 1906** – this became law during the days when most transport was still by horse and cart. How practical is it today to peacefully communicate with the driver of a motor vehicle such as a lorry without physically obstructing the path of that vehicle? Nevertheless, such obstruction will be outside the scope of lawful picketing.

   There is no right to physically stop anyone entering or leaving premises.

   Sometimes workers may argue that they are not engaged in a picket, but in a demonstration and therefore do not have to limit their numbers to six. 'Peaceful' picketing will be assessed objectively on the basis of the pickets' behaviour. Where a large group of workers (or former workers) show by their behaviour that their intention is to persuade others not to work then they will be deemed to be a picket.

(c) '...place of work...'

Should the worker not have a regular place of work they may picket the employer's premises from where the work is administered. Where a worker's normal place of work is closed-down then they may not picket any other premises of the former employer.

If a picket is set-up at the nearest point to the employer's entrance/exit but is adjacent to another's property it will not be unlawful provided it does not give rise to a breach of civil or criminal law.

17.3 Committing one or more torts

The general difficulty which organisers of picketing face is that even small numbers of pickets may constitute civil or criminal breaches of law.

Examples

(a) **Trespass to the highway**

Normally, travelling by foot along the highway to get from one place to another, or to stop and talk to another person is not a trespass of the highway. However, if it were to block the route of others it could be deemed to be a trespass.

(b) **Private nuisance**

This tort may be caused by unreasonable interference with another's enjoyment of his/her land.

17.4 Criminal liability for picketing

These include:

- Obstruction of the highway
- Assault
- Obstructing a constable in the course of duty
- Unlawful assembly
- Affray and riot
- Public nuisance
- Intimidation and conspiracy and
- Using violence to or intimidating the other person or his/her spouse or children or injuring his/her property.

18 Remedies for employers

Where unlawful industrial action takes place certain statutory and common law remedies will be available against the union.

18.1 Against the employee

- If there is a repudiatory breach of contract the employer may lawfully **dismiss** all those involved.

- **Disciplinary action** (including withholding of pay for part performance) may be taken

- **Damages** may be claimed, however, this is rarely used, not least because it will be difficult for the employer to prove loss due to the actions of one employee as opposed to the whole group on strike.

18.2 Against the union

Damages for actions in tort not protected by the 'immunities'. The damage must be 'foreseeable' to be actionable in law. It is limited in accordance with the numbers in membership of the union:

Limit for damages

Less than 5,000 members: £10,000
5,000 – 24,999 members: £50,000
25,000 – 99,999 members: £125,000
100,000 or more members: £250,000

18.3 Injunctions

Interim injunction: An order sought to (normally) prevent, restrict or prohibit the union from doing something (eg, unofficial industrial action) subject to a full hearing and a declaration of the rights of the parties. Prior to 1998 these were called interlocutory injunctions. These injunctions can be obtained at very short notice from a judge in Chambers, but will not be granted without proper consideration of the following:

(a) To grant or not grant the application '**on the balance of convenience**' test. This takes into account whether there is a serious matter to be tried – if it is decided there is, then injunctive relief will not be granted where a full hearing and damages would adequately compensate the complainant. Where the defendant union is likely to succeed in its defence of action 'in contemplation or furtherance of a trade dispute' the court may not grant the order.

(b) The party seeking the injunction must show they took all reasonable steps to notify the other party of the application for an injunction.

18.4 Enforcement

This is used where the defendant does not:

- Pay damages
- Obey the injunction

Such actions will be deemed to be contempt of court. Wilful disobedience will be treated seriously by the courts. The plaintiff must bring the contempt to the attention of the court. The defendant must purge their contempt by following court orders and acting to redress any unlawful actions.

Contempt of court is a deliberate failure by a union (or any party) to obey the terms of an injunction or other court order. The contempt may be punishable by the court as follows:

Punishment	Comment
A fine	May be concurrent with sequestration.
Sequestration of funds	The defendant is deprived of 'property' (goods or money). Because assets of unions are reported annually to the Certification Officer they are particularly vulnerable to specific sequestration. Sequestration may follow a fine where the defendant refuses to comply with the injunction.
Committal	This is a last resort enforcement, normally because of open defiance of the court. Maximum term of imprisonment: two years. Seldom used in industrial disputes.

18.5 Criminal liability

As the above section on picketing explains there are a number of criminal offences which pickets may commit in the course of their activities. These include:

(a) Obstruction of the highway

(b) Obstruction of a constable in the execution of duties (eg, refusal to obey a police officer)

(c) Offences under the **Public Order Act 1986** (as amended):

– Failure to comply with police instructions in organising or proceeding with 'public assemblies' and 'public processions'

- Riot, violent disorder, affray, causing fear of violence or provoking it, and causing harassment, alarm or distress. These may be carried out in a public or private place.

(d) The **TULR(C)A 1992 (s 241** – amended by the **Civil Partnership Act 2004)** makes it an offence to do one of five acts 'wrongfully and without legal authority......with a view to compelling another person to abstain from doing or to do any act which that person has a legal right to do or abstain from doing'.

These acts include:

- Using **violence** to (or intimidating) that person or their spouse or civil partner or children or injuring their property
- Persistently **following** that person about from place to place
- Hiding any tools, clothes or other property owned or used by that person, or depriving them or hindering them in the use
- **Watching** or besetting the house or other place where that person resides, works, carries on business or happens to be, or the approach to any such house or place
- **Following that person with two or more other persons** in a disorderly manner in or through any street or road.

These statutory breaches are in addition to those economic torts outlined above in earlier sections.

19 The meaning of industrial action and 'protected' industrial action

19.1 Definition

Until 2000 the dismissal of an employee participating in any type of industrial action (including 'other industrial action or action short of a strike') was **automatically fair** and an Employment Tribunal had no jurisdiction to hear a complaint. This situation included where the employer was operating a lock-out.

However, now during the first 12 weeks of an employee's participation in **official** industrial action, it will be **automatically unfair** to dismiss the employee for participating in the action. After the 12-week period has expired a dismissal may still be automatically unfair where the employer has failed to take reasonable steps (within the context of good industrial relations practice) to resolve the dispute. Any involvement in unofficial or secondary industrial action will be unprotected. Periods of lock out will **not** count towards the 12-week protected period.

The following definitions have been applied:

(a) **Strike**

    (i) 'A cessation of work by a body of persons employed acting in combination; or

    (ii) 'A concerted refusal of any number of persons to continue to work for an employer in consequence of a dispute...................in order to compel the employer to accept or not to accept terms and conditions.......'.

(b) **Lock-out**

    (i) 'Closing the place of employment; or

    (ii) suspending work; or

    (iii) refusal to continue to employ any number of persons employed by him in consequence of a dispute................done with a view to compelling persons employed by the employer to accept terms or conditions or with a view to otherwise affecting employment'.

19.2 Complaint of unfair dismissal

An employee dismissed under these circumstances may submit a claim for unfair dismissal *only if:*

(a) One or more relevant employees (also taking part in the industrial action) of the same employer have not been dismissed; or

(b) Any relevant employee (also taking part in the industrial action) has been offered re-engagement and that the employee complaining has not been offered re-engagement. The offer of re-engagement must have occurred before the expiry of the period of three months beginning with the effective date of dismissal of the relevant employee; or

(c) The reason or principal reason for the dismissal was one of those specified (ie, dismissal in jury service, family, health and safety, working time, employee representative and flexible working cases).

19.3 Participation in employment action

It is a **question of fact** for the tribunal to decide whether the relevant employee was taking part in employment action at the material time of the dismissal. Generally, where an employee allies himself/herself to the strike (and stays away from work) they are participating in the strike even though they may be absent from work for other reasons (eg, because of illness). Should an employee on the day of the strike take a day's holiday with the permission of the employer this will not of itself render the employee liable to dismissal. Where there is uncertainty a sensible employer will make contact with the employee and ask them whether or not they are ready and willing to work. Where the industrial action is **unofficial** then the relevant employee has no right of complaint. In these circumstances the employer **may** selectively dismiss or re-engage.

19.4 Selective dismissal and re-engagement

Selective re-engagement means that the employee will be re-offered the job held immediately before the date of dismissal or another job which is reasonably suitable. Where the employer offers selective re-engagement to some employees within a three-month period, all of the relevant employees dismissed and not re-engaged may complain of unfair dismissal.

Provided the employer offers re-engagement to all of the dismissed employees within the three month period there will be no right of complaint to the tribunal. It is for this reason that the period in which a complaint of unfair dismissal can be submitted is extended to six months.

20 Employee Information, Participation and Consultation with Employee Representatives – Pensions and the Companies Act 1985 (amended and repealed in part by the Companies Act 2006)

In addition, there are specific provisions for publishing information relating to pensions, and information in directors' annual reports.

20.1 Pensions

The employee's statement of principal terms and conditions must contain details of any occupational pension scheme to which the employee is entitled to have access. Part-time employees cannot be excluded from access to, or equal benefits arising out of an occupational pension scheme.

The trustees of the pension scheme must disclose to employees who are members certain information in writing, normally provided in a scheme booklet. The information must, *inter alia* include:

- A description of the procedures for handling disputes
- Contact details: Occupational Pensions Regulatory Authority
- Arrangements for AVCs, and
- On what basis the scheme has been contracted-out (if relevant).

Recognised trade unions may also receive a copy of the 'booklet' within two months of the request.

In addition, an annual statement must be provided to each member detailing matters such as a review of investment over the last year (and in a money purchase scheme – an annual benefit statement).

The **Occupational and Personal Pension Schemes (consultation by employers and miscellaneous amendment) Regulations 2006** oblige employers to consult with members on significant changes to their pension schemes.

20.2 Disability and employee involvement – Companies Act 1985

The **Companies Act 1985** specifies that certain information will be included in the directors' annual report where the company employs in excess of 250 employees, specifically:

- Information concerning the employment of disabled persons, and
- Information about employee involvement.

Also the report should:

- Encourage the involvement of employees in the company's performance through an employee share scheme, and

- Explain the methods for consulting employees or their representatives on a regular basis so that those views can be taken into account.

21 Employee participation and information

21.1 Main aspects

The two main aspects of this activity will be examined:

- European Works Councils
- National Works Councils

} Worker information and consultation

(a) **European Works Councils** (EWCs)

    (i) **Introduction**

        Although common throughout continental Europe, Works Councils have until recently not been a characteristic of traditional UK industrial or employment relations. British systems for informing and consulting 'employees' have developed piece-meal through the provision of specific rights found in legislation, eg, the right to be consulted on proposed redundancies. Such requirements direct information through or with **employee representatives**, *not* with the employees themselves. There are few exceptions for consultation, for example, the redundancy example above states that where no recognised trade union exists the employer must hold an election for the appointment of employee representatives. On the other hand, there are many examples where specific **information** must be communicated directly to the individual employee, eg, provision of a statement of principal terms and conditions.

Works Councils (or staff councils as they are more likely to be called in the UK) represent an organised and continuous form of information and consultation that is designed to create a more systematic way of allowing the workforce of each organisation to 'participate' in the employer's decision-making processes. Albeit conservative in scope, the introduction of Works Councils in the UK is still a significant step away from traditional processes which have never seriously included any form of real workforce participation in the organisation's decision-making.

It is important to realise that Works Councils do not officially constitute **employee participation**, only information and consultation. Full participation would include the following:

- Power to veto management decision-making, or at least the employer being obliged to consider the employees' views in his/her decision-making, and

- Employees having the power to introduce new matters or ideas for inclusion in management strategy through, say, a works council forum.

In some European countries, such as Germany, the Works Council system has embraced aspects of participation (eg, power to veto employee dismissals), but the EWCs and the 'National Works Councils' discussed below do not include such measures.

(ii) **Purpose of EWCs and their origins**

The **European Works Council Directive (EWCD) (EC/94/45)** came into force throughout the EU in 1996, but the UK was not subject to it because the government had negotiated an opt-out from its provisions through the general opt out of the Social Chapter of the Maastricht Treaty in 1991. Some UK companies were, however covered because they had substantial operations in continental Europe, or because they were subsidiaries of another company directly affected by the Directive in say, France or Germany. Because of this, many UK employers voluntarily implemented the Directive.

In 1997 the new Labour Government adopted the Social Chapter of Maastricht and formally withdrew the opt-out. Subsequently, the **Transnational Information and Consultation of Employees Regulations 1999** were introduced. The two-year gap was provided for in the Directive: **Article 13** of the Directive provided for a two-year period in which employers could negotiate voluntary agreements with employee representatives (including recognised trade unions) for a number of flexible provisions to apply. However, an Article 13 Agreement could not undermine the basic requirements of the EWCD.

The EWCD covers 'Community-scale undertakings' – any business organisation with at least 1,000 employees and a minimum of 150 employees located in two or more member states of the EU. The size of the workforce is based on the average number of employees, including part-timers, employed during the previous two years and calculated according to national law/practice.

The purpose of the EWCD is to reinforce the '**social dialogue**' between workers and employers to facilitate co-operation, protection of employees' rights and prospects, and the economic success of the enterprise. The EWC will comprise representatives of the workforce and from management. The EWC has the right to be informed by the employer of the following:

- The structure, economic and financial situation and probable development of the business
- Production and sales
- The situation and probable trend of employment
- Substantial organisational changes
- Introduction of new working methods or production processes
- Mergers, important cutbacks or closures
- Collective redundancies.

Further functions for the EWC are discussed directly below.

(iii) **Further functions of the EWC**

- **Initial request for an EWC**

    Negotiations to set-up a EWC can be triggered by either central management or a request from a minimum of 100 employees (or their representatives) from at least two member states. In the UK the employer can apply to CAC if they believe the request is not valid. Where the company refuses to respond appropriately the employees may complain directly to the EAT. Unless management has a 'reasonable excuse' a civil financial penalty of up to £75,000 may be imposed.

- **Articles 13 and 6 Agreements**

    In the first two years of the application of the EWCD, Article 13 allowed less prescriptive arrangements to be agreed for the provision of information and consultation. However, since 1999 any EWC must be established under **Article 6** through negotiations between central management and a **Special Negotiation Body** (SNB) – in the UK this will comprise between 3 and 18 employee representatives depending on size of enterprise.

    Membership of SNB: Members of any existing information and consultation body, or, if not in existence, through a balloted election of employee representatives.

(iv) **EWC terms of reference**

The SNB and management will then meet to agree the functioning details of the EWC. The agreement must include matters such as:

- Establishments to be covered by the EWC
- Venue, frequency/duration of meetings
- Resources allocated to the EWC, and
- Terms of reference of the EWC.

Once the SNB has completed its business the EWC will be formally established. Thereafter, the EWC must meet at least once a year to be informed and consulted by management through a report on the progress of business. The EWC may expand its membership to between 3 and 30 members; special committees may be elected to deal with specific matters, and certain specialists may be co-opted to assist the EWC. The employer must provide the EWC with necessary financial and material resources. EWC members must be given reasonable paid time-off to perform their duties.

(v) **Some reported benefits of EWCs**

- Catalyst for improving communications
- Symbolic value in demonstrating employers' concern for workforce morale and welfare
- Improvements in trust, employee involvement in business decision-making, a better understanding by the workforce of commercial pressures
- Development of a more cohesive corporate culture.

(vi) **Some reported problems with EWCs**

- Extra management time

- Costs (administration, management time, resources and lost staff time) (costs per employee representative range from £900 to £4,500 (*))

- Unnecessary duplication of information/consultation (particularly where there are National Works Councils)

- Management fear of transition to 'trans-national pay bargaining' and undermining of 'management's right to manage'

- Raising of unrealistic expectations among workforce.

((*) All the evidence in the two sections above is taken from: *Cost and Benefits of the European Works Councils Directive;* Weber, Foster & Egriboz, ECOTEC Research & Consulting. DTI Employment Relations Research Series No. 9, 2000.)

(vii) **Review of the EWC Directive**

In 2003 the European Commission under took a review of the working of the EWCD. The European Trade Union Confederation (ETUC) presented evidence to the European Commission that the EWC should be strengthened. Their main concern was the lack of clear remedies where an employer fails to provide proper information to or consultation for its EWC. Their proposals can be summarised as follows:

- Provision of sanctions against employers failing to honour EWC Agreements. Proposals include nullifying measures introduced in contravention to the respective Agreement, excluding the employer from the award of any public service contract and fines

- Addition of equal opportunities, environmental issues and health and safety to the list of subjects for Agreement

- Reduction of the employee threshold for the establishment of an EWC

- Requirement that information and consultation must take place 'in good time before decision-making'. (**NB**: At the moment there is no need for an employer to consult or inform the EWC before a decision is taken or to change it in any form after consultation.)

(b) **National Works Councils (NWC)**

    (i) **Introduction**

        EU Directive 2002/14/EC (the National Works Council Directive – NWCD) is a natural extension of the legislative work already in place through the EWCD.

        The European Commission decided that further rules must be laid-down to strengthen information and consultation mechanisms on a national basis. It failed to get the *Social Partners* to reach a *Framework Agreement*, and, therefore pressed ahead with draft legislation.

    (ii) **Implementation of the National Works Council Directive (NWCD) – EC Directive 2002/14/EC establishing a general framework for informing and consulting employees in the European Community – in the UK.**

        The Regulations were issued under powers set out in Section 42 of the Employment Relations Act 2004.

        Timetable

        The Directive was implemented into the UK as follows:

        By 23 March 2005: Undertakings with 150+ employees

        By 23 March 2007: Undertakings with 100+ employees

        By 23 March 2008: Undertakings with 50+ employees

        You will note that both private businesses and public sector organisations are equally covered, unlike the EWCD.

    (iii) **General purpose**

        UK employers are under an obligation to consult with their employees on an ongoing basis. This should allow the workforce to have a clear understanding of all the changes impacting on them and thereby give them the opportunity to put forward views and proposals that might ameliorate negative influences on them and improve their position within the enterprise.

    (iv) **Similarity between the EWCD and the NWCD – Voluntary Agreements**

        Article 13 of the EWCD provided that a Voluntary Agreement could be signed within the first two years of the Directive. An identical provision is contained in the NWCD. Article 5 permits employers and elected employee representatives to make flexible Agreements that, for example, can incorporate existing procedures/arrangements. This reflects the government's belief that implementation of the Directive must *not* be along the lines of a 'one size fits all' approach.

(v) **Triggering of NWCD process**

Provided 10 per cent of the workforce petition management (in one document or individually over any period of six months) the process will be triggered. The negotiation period would then commence. However, where existing information and consultation processes are already in place the employer can ballot the workforce to simply use those existing processes as the basis for the NWC (or staff council). Provided at least 40 per cent of the workforce endorse the arrangement this will remain valid under the new Regulations. However, where new arrangements require setting-up the equivalent of an SNB, a high degree of flexibility is envisaged, but if no Agreement is concluded within the specified timescale the **default model** provided for in the Regulations will apply.

(vi) **Default model**

Where a Voluntary Agreement cannot be concluded an information and consultation committee must be established representing all the employees in the organisation. This will take place through a ballot. The number of employee representatives will be one representative for every 50 employees, up to a maximum of 25.

The NWC (or staff council) will operate as follows:

The employer will have to provide the new information and consultation committee (ie, the NWC/staff council) with information on the following:

- Recent and probable development of the undertaking's activities and economic situation

- The situation, structure and probable development of job stability, employment levels and anticipatory measures, particularly where there might be a threat to employment, and

- Management decisions likely to lead to substantial changes in work organisation or in contractual relations, including collective redundancies/transfers of undertakings.

Example changes to work organisation or contractual

The Regulations will also contain rules on timing, method and content of the information/consultation; for example, where information is provided to representatives it should be in a format which enables them to properly study it, and if necessary appoint an expert to assist them in that analysis. Meetings between the committee and management must take place with a view to 'reaching agreement' on management decisions.

(vii) **Disputes**

Where the employer fails to abide by the Regulations by not establishing a proper NWC/staff council the employees may complain to the CAC, which may order rectification; a similar complaint can be brought by the employer against the employee representatives where there is an alleged breach of the Agreement. Where a complaint is upheld against the employer, the representatives may apply to the EAT for a penalty to be imposed.

(viii) **Confidentiality**

This has been a matter of concern for many employers. What should an employer do if time-sensitive or share-sensitive information needs to be imparted to employee representatives?

The Regulations state that representatives or assisting experts may not disclose to any third party any information entrusted to them in confidence by the employer in the course of exercising the information or consultation Agreement. Where this occurs, the employer may sue for damages.

Representatives may apply to the CAC for an order for information to be released to them because they believe it would not breach confidentiality. This provision exists because the Regulations permit employers not to disclose information which could 'harm the functioning of the undertaking or be prejudicial to it.' CAC will also act as arbiter in such matters.

(ix) **Protection of employee representatives**

A number of measures are proposed which would grant employee representatives:

- Reasonable paid time-off to carry out their duties
- The power to stand for election as a representative, and
- Protection against unfair dismissal or other detriment when acting in accordance with the legislation.

Complaint will be by way of an application to the employment tribunal.

(x) **Outstanding matters**

At the time of writing a series of matters are not yet decided.

Examples:

- How and in what circumstances should information and consultation be undertaken, not just at the level of the undertaking, but extended to individual establishments? The government notes that in some business organisations it may be more appropriate for the legislation to apply to **separate establishments**, rather than **undertakings as a whole** (which is the basic term of reference for a NWC/staff council in the Regulations).

- Interaction with other existing information and consultation mechanisms, eg, EWCs and consultation for redundancies and transfer of undertakings.

Index

A

Absenteeism, 237
Access to Health Records Act 1990, 100
Access to Medical Reports Act 1988, 100
Additional adoption leave, 158
Additional Maternity Leave, 144
Additional paternity leave, 151
Adoption leave, 155
Age-related discrimination, 192
Annual hours contracts, 57
Annual leave, 181
Application forms, 15
Atypical contracts, 53
Automated data, 63

B

Ballots for industrial action, 293
Band of reasonable responses, 254
Binding contract, 21
Bonuses on termination, 116
Breach of contract, 168
Business Transfer test, 211

C

Capability, 233
Car allowances, 116
Cashless pay, 110
Category 1 workers, 185
Category 2 workers, 185
Category 3 workers, 186
Category 4 workers, 186
Central Arbitration Committee, 279
Citizen's Right of Action, 297
Codes of practice, 33
Collective agreements, 34, 42
Collective bargaining, 270, 284
Common law implied terms, 33
Competency frameworks, 13
Compulsory maternity leave, 144
Conduct, 233, 236
Conduct outside employment, 238
Confidential sensitive information, 42
Confidentiality, 48
Conspiracy, 290
Constructive dismissal, 231
Consultation, 209
Continuity of employment, 174
Contract changes, 167
Criminal convictions, 253
Criminal Records Bureau, 97
Custom and practice, 34

D

Damages, 267
Data Protection Act 1998, 61
Data protection principles, 69
Deduction of wages - redress, 116
Deductions in wages, 111
De-recognition, 285
Diet, 198
Disciplinary sanctions, 258
Discretionary bonuses, 115
Discrimination legislation, 189
Dishonesty, 237
Dismissal, 219
Dismissal and waiver clauses, 55

Dismissals connected with a transfer, 209
Dress, 198
Dress or appearance, 204
Duties of the employer, 43
Duty to inform and consult, 217
Duty to pay wages, 110

E

Economic torts, 289
Effective date of termination, 220
E-mail, 77
Employee – who is an employee?, 25
Employee/worker status, 25
Employees' duties, 47
Employer's duties, 44
Employment Practices Data Protection Code, 72
Employment Rights Act 1996, 108
Equal pay, 129
Equality, 102
Equality Act 2010, 1
Errors of computation, 112
ETO reason defence, 216
European Economic Area, 81
Express terms, 33
Express terms of the contract, 35

F

Fair dismissals, 224
Fixed-term contracts, 40, 54
Fixed-term employees (Prevention of Less Favourable Treatment) Regulations, 55
Flexibility and mobility clauses, 40
Flexible working, 161
Freedom of Information Act 2000, 71
Frustration of the contract, 261

G

Garden leave, 52
Genuine Occupational Requirement, 196, 203

Global contracts, 57
Guarantee payments, 117

H

Health and safety, 45
Health and Safety at Work Act 1974, 273
Health records, 71
Holiday pay, 117
Homophobia, 204

I

Ill health, 235
Immigration, Asylum and Nationality Act 2006, 87
Implied duties, 47
Imprisonment of the employee, 262
Indefinite contracts, 39
Individual rights for time off, 137
Inducement to break a contract, 290
Industrial action, 288
Information, 61
Information and Consultation of Employees Regulations 2004, 218
Information Commissioner, 71
Injunctions, 300
Integration test, 28
Interviews, 16
Inventions, copyright and discoveries, 41

J

Job advertisements, 14
Job descriptions, 13

K

Keeping-in-touch (KIT) days, 145, 158

L

Leave for religious observance, 197

M

Mandatory retirement ages, 192
Marriage and civil partnerships, 193
Maternity leave, 56
Maternity rights, 141
Medical information, 98
Mutual agreement, 263
Mutual trust and confidence, 44

N

National Minimum Wage Act 1998, 125
Night work, 186
Non-contractual payments, 115

O

Occupational pension schemes, 103
Occupational Pension Schemes (Equal Treatment) Regulations 1995, 131
Offensive remarks, 198
Ordinary adoption leave, 155
Ordinary Maternity Leave, 143
Ordinary paternity leave, 150
Overpayments of wages, 115

P

Part-time workers, 58
Paternity leave, 149
Pay, 107
Pay in lieu of notice, 41
Pay in lieu of notice payments, 113
Pensions, 304
Period of continuous employment, 174
Person specifications, 13
Personal data, 61, 62
Picketing, 297
Positive action, 204
Posting of Workers Directive 1996 (96/71), 86
Pragmatic test, 28
Pre-employment health checks, 19
Privity of contract, 24
Probationary period, 41
Procedural fairness, 256
Proposed redundancies, 273
'Protected' industrial action, 302
Public Interest Disclosure Act 1998, 103

R

Reasonable orders, 237
Recovery of wages, 114
Recruitment and selection, 11
Redundancy, 238
References, 44, 92
Regulation of Investigatory Powers Act 2000, 73
Rehabilitation period, 95
Relevant transfers, 211
Religion and belief, 195
Resignation of the employee, 263
Rest and break periods, 187
Restraint of trade, 50
Retirement, 251
Retirement ages, 251
Right of accompaniment, 259

S

Secondary industrial action, 292
Selection tests, 18
Self-certification, 124
Sensitive personal data, 61
Service Provision Change, 212, 213
Sex, 199
Sexual harassment, 201
Sexual orientation, 202, 204
Sick pay, 54, 117, 119
Specific express clauses, 39
Spent convictions, 97
Statutorily imposed terms, 34
Strike, 288
Summary dismissal, 220, 266
Sunday Trading Act 1994, 189
Sunday working, 189

T

Telecommunications (Lawful Business Practice) (Interception of Communications) Regulations 2000 (SI 2000/2699) (Regulation 3 amended by Regulation 34 of The Privacy and Electronic Communications (EC Directive) Regulation 2003), 75
Temporary and casual contracts of employment, 56
Termination of employment, 219
Terms of the contract, 33
Time off for dependants, 152
Time off for education/training, 139
Time off for employee representatives, 139
Time off for employees who are trustees of occupational pension schemes, 140
Time off for public duties, 138
Tort, 289, 299
Trade union, 269
Transfer of Undertakings, 205
TUPE Regulations, 208

U

Unfair dismissal, 192, 222, 228, 303
Unilateral variation, 171
Union recognition, 271
Unjustified dismissal without notice, 267
Unofficial industrial action, 293

V

Vitiating factors, 24

W

Wages Act 1986, 110
Work and Families Act 2006, 155
Working hours, 179
Working Time Regulations 1998, 176
Working under protest, 171
Works rules, 33
Wrongful dismissal, 265

Z

Zero-hours contracts, 57

Notes

Notes

Notes

Notes